Fodor's

THE BERKSHIRES & PIONEER VALLEY

1ST EDITION

Where to Stay and Eat
for All Budgets

Must-See Sights
and Local Secrets

Ratings You Can Trust

Fodor's Travel Publications   New York, Toronto, London, Sydney, Auckland
www.fodors.com

MAY   2005

FODOR'S BERKSHIRES & PIONEER VALLEY
Editors: Mark Sullivan, William Travis

Editorial Production: David Downing
Editorial Contributors: Gail M. Burns, Andrew Collins, Dr. Carole Owens, Eileen Pierce, David Simons
Maps: David Lindroth Inc., *cartographer;* Rebecca Baer and Bob Blake, *map editors*
Design: Fabrizio La Rocca, *creative director;* Guido Caroti, *art director;* Moon Sun Kim, *cover designer;* Melanie Marin, *senior picture editor*
Production/Manufacturing: Colleen Ziemba
Cover Photo: Kindra Clineff/Index Stock Imagery

COPYRIGHT

First Edition

ISBN 1–4000–1467–0

SPECIAL SALES

This book is available for special discounts for bulk purchases for sales promotions or premiums. Special editions, including personalized covers, excerpts of existing books, and corporate imprints, can be created in large quantities for special needs. For more information, write to Special Markets/Premium Sales, 1745 Broadway, MD 6-2, New York, New York 10019, or e-mail specialmarkets@randomhouse.com.

AN IMPORTANT TIP & AN INVITATION

Although all prices, opening times, and other details in this book are based on information supplied to us at press time, changes occur all the time in the travel world, and Fodor's cannot accept responsibility for facts that become outdated or for inadvertent errors or omissions. So **always confirm information when it matters,** especially if you're making a detour to visit a specific place. Your experiences—positive and negative—matter to us. If we have missed or misstated something, **please write to us.** We follow up on all suggestions. Contact the Berkshires & Pioneer Valley editor at editors@fodors.com or c/o Fodor's at 1745 Broadway, New York, New York 10019.

DESTINATION THE BERKSHIRES & PIONEER VALLEY

In so much of New England, you must choose between natural beauty and cultural stimulation, but the Berkshires and Pioneer Valley offer astounding riches on all fronts: Massachusetts' highest mountain peaks and most dramatic river, a seemingly limitless supply of refined country inns and stellar dining options, performance festivals and art museums that rival those in any big city in the country, and the academic stimulation of some of the Northeast's most respected colleges and universities. Although western Massachusetts sits happily away from the congestion and fast pace of other parts of the state, it's still just an afternoon's drive from Boston and New York City. Countless artists, writers, musicians, and wealthy business barons have been lured to the area over the years—people with the means to live virtually anywhere. Come see for yourself why the Berkshires and Pioneer Valley possess a mystical allure and creative spirit unrivaled elsewhere in the Northeast. Whether you visit for an afternoon or a full season, you're in for a magical experience.

Tim Jarrell, Publisher

CONTENTS

(1) South County   *1*

(2) Central County   *38*

(3) North County   *67*

(4) The Pioneer Valley   *111*

Index   *153*

Maps

CloseUps

ON THE ROAD WITH FODOR'S

A trip takes you out of yourself. Concerns of life at home completely disappear, driven away by more immediate thoughts—about, say, what marvels will beguile the next day or where you'll have dinner. That's where Fodor's comes in. We make sure that you know all your options, so that you don't miss something that's around the next bend just because you didn't know it was there. Mindful that the best memories of your trip might have nothing to do with what you came to the Berkshires or Pioneer Valley to see, we guide you to sights large and small all over town. With Fodor's at your side, serendipitous discoveries are never far away.

Our success in showing you every corner of the Berkshires and Pioneer Valley is a credit to our extraordinary writers. Although there's no substitute for travel advice from a good friend who knows your style, our contributors are the next best thing—the kind of people you would poll for travel advice if you knew them.

A freelance writer, **Gail M. Burns** has lived in northern Berkshire County for almost 25 years. She came to know and love the area through her work as a journalist and a theater critic. A member of the American Theatre Critics Association and the International Association of Theatre Critics, Gail maintains a Web site www.gailsez.com which lists and reviews area theatre productions. She recently authored the 50-year update to the bicentennial history of Williamstown and edited the centennial history of the Episcopal Diocese of Western Massachusetts.

Former Fodor's editor and New Englander **Andrew Collins,** who compiled the Smart Travel Tips section as well as portions of the book's front section and also acted as copyeditor, is the author of several books on travel in New England, including guides to Connecticut, Rhode Island, and New Orleans. He's also a frequent contributor to *Travel + Leisure,*

Sunset and numerous other newspapers and magazines.

Eileen Pierce, a freelance writer for 25 years, has lived in the Berkshires since 1973. She is the PR/Marketing director at the Berkshire Theatre Festival, and when she's not composing press releases, she is busy writing a memoir.

Carole Owens is the author of seven books, five of which are about the Berkshires, her home for 30 years. She has written articles about the Berkshires for *Country Inns, Victoria, New England Travel and Life, the Boston Globe Magazine, the Berkshire Eagle, Berkshire Magazine,* and *Berkshire Living.* She has been consultant on television shows for HGTV, A & E, and the History and Travel hannels. Teacher and lecturer, Owens loves her topic: the Beautiful Berkshires now and then.

Author **David Simons** spent his formative years roaming the streets of Boston before joining the ranks of the "hayseeds" in the Pioneer Valley back in the '70s. Alongside continuing contributions to a range of music and business publications, he has written several books including his latest, *Studio Stories: How the Great New York Records Were Made.*

ABOUT THIS BOOK

The best source for travel advice is a like-minded friend who's just been where you're headed. But with or without that friend, you'll be in great shape to find your way around your destination once you learn to find your way around your Fodor's guide.

SELECTION
Our goal is to cover the best properties, sights, and activities in their category, as well as the most interesting communities to visit. We make a point of including local food-lovers' hot spots as well as neighborhood options, and we avoid all that's touristy unless it's really worth your time. You can go on the assumption that everything in this book is recommended wholeheartedly by our writers and editors. Flip to On the Road with Fodor's to learn more about who they are. It goes without saying that no property pays to be included.

RATINGS
Orange stars ★ denote sights and properties that our editors and writers consider the very best in the area covered by the entire book. These, the best of the best, are listed in the Fodor's Choice section in the front of the book. Black stars ★ highlight the sights and properties we deem Highly Recommended, the don't-miss sights within any region.

SPECIAL SPOTS
Pleasures & Pastimes and text on chapter-title pages focus on experiences that reveal the spirit of the destination. Also watch for Off the Beaten Path sights. Some are out of the way, some are quirky, and all are worthwhile. When the munchies hit, look for Need a Break? suggestions.

TIME IT RIGHT
Check On the Calendar up front and chapters' Timing sections for weather and crowd overviews and best days and times to visit.

SEE IT ALL
Use Fodor's exclusive Great Itineraries as a model for your trip. In cities, Good Walks guide you to important sights in each neighborhood; ⌐ indicates the starting points of walks and itineraries in the text and on the map.

BUDGET WELL
In the hotel and restaurant price categories, from ¢ to $$$$, we provide a balanced selection for every budget. For attractions, we always give standard adult admission fees; reductions are usually available for children, students, and senior citizens. Look in Discounts & Deals in Smart Travel Tips for information on destination-wide ticket schemes. Want to pay with plastic? AE, D, DC, MC, V following restaurant and hotel listings indicate whether American Express, Discover, Diner's Club, MasterCard, or Visa are accepted.

BASIC INFO
Smart Travel Tips lists travel essentials for the entire area covered by the book. To find the best way to get around, see the transportation section; see individual modes of travel ("Car Travel," "Train Travel") for details.

ON THE MAPS	**Maps** throughout the book show you what's where and help you find your way around. Black and orange numbered bullets **❶ ❶** in the text correlate to bullets on maps.
BACKGROUND	We give background information within the chapters in the course of explaining sights as well as in **CloseUp** boxes.
FIND IT FAST	Chapters are divided into small regions, within which towns are covered in logical geographical order; attractive routes and interesting places between towns are flagged as **En Route**. Heads at the top of each page help you find what you need within a chapter.
DON'T FORGET	**Restaurants** are open for lunch and dinner daily unless we state otherwise; we mention dress only when there's a specific requirement and reservations only when they're essential or not accepted— it's always best to book ahead. **Hotels** have private baths, phone, TVs, and air-conditioning and operate on the European Plan (aka EP, meaning without meals). We always list facilities but not whether you'll be charged extra to use them, so when pricing accommodations, find out what's included.
SYMBOLS	

Many Listings

★ Fodor's Choice
★ Highly recommended
⊠ Physical address
⊹ Directions
⌖ Mailing address
☏ Telephone
🖷 Fax
⊕ On the Web
✐ E-mail
🎟 Admission fee
◷ Open/closed times
► Start of walk/itinerary
Ⓜ Metro stations
⊟ Credit cards

Outdoors

⛳ Golf
⛺ Camping

Hotels & Restaurants

🏨 Hotel
🛏 Number of rooms
⚐ Facilities
🍽 Meal plans
✕ Restaurant
⚑ Reservations
🏛 Dress code
⚞ Smoking
🍷 BYOB
✕🏨 Hotel with restaurant that warrants a visit

Other

☺ Family-friendly
🛈 Contact information
⇨ See also
⊠ Branch address
☞ Take note

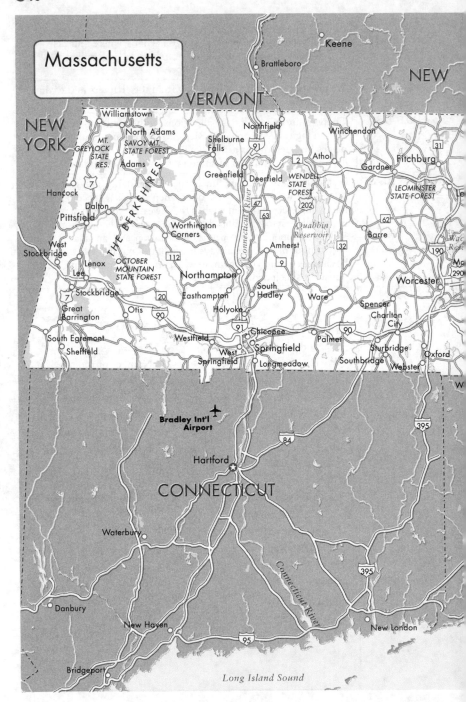

Massachusetts

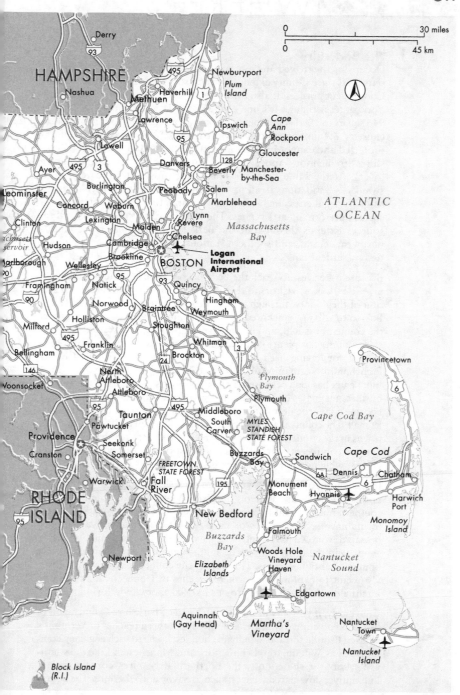

0   30 miles
0   45 km

Derry

93

HAMPSHIRE
Nashua   495   Newburyport
        Haverhill   Plum
Methuen   1   Island
                              Cape
Lawrence   Ipswich   Ann
        95   Rockport
Lowell   Gloucester
Ayer   495   3   128   Manchester-
    Burlington   Danvers Beverly by-the-Sea
Leominster   Peabody Salem
Concord   Woburn   Marblehead
Clinton Lexington   ATLANTIC
    Malden   Lynn   OCEAN
ichusetts Hudson Cambridge Revere
servoir   Brookline Chelsea Massachusetts
Marlborough Wellesley BOSTON   Bay
20   Logan
Framingham Natick   95   93 Quincy International
90   Airport
    Norwood   Braintree Hingham
Milford Holliston Stoughton Weymouth
    495   Franklin   Whitman
Bellingham   Brockton   3
146   North   24   Provincetown
        Attleboro
Woonsocket   Attleboro Plymouth
        95   Bay
    95   495 Middleboro Plymouth Cape Cod Bay
    Taunton   South   MYLES
Providence Pawtucket Carver STANDISH
Cranston Seekonk   STATE FOREST   Cape Cod
        Somerset   Sandwich
            FREETOWN Buzzards   6A Dennis   6 Chatham
            STATE FOREST Bay
    Warwick Fall   195   Monument   Hyannis   Harwich
RHODE   River   Beach   Port
ISLAND   New Bedford   Monomoy
95   Falmouth   Island
        Buzzards
Newport   Bay   Woods Hole Nantucket
        Elizabeth Vineyard Sound
        Islands   Haven
                    Edgartown
    Aquinnah   Nantucket
    (Gay Head) Martha's   Town
            Vineyard   Nantucket
Block Island   Island
(R.I.)

WHAT'S WHERE

① The Berkshires

Occupying the rugged and mountainous western reaches of Massachusetts, Berkshire County extends north to south from the Vermont to the Connecticut borders; it also forms the state's western border with New York state. Although it's one of the state's largest counties in area, at 946 square mi, Berkshire County is home to only about 133,000 of Massachusetts' 6.4 million residents. More than 25% of the county's land is protected and cannot be developed, which helps account for the Berkshires' tremendous appeal among outdoors enthusiasts and nature lovers. At the same time, it's one of the most sophisticated—even swanky—destinations in all of New England, abundant with antiques shops, art galleries, high-end country inns, fine restaurants, and respected performing arts venues. The wealth of natural and cultural resources extends throughout the Berkshires, although the county's northern, central, and southern sections each have distinct personalities and ardent fans.

Because it's easiest to reach the Berkshires via the Massachusetts Turnpike (I–90), most visitors to the region first lay eyes on the central section of the county, through which the interstate passes, en route from Boston to Albany. Anchored by both the most populous community in the county, Pittsfield, and its fanciest small town, Lenox, central Berkshire County has plenty going on and lots to see and do. Stockbridge is famous for having been home to Norman Rockwell, Daniel Chester French, and Norman Mailer and also contains the vaunted Red Lion Inn; Lenox has long been western Massachusetts' playground for wealthy business magnates and their families; and the old mill town of Lee has become a favorite destination of bargain hunters owing to its huge outlet mall. The county seat of Pittsfield lacks the high quaint factor of smaller towns in the county, but downtown has been experiencing a gradual renaissance in recent years; it's also just east of the county's only Shaker village, which is now a living-history museum.

In the southern Berkshires you'll find such sleepy but stunning picture-postcard villages as Monterey and New Marlborough. The Berkshires southern hub is Great Barrington, where a slew of New York City residents have second homes or have relocated permanently. The once prosaic downtown has recently blossomed with hip restaurants and trendy shops, and the nearby towns of South Egremont and Sheffield have a bounty of antiques stores. This part of the county is a good base if you also want to explore the northern reaches of Connecticut's charming Litchfield County, including towns like Salisbury and Norfolk.

Conversely, if you stay in the northern end of Berkshire County, you're in a good position to wander around the southern reaches of Vermont's alluring Bennington and Windham counties, home to such engaging communities as Wilmington, Bennington, and Manchester. Like the southern section of the county, the northern Berkshires contain mostly diminutive, slow-paced villages, such as Savoy and Cheshire. The largest town, North Adams, had been an industrial powerhouse until its fortunes waned following World War II; the opening in 1999 of Mass MoCA (Massachusetts Museum of Contemporary Arts) almost immediately transformed the town into an arts center, and its success has spilled over into its smaller neighbor, the town of Adams. The region's truest cultural and educational center is the handsome community of Williamstown, the home to prestigious Williams College and the venerable Berkshire Theatre Festival, which runs throughout July and August. You'll find great shopping and dining in the compact, walkable downtown.

② The Pioneer Valley

Less remote and more densely populated than the Berkshires, the Pioneer Valley offers tremendous variety as it extends southward from the Vermont to the Connecticut borders. At the northern end, the peaceful and hilly towns of Northfield, Greenfield, Deerfield, and Ashfield chug along at an easy pace, refreshingly free of major development and bearing a certain resemblance to the Berkshires, albeit with fewer fancy shops, restaurants, and inns. This is an easygoing, unpretentious section of the Pioneer Valley that's best-known for its superb opportunities for outdoors adventures.

Bearing little resemblance to the northern reaches of the valley, the southern Pioneer Valley comprises western Massachusetts' largest city, Springfield, along with such densely settled semi-industrial communities as Westfield, Chicopee, and Holyoke. A region that fell on hard times during the mid- to late 20th century, the southern Pioneer Valley has begun to show signs of a comeback in recent years. About 30 mi east lies Sturbridge, home to one of the state's leading attractions, Old Sturbridge Village. Finally, there's the central Pioneer Valley, arguably the most popular part of the region among visitors. Comprising the youthful but sophisticated college towns of Northampton, Amherst, and South Hadley, this generally liberal and diverse area has developed considerable cachet of late among academics, telecommuters, empty nesters, and young people seeking the cultural you'd expect of a big city balanced with the relaxed demeanor and bewitching natural scenery of rural New England.

GREAT ITINERARIES

Art & Antiques
4 or 5 days

GREAT BARRINGTON & SHEFFIELD 1 day. South County is the best place for antiques shopping in the Berkshires, with Great Barrington and nearby Sheffield leading the way; nearby Stockbridge and Egremont also contain a few notable shops, such as Geffner-Schatzky, which specializes in 19th- and 20th-century French pieces. Great Barrington's Bella Collections is a leader in fine jewelry, and multidealer showrooms such as Great Barrington Antiques Center and Jennifer Commons can keep bargain hunters busy for hours.

LENOX 1 day. In summer, sophisticated Lenox hosts the famous Tanglewood music festival; year-round, many of its lavish old inns—the former summer "cottages" of 19th-century barons of industry—contain priceless artwork in guest rooms and even common areas. The town also has some excellent art galleries and antiques shops. Also stop by the modernist Frelinghuysen Morris House Museum, whose collection of artwork includes originals by Picasso, Braque, and Gris. Pittsfield's Berkshire Museum contains a fine collection of paintings by members of the Hudson River School (including Frederic Church and Thomas Cole).

NORTH ADAMS 1 or 2 days. What had been a depressed industrial town until the mid-1990s, North Adams was transformed into the Berkshires' most provocative arts center with the opening in 1999 of the Massachusetts Museum of Contemporary Art (MASS MoCA), a stunning facility fashioned out of a Victorian textile factory (some of the old houses formerly inhabited by factory workers have been converted into the luxurious Porches Inn). The nearby college town of Williamstown is home to a similarly important repository of fine paintings, the Clark Art Institute, which contains works by Degas, Renoir, Monet, and many other masters.

STURBRIDGE 1 day. Although it's most famous as the home of Old Sturbridge Village, a wonderful living-history museum, Sturbridge is also just east of one of the nation's great antiques meccas, Brimfield. U.S. 20 is lined with antiques shops throughout this small town, which also hosts three absolutely mammoth antiques shows each year, one in mid-May, one in mid-July, and the last one over Labor Day weekend. On your way to Sturbridge from the Berkshires, be sure to stop in the largest city in the region, Springfield, to visit the Springfield Museums at the Quadrangle; two of the four excellent museums here focus on fine art.

Highlights of Western Massachusetts
6 or 7 days

SOUTH COUNTY 1 day. Spend the night at one of the great historic stagecoach taverns in the region, such as Stockbridge's Red Lion Inn, and visit this rural part of the Berkshires' most prominent attractions, such as Berkshire Botanical Gardens, Chesterwood, and the Norman Rockwell Museum. There's great shopping in Sheffield, Egremont, and Great Barrington, the latter community also being the area's hub of fine dining.

CENTRAL COUNTY 2 or 3 days. Try to spend at least two nights in the jewel of the Berkshires, Lenox, home to scads of luxurious inns and B&Bs (some of them fashioned out of grand summer "cottages" of yesteryear), and some of the leading restaurants in the county. In nearby Pittsfield, be sure to visit the Berkshire Museum and the former home of author Herman Melville, Arrowhead. Nearby Hancock is home to one of the most impressive living-history museums in the state, Hancock Shaker Village.

NORTH COUNTY 1 day. The following day, drive north to tony Williamstown, the dapper community that's home to prestigious Williams College and the access road to the area's highest peak, Mt. Greylock. The community's downtown has numerous fine shops and desirable eateries, and from here you're a short drive to North Adams, a former industrial town that's now home to the Massachusetts Museum of Contemporary Art (MoCA).

PIONEER VALLEY 2 days. From North County, drive east into the Pioneer Valley, where you then want to make your way south to the region's most dynamic communities, Northampton and Amherst. In both you'll find plenty of appealing lodging and dining options as well as the stately campuses of Smith College and Amherst College. In the town of Amherst, you can also tour the Emily Dickinson Homestead. The next day, venture still farther east to one of the nation's most famous historical attractions, Old Sturbridge Village, which merits a full day of exploration.

The Berkshires and Pioneer Valley are largely year-round destinations. Summer through the fall foliage period (roughly early October) marks the busiest time in the region, when hotel rates are high and restaurants and attractions can be crowded. The foliage season runs a week or two later in the Pioneer Valley, which is at a lower elevation, but by the third week or so in October, most of the leaves in western Massachusetts have fallen.

Although western Massachusetts lacks the ski facilities of Vermont and New Hampshire, the region does offer cross-country skiing, snowshoeing, and other winter sports, and visiting at this time can be a real joy, especially considering how many of the area's inns and hotels have rooms with fireplaces, whirlpool tubs, and huge beds with fluffy down comforters.

Climate
The hilly Berkshires experience the chilliest weather in Massachusetts, with relatively cool summers and downright frigid winters that see plenty of snow. Temperatures are lowest in the communities with the highest elevations. Down in the Pioneer Valley, which sits at a much lower elevation, temperatures average several degrees warmer than in the Berkshires. Spring in western Massachusetts is often windy and rainy; in many years it appears as if winter segues almost immediately into summer. One of the delights of the region, particularly at higher elevations, is the prevalence of cool summer nights.

Forecasts **Weather Channel** ⊕ www.weather.com

PITTSFIELD, MA

Jan.	32F	1C	May	70F	21C	Sept.	71F	22C
	13	− 11		43	6		48	9
Feb.	36F	2C	June	77F	25C	Oct.	60F	16C
	14	− 10		52	11		37	3
Mar.	45F	7C	July	81F	27C	Nov.	48F	9C
	23	− 5		57	14		30	− 1
Apr.	58F	14C	Aug.	79F	26C	Dec.	37F	3C
	34	1		56	13		19	− 7

SPRINGFIELD, MA

Jan.	35F	2C	May	72F	22C	Sept.	76F	24C
	17	− 8		48	6		52	11
Feb.	39F	4C	June	80F	27C	Oct.	65F	18C
	20	− 7		57	14		42	6
Mar.	48F	9C	July	85F	29C	Nov.	52F	11C
	28	− 2		62	17		34	1
Apr.	61F	16C	Aug.	83F	28C	Dec.	39F	4C
	38	3		61	16		22	− 6

ON THE CALENDAR

The region's top seasonal events are listed below. Reserve rooms far in advance for many of these events, especially those that fall during the busy summer and fall high seasons.

WINTER & SPRING

December

Over two days, you can partake of a variety of holiday festivities at the **Williamstown Holiday Walk**, which includes a juried crafts fair at Williams College, horse-drawn carriage rides, and Christmas caroling.

March

Over four days in the early part of the month, you can attend the **Springfield Boat Show**, the largest such event in western New England. It's held at Springfield's Eastern States Exposition and features a wealth of boats in all shapes, sizes, and price ranges. This is one of the many trade shows held here throughout the year, from bridal shows to golf expos.

The Pioneer Valley city of Holyoke throws the largest and most festive **St. Patrick's Day Parade** in western New England. The procession winds through downtown and celebrates the region's dynamic Irish heritage.

As the sap begins to trickle from maple trees throughout central Massachusetts, it's time to attend **Sturbridge Area Maple Days**, which includes some 10 days of sugaring demonstrations at sugar houses throughout the region. There are also special dinners, theater events, crafts shows, pancake breakfasts, and myriad opportunities to learn about this rich—and sweet—New England tradition.

April

One of the few events in the Berkshires during the region's infamous "mud season," the **Williamstown Jazz Festival** continues to grow in prestige each year. Concerts are held over four days at different venues on the campus of Williams College.

The **Eastern States Antique & Collectibles Show and Sale**, held at the Eastern States Exposition, shows wares from more than 300 dealers, making it the largest indoor antique show in New England.

May

Near Sturbridge Village, the **Brimfield Antiques and Collectibles Show**, known locally as the "Brimfield Flea Markets," has been going strong since the 1950s and draws as many as 4,500 dealers from across the country for its five-day shows. The first show takes place in May, the second in July, and the third in September. This is the foremost antiques show in the country.

Grab the maple syrup: each May Springfield hosts the **World's Largest Pancake Breakfast**, which is set along a massive continuous table that runs down Main Street for several blocks.

Toward the end of the month, head to Northampton's Three County Fair Ground for the **Springtime in Paradise: Arts Festival.** The three-day event includes great food provided by some of NoHo's most esteemed restaurants, live jazz, a sculpture garden and courtyard, and artwork displays by more than 200 artists and artisans. The event is held again each year in October.

SUMMER

June

The summer season gets off to a great start with the **Old Deerfield Summer Craft Fair,** which is held on the lawn of the Memorial Hall Museum, in Old Deerfield Village. The show draws some 200 juried exhibitors, who hail from some 20 states.

Learn everything you could ever want to know about lavender at Greenfield's **Annual Lavender Festival.** The event takes place at several private lavender gardens and farms in the upper Pioneer Valley and includes educational workshops, culinary demonstrations, and live music.

July

More than 200 artists present their handcrafted creations at the **Berkshires Arts Festival,** which runs over July 4th weekend and is held at Great Barrington's Butternut Basin. The juried event is held rain or shine, in tents, and includes great food and music. It's one of the best-attended arts fairs in the Northeast.

Few places throw a more rousing and patriotic Independence Day celebration than Old Sturbridge Village, host of the **Great American Picnic.** Over three days, thousands of visitors come to listen to music, watch marching and mustering, feast on a grand picnic, and watch 1830s-style baseball and other old-time games.

Drop by downtown Northampton for **SummerFest,** a three-day shopping-and-entertainment fair that includes a massive sidewalk sale all through town. It's a real bargain-hunter's delight.

One of the best agricultural fairs in the region, the **Hampden County 4-H Fair** takes place in late July at the Eastern States Exposition complex in Springfield. There's a horse show, youth fair, livestock exhibits, arts and crafts, a pet show, talent contest, and pedal-tractor pull.

August

At the Berkshire Botanical Garden, the **Stockbridge Summer Arts & Crafts Show** draws some 50 arts and crafts exhibitors. This juried show runs for two days during the latter part of the month.

A favorite event since the early '70s, the juried **Berkshire Crafts Fair** pulls in arts-and-crafts lovers from all over. The three-day event features nearly 100 exhibitors, offering both contemporary and traditional creations. It's held in Great Barrington at Monument Mountain Regional High School.

For three days in early August, hundreds of cyclists head to Lanesboro to partake of **Pedro's Mountain Bike Festival.** In addition to trail and road rides, there's a big mountain-bike expo, a marathon ride to raise money for lymphoma research, children's activities, and live music. Many participants camp out in the field adjacent to the festival.

Come hunting for great shopping bargains and treasures at the **Sheffield Antiques Show,** held for two days in mid-August at the Mount Everett Regional School. Dozens of dealers from throughout the Northeast attend this popular event.

FALL

September

Northampton's **Three County Fair** is a huge four-day gathering held over Labor Day Weekend at Three County Fairgrounds. This is the longest-running agricultural fair in the country, having begun in 1819. There's thoroughbred horse–racing, a games midway, two demolition derbies, a Polish festival with great food and polka dancing, and a Wild West Show. It's truly the mother of all "aggie" fairs.

October

Head to downtown Amherst in the early part of the month for the **Annual Apple Harvest & Crafts Festival.** Artisans specializing in folk art, furniture, jewelry, and wooden toys exhibit their wares, and there's also music, great food, and a children's fair.

North Adams is the site of the **Fall Foliage Festival,** a weeklong flurry of arts, outdoors, and cultural events that culminates with a parade. This gathering has been going strong since the 1940s and now includes such activities as children's fair, ziti supper, blessing of the animals, crafts show, and 5K road race.

The town of Lee celebrates its heritage with an annual **Founder's Weekend Celebration** early in October. Come and listen to live music, observe live-history reenactments, and watch a parade pass through downtown. There's a pancake breakfast to kick things off.

Usher in Autumn at the **Harvest Festival,** which takes place each year at the Berkshire Botanical Garden. This is one of the best-attended and longest-running events in the region, with amusement rides and games, live music, a crafts fair, a huge tag sale, pumpkin carving, and plenty of other family-friendly activities.

The ultimate gathering for anybody passionate about pumpkins, the **Great Pumpkinfest** takes place at South Deerfield's Yankee Candle store and features a display of some 24,000 carved pumpkins illuminated by 24,000—you guessed it—Yankee Candles. The first 500 guests to bring a carved pumpkin receive a free ticket to Fright-Fest at Six Flags New England amusement park (near Springfield).

November

Pittsfield's Berkshire Museum hosts the **Festival of Trees** from mid-November through the end of December. Some 200 trees are decorated creatively for the holiday season and displayed throughout the museum's galleries. The displays reflect decorative traditions from around the world, from Germany to Nicaragua to Russia. It's great fun to watch the magnificent displays at Springfield's **Bright Nights at Forest Park**, a holiday display that's up from the last week in November to the first week in January.

PLEASURES & PASTIMES

Outdoor Adventures With its rugged terrain and spectacular beauty, western Massachusetts is the perfect locale to satisfy your yearnings for an adrenalin rush. Generally, you don't have to risk life and limb to enjoy the great outdoors here, either. An abundance of lakes and rivers affords ample opportunities for canoeing, kayaking, paddleboating, and either "mild or wild" river rafting. Bicycling has been popular in these parts since Emily Vanderbilt pedaled her way to the Lenox post office in the 1890s. The Ashuwillticook Rail Trail provides a paved 10-foot trail along a former rail bed—it's great for strolling and jogging, too.

If you prefer horsepower, contact the many stables throughout the Berkshires and Pioneer Valley; these offer both scenic trail rides and instruction. Hiking is perhaps the favorite outdoorsy pastime, however; the Appalachian Trail runs the length of Berkshire County, and numerous preserves and parksprovide hundreds of miles of trails throughout western Massachusetts. For the ultimate vertical challenge, head up to the peak of Mt. Greylock, the highest mountain in the state. Other great ways to get a workout include llama trekking, cross-country skiing, hot-air ballooning, and snowshoeing. The possibilities are endless.

Spa Getaways The Berkshires enjoy a long and proud history as a center for the rejuvenation of the mind and body. It's said that Native Americans long ago began stopping at Sand Springs (now Williamstown) to drink from the healing waters. As early as 1776, Hancock was known for its curative Warm Springs spa. More recently, resorts and hotels throughout the region have added luxury spas, including Cranwell Resort and Wheatleigh. And a few establishments thrive as full-immersion spa destinations, such as Canyon Ranch and Kripalu Center for Yoga and Health. You'll also find an abundance of day spas that provide a variety of spa experiences.

Culture in the Country It's never a challenge satisfying your appetite for cultural enrichment in the rural western reaches of Massachusetts. In fact, the Berkshires and Pioneer Valley have as much in the way of fine visual and performing arts as most big cities, in part because the area is or has been home to countless writers, artists, and musicians, from Edith Wharton to Herman Melville to Norman Rockwell. The region abounds with excellent art museums and historic homes, not to mention dozens of commercial art galleries. The Pioneer Valley's several colleges have art museums and exhibitions plus theater, music, dance, and film events throughout the academic year. In summer the Berkshires come alive with such performing arts events as Tanglewood, Jacob's Pillow, Shakespeare and Company, the Williamstown Theatre Festival, and the Berkshire Theatre Festival.

Homes Away from Home
Stagecoach inns began to appear very early in Berkshires history. At the crossroads of Connecticut, New York, and Massachusetts, Berkshire County saw a constant flow of travelers, which spurred the opening of some of New England's earliest stagecoach inns. At the point where U.S. 7 meets Main Street in Stockbridge, Anna Bingham became one of the first women to own and operate such an establishment—today we know Bingham's hostelry as the famed Red Lion Inn. The Merrell Inn in Lee began providing succor to travelers at a time when it took 17 hours to get from Hartford to Albany—at that rate, a place to stop, eat, and rest the horses was necessary. These are just two of the many esteemed taverns in western Massachausetts that have been welcoming travelers for years.

Fall Foliage
People travel from as far as Europe and Asia to watch Mother Nature strut her stuff each October in western Massachusetts, one of the world's most scenic places to witness the annual rite of fall foliage. It's usually the very end of September or beginning of October that the Berkshire Hills and Pioneer Valley are set alight in a brilliant blaze of yellows, reds, coppers, purples, and oranges. Even the locals who witness this spectacle year-in and year-out seem never to grow jaded. They gape at the dramatic autumn displays just as the tourists do. It's quite easy to soak up these scenes each fall. Just motor along the region's major roads, such as U.S. 7 and Route 2, and you'll be treated to expansive views throughout the region. Some particularly alluring and less-crowded highways worth driving at this time include Route 116 west from Amherst to Adams, Route 23 west from Blandford to South Egremont, and Route 143 west from Williamsburg to Hinsdale.

Shopping
From Sturbridge west through the Pioneer Valley and up into the Berkshires, it's easy to find exceptional shopping in western Massachusetts, including some of the best antiques shops and farmers' markets in New England. Additionally, lively downtowns such as Northampton, Lenox, Amherst, Great Barrington, and Williamstown abound with distinctive independent shops—tony clothiers, funky crafts shops, prestigious art galleries, well-stocked bookstores, and one-of-a-kind gift emporia. Great Barrington, Lenox, and Sheffield claim among the best farmers' markets in the region; these are great places to find not just locally raised produce but cheeses, jams, baked goods, and fine prepared foods. Just west of Sturbridge, the town of Brimfield is one of New England's premier antiques-shopping hubs, with numerous stores and three massive regional antiques shows each year. But just about all the larger towns in these parts have a few good antiques shops, with Great Barrington among the best. Finally, outlet shoppers can search for bargains in Lee at Prime Outlets, which contains some 65 stores.

The Gilded Age Resorts

The Berkshires during the Gilded Age (from about the 1870s until the early 1910s) was one of the nation's great summer playgrounds among the princes of industry and barons of banking, and many of these spectacular homes still stand today, some of them having been converted into hotels, and others open as house museums. These mansions were, to some extent, built throughout the region, but the highest concentration of them is in Lenox, the "Queen of Gilded Age Resorts." The town's artsy, literary reputation helped to attract the rich and powerful. Although these houses were typically occupied for no more than a few weeks each year, they often contained as many as 75 to 100 rooms and were surrounded by acres of manicured gardens. In the ultimate act of verbal understatement, the owners of these behemoths called them "cottages." Among them, Elm Court, Blantyre, Cranwell, and Wheatleigh are now inns where you can stay the night or dine. The Mount, the former home of Edith Wharton who chronicled the Gilded Age; Naumkeag, the home of Joseph Hodges Choate, attorney to elite; and Chesterwood, home of extraordinary sculptor Daniel Chester French, can all be visited today as house museums.

FODOR'S CHOICE

The sights, restaurants, hotels, and other travel experiences on these pages are our editors' top picks—our Fodor's Choices. They're the best of their type in the area covered by the book—not to be missed and always worth your time. In the chapters that follow, you will find all the details.

LODGING

$$$$	**Canyon Ranch,** Lenox. This world-class spa resort provides a full slate of vigorous activities and beauty-and-body treatments, along with Colonial-style rooms
$$$$	**Deerfield Inn,** Deerfield. Period wallpaper decorates the rooms at this lovely lodging, which was built in 1884.
$$$–$$$$	**Devonfield Inn,** Lee. This grand, pale yellow-and-cream Federal house sits atop a birch-shaded hillside amid 29 acres of rolling meadows.
$$$–$$$$	**Gateways Inn,** Lenox. The rooms as the former summer cottage of Harley Proctor (as in Proctor and Gamble) come in a variety of configurations and styles, most with working fireplaces, detailed moldings, and plush carpeting.
$$–$$$$	**Inn at Stockbridge,** Stockbridge. Antiques and feather comforters are among the accents in the rooms of this 1906 Georgian Revival inn.
$$–$$$$	**Porches Inn,** North Adams. One of New England's quirkiest hotels, Porches strikes a perfect balance between high-tech and historic— rooms have a mix of retro '40s and '50s lamps and bungalow–style furnishings.
$–$$$$	**Red Lion Inn,** Stockbridge. An inn since 1773, the historic Red Lion has hosted presidents, senators, and celebrities inside its historic, antique enriched buildings.
$–$$	**Publick House Historic Inn,** Sturbridge. A blend of Colonial and modern enrich the three inns and the motel at this complex, which also houses big, bustling Publick House restaurant.

RESTAURANTS

$$–$$$$	**Shiro,** Great Barrington. Sushi and other Japanese fare top the menu in this warmly lit, art-filled space
$$$	**Mezze Bistro & Bar,** Williamstown. At this hot spot, the interior mixes urban chic and rustic charm with an equally creative menu.
$$–$$$	**Cedar Street,** Sturbridge. This eatery, housed in a modest but charming Victorian house, serves simple, heathful creations.
$$–$$$	**Hobson's Choice,** Williamstown. Resembling an early 19th-century tavern, this chef-owned restaurant is known for its expertly prepared seafood and steaks.

$$–$$$	**Rouge,** West Stockbridge. At this country French spot, owner–chef William Merelle intends that the food, wine, and surroundings should evoke pleasure.
$$–$$$	**Spigalina,** Lenox. Spigalina serves high-quality cuisine, reflecting the flavors of Spain, Southern France, Greece, and Morocco.
$$–$$$	**Spoleto,** Northampton. A Noho mainstay since the '80s, busy Spoleto delivers top-flight Italian fare and an excellent Sunday brunch.
$–$$	**Judie's,** Amherst. Stop here for the best bowl of French onion soup the town has to offer. The atmosphere is hip and artsy; a painting covers each tabletop.

HISTORIC TOWNS AND VILLAGES

Hancock Shaker Village, Hancock. Founded in the 1790s, the third Shaker community in America is now a living-history museum, with many period artifacts and buildings on display.

Historic Deerfield, Deerfield. With 52 buildings on 93 acres, this village provides a vivid glimpse into 18th- and 19th-century America.

Old Sturbridge Village, Sturbridge. One of the country's finest recreations of a Colonial-era village is modeled on an early-19th-century New England town, with more than 40 historic buildings that were moved here from other communities.

MUSEUMS

Magic Wings Butterfly Conservatory & Gardens, Deerfield. Stroll among thousands of fluttering butterflies, as well as an extensive three-season outdoor garden filled with plants that attract local species at this popular attraction.

Naismith Memorial Basketball Hall of Fame, Springfield. This 80,000-square-foot facility includes a soaring domed arena, dozens of high-tech interactive exhibits, and video footage and interviews with former players.

NATURE

Appalachian Trail, Cheshire. Berkshire County is the only county in the state of Massachusetts traversed by the 2,100-mi Appalachian Trail, which winds from Georgia to Maine. The spot where the Ashuwillticook and Appalachian trails cross is Cheshire makes a perfect place for a day hike filled with lovely views.

Mohawk Trail, Florida. There is no more beautiful stretch of highway in Berkshire County than Route 2 as it traverses the town of Florida.

Mt. Greylock State Reservation, Adams. At 3,491 feet, Mt. Greylock is the highest peak in Massachusetts.

STATELY HOMES

Chesterwood, Stockbridge. At summer home of the sculptor Daniel Chester French (1850–1931), you can view the casts and models French used to create the Lincoln Memorial and stroll the beautifully landscaped 122-acre grounds.

The Mount, Lenox. The house and grounds of Novelist Edith Wharton's home were designed by Wharton herself, who is considered by many to have set the standard for 20th-century interior decoration.

WHERE ART COMES FIRST

Clark Art Institute, Williamstown. One of the nation's notable small art museums, the Clark has more than 30 paintings by Renoir as well as canvases by Monet and Pissarro.

Springfield Museums at the Quadrangle, Springfield. Four museums make up this complex including the Museum of Fine Arts, which exhibits paintings by Gauguin, Monet, Renoir, and Degas as well as contemporary works by Georgia O'Keeffe, Frank Stella, and George Bellows.

Tanglewood, Lenox. The 200-acre summer home of the Boston Symphony Orchestra attracts thousands every year to concerts by world-famous performers from mid-June to Labor Day.

Williams College Museum of Art, Williamstown. Comprising one of the finest college art museums in the country, the collection contains approximately 12,000 pieces.

Williamstown Theatre Festival, Williamstown. From June to August, the long-running production presents well-known theatrical works with famous performers.

Massachusetts Museum of Contemporary Art (MASS MoCA), North Adams. Six factory buildings have been transformed into more than 250,000 square feet of galleries, studios, performance venues, cafés, and shops.

SMART TRAVEL TIPS

Finding out about your destination before you leave home means you won't squander time organizing everyday minutiae once you've arrived. You'll be more streetwise when you hit the ground as well, better prepared to explore the aspects of the Berkshires and the Pioneer Valley that drew you here in the first place. The organizations in this section can provide information to supplement this guide; contact them for up-to-the-minute details. Happy landings!

AIR TRAVEL TO & FROM THE BERKSHIRES & PIONEER VALLEY

Although there are no major airports in this part of Massachusetts, the Berkshires and the Pioneer Valley are within a two- to three-hour drive of numerous major airports, the closest being Bradley International Airport (in Windsor Locks, CT, about a 30-minute drive south of Springfield) and Albany International Airport (in Albany, NY, an hour northwest of Pittsfield). However, it's also worth checking fares into Logan (in Boston, a 90-minute drive east of Springfield), which is one of the country's major airports, with directs flights from all over the United States, Canada, and Europe.

International fares into Boston are among the least expensive in the country. For domestic flights, compare fares and flying times into the aforementioned three airports that serve the region. If you're not spending time in Boston, it's best to avoid the often chaotically busy facilities at Logan, where car-rental rates also tend to be a bit higher and traffic in and out of Boston congested. Your best strategy is to shop around and be sure to factor in differences in local car-rental rates and the number of connections required to reach different airports from wherever you're flying.

BOOKING

When you book, look for nonstop flights and remember that "direct" flights stop at least once. Try to avoid connecting flights, which require a change of plane. Two airlines may operate a connecting flight jointly, so ask whether your airline operates every segment of the trip; you may find that the carrier you prefer flies you only part of the way. To find more booking tips and to check prices and make online flight reservations, log on to www.fodors.com.

CARRIERS

There's an abundance of large and small airlines with flights to and from Boston; additionally, the discount carrier Southwest Airlines flies to both Albany International and Bradley International, as does the new (in 2004) low-cost carrier Independence Air, which flies direct from Dulles, outside Washington, D.C. Smaller or discount airlines serving Boston include AirTran, ATA, Cape Air, Independence Air, jetBlue, and Midwest.

⁊ Major Airlines Domestic carriers: **America West** ☎ 800/235-9292 ⊕ www.americawest.com. **American** ☎ 800/433-7300 ⊕ www.americanairlines.com. **Continental** ☎ 800/525-0280 ⊕ www.continental.com. **Delta** ☎ 800/221-1212 ⊕ www.delta.com. **Northwest/KLM** ☎ 800/225-2525 ⊕ www.nwa.com. **United** ☎ 800/241-6522 ⊕ www.united.com. **US Airways** ☎ 800/428-4322 ⊕ www.usairways.com.

⁊ International Carriers Aer Lingus ☎ 800/474-7424 ⊕ www.aerlingus.ie. **Air Canada** ☎ 888/247-2262 ⊕ www.aircanada.ca. **Air France** ☎ 800/237-2747 ⊕ www.airfrance.com. **Alitalia Airlines** ☎ 800/223-5730 ⊕ www.alitalia.com. **British Airways** ☎ 800/247-9297, 0870/85-098-50 in U.K. ⊕ www.ba.com. **Lufthansa** ☎ 800/645-3880 ⊕ www.lufthansa.com. **Virgin Atlantic Airways** ☎ 800/862-8621, 01293/450-150 in U.K. ⊕ www.virgin-atlantic.com.

⁊ Smaller Airlines AirTran Airways ☎ 800/247-8726 ⊕ www.airtran.com. **ATA Airlines** ☎ 800/225-2995 ⊕ www.ata.com. **Cape Air** ☎ 800/352-0714 ⊕ www.flycapeair.com. **Independence Air** ☎ 800/359-3594 ⊕ www.flyi.com. **jetBlue** ☎ 800/538-2583 ⊕ www.jetblue.com. **Midwest** ☎ 800/452-2022 ⊕ www.midwestairlines.com. **Southwest Airlines** ☎ 800/435-9792 ⊕ www.southwest.com.

CHECK-IN & BOARDING

Always **find out your carrier's check-in policy.** Plan to arrive at the airport about two hours before your scheduled departure time for domestic flights and 2½ to 3 hours before international flights. You may need to arrive earlier if you're flying from one of the busier airports or during peak air-traffic times. If you're flying from Albany and Bradley, which are smaller and more manageable than Logan International, you may be able to get away with arriving a bit later (60 to 90 minutes ahead of departure). To avoid delays at airport-security checkpoints, try not to wear any metal. Jewelry, belt and other buckles, steel-toe shoes, barrettes, and underwire bras are among the items that can set off detectors.

Assuming that not everyone with a ticket will show up, airlines routinely overbook planes. When everyone does, airlines ask for volunteers to give up their seats. In return, these volunteers usually get a several-hundred-dollar flight voucher, which can be used toward the purchase of another ticket, and are rebooked on the next flight out. If there are not enough volunteers, the airline must choose who will be denied boarding. The first to get bumped are passengers who checked in late and those flying on discounted tickets, so get to the gate and check in as early as possible, especially during peak periods.

Always **bring a government-issued photo ID** to the airport; even when it's not required, a passport is best.

CUTTING COSTS

The least expensive airfares to this part of the country are priced for round-trip travel and must usually be purchased in advance. Airlines generally allow you to change your return date for a fee; most low-fare tickets, however, are nonrefundable. It's smart to call a number of airlines and check the Internet; when you are quoted a good price, book it on the spot—the same fare may not be available the next day, or even the next hour. Always check different routings and look into using alternate airports. Also, price off-peak flights, which may be significantly less expensive than others. Travel agents, especially low-fare specialists (⇨ Discounts & Deals), are helpful.

Consolidators are another good source. They buy tickets for scheduled flights at reduced rates from the airlines, then sell them at prices that beat the best fare available directly from the airlines. (Many also offer reduced car-rental and hotel rates.) Sometimes you can even get your money back if you need to return the ticket. Carefully read the fine print detailing penalties for changes and cancellations, purchase the ticket with a credit card, and confirm your consolidator reservation with the airline.

When you fly as a courier, you trade your checked-luggage space for a ticket deeply subsidized by a courier service. There are restrictions on when you can book and how long you can stay. Some courier companies list with membership organizations, such as the Air Courier Association and the International Association of Air Travel Couriers; these require you to become a member before you can book a flight.

🛪 Consolidators AirlineConsolidator.com
☎ 888/468-5385 ⊕ www.airlineconsolidator.com, for international tickets. **Best Fares** ☎ 800/880–1234 or 800/576-8255 ⊕ www.bestfares.com; $59.90 annual membership. **Cheap Tickets** ☎ 800/377-1000 or 800/652-4327 ⊕ www.cheaptickets.com. **Expedia** ☎ 800/397-3342 or 404/728-8787 ⊕ www.expedia.com. **Hotwire** ☎ 866/468-9473 or 920/330-9418 ⊕ www.hotwire.com. **Now Voyager Travel** ✉ 45 W. 21st St., Suite 5A, New York, NY 10010 ☎ 212/459-1616 🖷 212/243-2711 ⊕ www.nowvoyagertravel.com. **Onetravel.com** ⊕ www.onetravel.com. **Orbitz** ☎ 888/656-4546 ⊕ www.orbitz.com. **Priceline.com** ⊕ www.priceline.com. **Travelocity** ☎ 888/709-5983, 877/282-2925 in Canada, 0870/876-3876 in U.K. ⊕ www.travelocity.com.
🛪 Courier Resources Air Courier Association/Cheaptrips.com ☎ 800/280-5973 or 800/282-1202 ⊕ www.aircourier.org or www.cheaptrips.com; $34 annual membership. **International Association of Air Travel Couriers** ☎ 308/632-3273 ⊕ www.courier.org; $45 annual membership. **Now Voyager Travel** ✉ 45 W. 21st St., Suite 5A, New York, NY 10010 ☎ 212/459-1616 🖷 212/243-2711 ⊕ www.nowvoyagertravel.com.

ENJOYING THE FLIGHT

State your seat preference when purchasing your ticket, and then repeat it when you confirm and when you check in. For more legroom, you can request one of the few emergency-aisle seats at check-in, if you're capable of moving obstacles comparable in weight to an airplane exit door (usually between 35 pounds and 60 pounds)—a Federal Aviation Administration requirement of passengers in these seats. Seats behind a bulkhead also offer more legroom, but they don't have under-seat storage. Don't sit in the row in front of the emergency aisle or in front of a bulkhead, where seats may not recline.

Ask the airline whether a snack or meal is served on the flight. If you have dietary concerns, request special meals when booking. These can be vegetarian, low-cholesterol, or kosher, for example. It's a good idea to pack some healthful snacks and a small (plastic) bottle of water in your carry-on bag. On long flights, try to maintain a normal routine, to help fight jet lag. At night, get some sleep. By day, eat light meals, drink water (not alcohol), and **move around the cabin** to stretch your legs. For additional jet-lag tips consult *Fodor's FYI: Travel Fit & Healthy* (available at bookstores everywhere).

Smoking policies vary from carrier to carrier. Most airlines prohibit smoking on all of their flights; others allow smoking only on certain routes or certain departures. Ask your carrier about its policy.

FLYING TIMES

Some sample flying times to Boston are: from Chicago (2½ hours), London (6½ hours), and Los Angeles (6 hours). Times from U.S. destinations are similar, if slightly shorter, to Albany and Hartford, assuming you can find direct flights.

HOW TO COMPLAIN

If your baggage goes astray or your flight goes awry, complain right away. Most carriers require that you **file a claim immediately.** The Aviation Consumer Protection Division of the Department of Transportation publishes *Fly-Rights,* which discusses airlines and consumer issues and is available online. You can also find articles and information on mytravelrights.com, the Web site of the nonprofit Consumer Travel Rights Center.

🔀 Airline Complaints Aviation Consumer Protection Division ✉ U.S. Department of Transportation, Office of Aviation Enforcement and Proceedings, C-75, Room 4107, 400 7th St. SW, Washington, DC 20590 ☎ 202/366-2220 ⊕ airconsumer.ost.dot.gov. **Federal Aviation Administration Consumer Hotline** ✉ For inquiries: FAA, 800 Independence Ave. SW, Washington, DC 20591 ☎ 800/322-7873 ⊕ www.faa.gov.

RECONFIRMING

Check the status of your flight before you leave for the airport. You can do this on your carrier's Web site, by linking to a flight-status checker (many Web booking services offer these), or by calling your carrier or travel agent. Always confirm international flights at least 72 hours ahead of the scheduled departure time.

AIRPORTS

The major air gateways to Berkshires and the Pioneer Valley are Hartford/Springfield's Bradley International (BDL), Albany International (ALB), and Boston's Logan International (BOS). Albany is closest to the Berkshires, and Hartford/Springfield and Boston are closer to the Pioneer Valley, but any of these three airports is relatively convenient to the entire region.

For the most part, fares are quite competitive among all three airports. However, discount airlines—such as Southwest, jet-Blue, and Independence Air—spur competition among other airlines serving similar routes. For example, it's often cheaper to fly to Bradley or Albany from other cities served by Southwest Airlines (such as Kansas City or Albuquerque) than to Boston. And it can be cheaper to fly into Boston from other cities served by jetBlue, ATA, and so on.

BIKE TRAVEL

BIKES IN FLIGHT

Most airlines accommodate bikes as luggage, provided they are dismantled and boxed; check with individual airlines about packing requirements. Some airlines sell bike boxes, which are often free at bike shops, for about $20 (bike bags can be considerably more expensive). International travelers often can substitute a bike

for a piece of checked luggage at no charge; otherwise, the cost is about $100. Most U.S. and Canadian airlines charge $40–$80 each way.

BUSINESS HOURS

Hours differ little in the western Massachusetts from other parts of the United States. Within the state, shops and other businesses tend to keep slightly later hours in Northampton, Pittsfield, Springfield, and other larger communities than in rural parts of the region.

MUSEUMS & SIGHTS

Most major museums and attractions are open daily or six days a week (with Monday being the most likely day of closing). Some prominent museums stay open late one or two nights a week, usually Tuesday, Thursday, or Friday; hours are often shorter on Saturday and especially Sunday. The Berkshires and the Pioneer Valley also have quite a few smaller museums—historical societies, small art galleries, highly specialized collections—that open only a few days a week in summer, and sometimes only by appointment in winter or shoulder seasons.

SHOPS

Banks are usually open weekdays from 9 to 3 and some Saturday mornings; the post office is open from 8 to 5 weekdays and often on Saturday morning. Shops in urban and suburban areas, particularly in indoor and strip malls, typically open at 9 or 10 daily and stay open until anywhere from 6 PM to 10 PM on weekdays and Saturday, and until 5 or 6 on Sunday. Hours vary greatly, so call ahead when in doubt.

On major highways and in densely populated areas you'll usually find at least one or two supermarkets, pharmacies, and gas stations open 24 hours, and in a few big cities and also some college towns you'll find a smattering of all-night fast-food restaurants, diners, and coffeehouses.

BUS TRAVEL

Regional bus service is relatively plentiful throughout western Massachusetts. It can be a handy and somewhat affordable means of getting around, as buses travel many routes that trains do not; however, this style of travel prevents the sort of spontaneity and freedom to explore than what you're afforded if traveling by car. It's a good idea to compare travel times and costs between bus and train routes to and within the Berkshires and Pioneer Valley; in many cases, it's faster to take the train.

Bonanza Bus Lines connects Sheffield, Great Barrington, Stockbridge, Lenox, Lee, Pittsfield, Brodie Mountain, and Williamstown with Albany, New York City, and Providence. Peter Pan Bus Lines serves Lee, Lenox, and Pittsfield from Boston, Hartford, and Albany. Berkshire Regional Transit Authority provides transportation throughout the Berkshires.

Reservations are not required on buses serving the region, but they're a good idea for just about any bus trip.

Within the Pioneer Valley, it's possible to use municipal bus service (on the Pioneer Valley Transit Authority) to get around—service is especially convenient and pervasive at the southern end of the valley. Still, relatively few nonlocals use municipal buses extensively, as bus schedules and routes take a bit of learning (⇨ Pioneer Valley A to Z).

CUTTING COSTS
Greyhound offers the **North America Discovery Pass**, which allows unlimited travel in the United States (and certain parts of Canada and Mexico) within any 7-, 10-, 15-, 21-, 30-, 45-, or 60-day period ($209–$569, depending on length of the pass). You can also buy similar passes covering different areas (America and Canada, the West Coast of North America, the East Coast of North America, Canada exclusively). International travelers can purchase international versions of these same passes, which offer a greater variety of travel periods and cost considerably less. Greyhound also has senior-citizen, military, children's, and student discounts, which apply to individual fares and to the Discovery Pass.

FARES & SCHEDULES
Approximate standard sample one-way fares (based on 7-day advance purchase—

prices can be 10% to 50% higher otherwise), times, and routes on major carriers to Springfield are: from Boston, 2½ hours, $30; from New York City, 4–5 hours, $30; from Philadelphia, 7–9 hours, $40; from Montréal, 8–10 hours, $40; from Toronto, 12–15 hours, $85; and from Cleveland, 14–16 hours, $60. (Note that times vary greatly depending on the number of stops.)

Approximate standard sample one-way fares (based on 7-day advance purchase—prices can be 10% to 50% higher otherwise), times, and routes on major carriers to Pittsfield are: from Boston, 3–4 hours, $38; from New York City, 4–5 hours, $30; from Philadelphia, 7–9 hours, $30; from Montréal, 7 hours, $40; from Toronto, 11–13 hours, $60; and from Cleveland, 12–13 hours, $60.

🚌 **Bus Information** Berkshire Regional Transit Authority ☎ 800/292-2782. **Bonanza Bus Lines** ☎ 800/556-3815 ⊕ www.bonanzabus.com. **Greyhound Lines Inc.** ☎ 800/231-2222 ⊕ www.greyhound.com. **Peter Pan Bus Lines** ☎ 413/781-2900 or 800/343-9999 ⊕ www.peterpanbus.com.

CAR RENTAL
Because a car is the most practical way to get around the region, it's wise to rent one if you're not bringing your own. The three major airports serving the region—Albany, Logan, and Bradley International—all have myriad on-site car-rental agencies. If you're traveling to the area by bus or train, you might consider renting a car once you arrive. The following communities have branches of Enterprise car-rental agency: Amherst, Great Barrington, Greenfield, North Adams, Northampton, Pittsfield, Springfield, and West Springfield. Springfield is also served by Budget.

🚌 **Major Agencies Alamo** ☎ 800/327-9633 ⊕ www.alamo.com. **Avis** ☎ 800/331-1212, 800/879-2847 or 800/272-5871 in Canada, 0870/606-0100 in U.K., 02/9353-9000 in Australia, 09/526-2847 in New Zealand ⊕ www.avis.com. **Budget** ☎ 800/527-0700, 0870/156-5656 in U.K. ⊕ www.budget.com. **Dollar** ☎ 800/800-4000, 0800/085-4578 in U.K. ⊕ www.dollar.com. **Enterprise** ☎ 800/261-7331 ⊕ www.enterprise.com. **Hertz** ☎ 800/654-3131, 800/263-0600 in Canada, 0870/844-8844 in U.K., 02/9669-2444 in Australia, 09/256-8690 in New Zealand ⊕ www.hertz.com. **Na-**

tional Car Rental ☎ 800/227-7368, 0870/600-6666 in the U.K. ⊕ www.nationalcar.com.

CUTTING COSTS

Rates at the area's major airports begin at around $35 a day and $150 a week for an economy car with air-conditioning, automatic transmission, and unlimited mileage. These rates do not include state tax on car rentals, which varies depending on the airport but generally runs 12% to 15%. The various Enterprise agencies around western Massachusetts charge similar rates.

For a good deal, book through a travel agent who will shop around. Also, price local car-rental companies—whose prices may be lower still, although their service and maintenance may not be as good as those of major rental agencies—and research rates on the Internet. Consolidators that specialize in air travel can offer good rates on cars as well (⇨ Air Travel). Remember to ask about required deposits, cancellation penalties, and drop-off charges if you're planning to pick up the car in one city and leave it in another. If you're traveling during a holiday period, also make sure that a confirmed reservation guarantees you a car.

INSURANCE

When driving a rented car you are generally responsible for any damage to or loss of the vehicle. You also may be liable for any property damage or personal injury that you may cause while driving. Before you rent, see what coverage you already have under the terms of your personal auto-insurance policy and credit cards.

For about $9 to $25 a day, rental companies sell protection, known as a collision- or loss-damage waiver (CDW or LDW), which eliminates your liability for damage to the car; it's always optional and should never be automatically added to your bill. In Massachusetts the car-rental agency's insurance is primary; therefore, the company must pay for damage to third parties up to a preset legal limit, beyond which your own liability insurance kicks in. However, **make sure you have enough coverage to pay for the car.** If you do not have auto insurance or an umbrella policy that covers damage to third parties, purchasing liability insurance and a CDW or LDW is highly recommended.

REQUIREMENTS & RESTRICTIONS

Most agencies won't rent to you if you're under the age of 21. When picking up a car, non-U.S. residents will need a reservation voucher for any prepaid reservations that were made in the traveler's home country, a passport, a driver's license, and a travel policy that covers each driver.

SURCHARGES

Before you pick up a car in one city and leave it in another, ask about drop-off charges or one-way service fees, which can be substantial. Also inquire about early-return policies; some rental agencies charge extra if you return the car before the time specified in your contract while others give you a refund for the days not used. To avoid a hefty refueling fee, fill the tank just before you turn in the car, but be aware that gas stations near the rental outlet may overcharge. It's almost never a deal to buy the tank of gas that's in the car when you rent it; the understanding is that you'll return it empty, but some fuel usually remains. Surcharges may apply if you're under 25 or if you take the car outside the area approved by the rental agency. You'll pay extra for child seats (about $8 a day), which are compulsory for children under five, and usually for additional drivers (up to $25 a day, depending on location).

CAR TRAVEL

Western Massachusetts is best explored by car. The region is largely without heavy traffic and congestion, and parking is consistently easy to find, even in larger communities, such as Springfield and Pittsfield. Some parts of the area can be reached fairly easily using public transportation, and can be explored on foot, using bicycles, or using local transit and cabs once you arrive. These communities include Great Barrington, Lenox, Pittsfield, Williamstown, and North Adams in the Berkshires, and Springfield, Northampton, Amherst, and Greenfield in the Pioneer Valley. In these areas, it's great to have a car for maximum flexibility and freedom, but if you're not a fan of car travel, you can still enjoy your visit.

The Massachusetts Turnpike (I–90) connects Boston with Lee and Stockbridge and continues into New York, where it becomes the New York State Thruway. To reach the Berkshires from New York City take either I–87 or the Taconic State Parkway. The main north–south road within the Berkshires is U.S. 7. Route 23 crosses south county east–west. Route 2 runs from the northern Berkshires to Greenfield at the head of the Pioneer Valley and continues across Massachusetts into Boston. The scenic section of Route 2 known as the Mohawk Trail runs from Williamstown to Orange.

Morning and evening rush-hour traffic isn't usually much of a problem in western Massachusetts, although you may encounter some congested driving up and down I–91 in the lower Pioneer Valley. More problematic is I–91 and I–90 (Mass Pike) traffic on Friday afternoons and evenings and again on Sunday, when many visitors to western Massachusetts and elsewhere in New England pass through the region.

Western Massachusetts does offer quite a few scenic drives, even along certain spans of interstate (notably I–91, once you're north of Northampton, and I–90 west of Springfield to the New York state border). More breathtaking are the many miles of U.S. and state highways that pass through dense forests, by verdant open farmland, and through pastoral historic hamlets. When time permits, it's worth venturing off the interstate system and beholding some of the delightful scenery fringing the state's country roads. Favorite routes include Route 9, from Northampton west to the New York border; Route 2, from Greenfield west to the New York border; U.S. 7, north from the Connecticut to the Vermont borders; and Route 8, north from the Connecticut to the Vermont borders.

Here are some common distances and approximate travel times between the Berkshires and Pioneer Valley and several popular destinations: Boston is 110 mi and 2 hours; Providence is 125 mi and 2½ hours; New York City is about 150 mi and 3 hours; Philadelphia is 250 mi and 4½ hours; Montréal is about 270 mi and 5 hours; Washington, D.C. is 385 mi and 6½ hours; Toronto is 430 mi and 8 hours; Pittsburgh is 480 mi and 8½ hours; and Cleveland is 500 mi and 9 hours.

PARKING

In most of western Massachusetts, parking is not a serious problem—this is true even for larger cities, such as Springfield, which has a number of parking garages. Amherst, Northampton, Lenox, and some other communities in the region have tight parking in their downtowns during busy weekends, but it's nearly always possible to find a space if you're persistent. Just pack plenty of spare change, as many communities in the area have meter parking.

RULES OF THE ROAD

On city streets the speed limit is 30 mph unless otherwise posted; on rural roads, the speed limit ranges from 40 to 50 mph unless otherwise posted. Interstate speeds range from 50 to 65 mph, depending on congestion. Throughout the region, you're permitted to make a right on red except where posted. Be alert for one-way streets in some of the more congested communities, such as Springfield and Northampton.

State law requires that front-seat passengers wear seat belts at all times. Children under 16 must wear seat belts in both the front and back seats. Always **strap children under age five into approved child-safety seats.**

CHILDREN IN THE BERKSHIRES & PIONEER VALLEY

Most of the region is ideal for travel with kids. It's an enjoyable part of the country for family road trips, and it's also relatively affordable, apart from some of the fancier resort towns in the Berkshires. Throughout most of the Berkshires and the Pioneer Valley, however, you'll have no problem finding comparatively inexpensive kid-friendly hotels and family-style restaurants. The Pioneer Valley and Sturbridge have some of the top kid-oriented attractions in the state. Just keep in mind that a number of fine, antiques-filled

B&Bs and inns punctuate the landscape, and these places are less suitable for kids—many flat-out refuse to accommodate children. Also, some of the quieter and more rural parts of the region—although exuding history—lack kid-oriented attractions.

Favorite destinations for family vacations in western Massachusetts include Springfield, which has several youthful attractions including Six Flags, the Basketball Hall of Fame, the Springfield Science Museum; Sturbridge Village; Holyoke, which has a children's museum; Deerfield, with the Yankee Candle Company and Deerfield Village; Old Greenfield Village in Greenfield; and the Railway and Berkshire museums in Pittsfield.

If you are renting a car, don't forget to arrange for a car seat when you reserve. For general advice about traveling with children, consult *Fodor's FYI: Travel with Your Baby* (available in bookstores everywhere).

FLYING

If your children are two or older, ask about children's airfares. As a general rule, infants under two not occupying a seat fly at greatly reduced fares or even for free. But if you want to guarantee a seat for an infant, you have to pay full fare. Consider flying during off-peak days and times; most airlines will grant an infant a seat without a ticket if there are available seats.

Experts agree that it's a good idea to use safety seats aloft for children weighing less than 40 pounds. Airlines set their own policies: if you use a safety seat, U.S. carriers usually require that the child be ticketed, even if he or she is young enough to ride free, because the seats must be strapped into regular seats. And even if you pay the full adult fare for the seat, it may be worth it, especially on longer trips. Do **check your airline's policy about using safety seats during takeoff and landing.** Safety seats are not allowed everywhere in the plane, so get your seat assignments as early as possible.

When reserving, request children's meals or a freestanding bassinet (not available at all airlines) if you need them. But note that bulkhead seats, where you must sit to use the bassinet, may lack an overhead bin or storage space on the floor.

LODGING

Most hotels in western Massachusetts allow children under a certain age to stay in their parents' room at no extra charge, but others charge for them as extra adults; be sure to find out the cutoff age for children's discounts.

SIGHTS & ATTRACTIONS

Places that are especially appealing to children are indicated by a rubber-duckie icon (🐤) in the margin.

CONSUMER PROTECTION

Whether you're shopping for gifts or purchasing travel services, **pay with a major credit card** whenever possible, so you can cancel payment or get reimbursed if there's a problem (and you can provide documentation). If you're doing business with a particular company for the first time, contact your local Better Business Bureau and the attorney general's offices in your state and (for U.S. businesses) the company's home state as well. Have any complaints been filed? Finally, if you're buying a package or tour, always consider travel insurance that includes default coverage (⇨ Insurance).

🌐 BBBs **Council of Better Business Bureaus** ✉ 4200 Wilson Blvd., Suite 800, Arlington, VA 22203 ☎ 703/276-0100 🖨 703/525-8277 ⊕ www.bbb.org.

DISABILITIES & ACCESSIBILITY

Although rural and historic in many places, the Berkshires and Pioneer Valley have come a long way in making life easier for people with disabilities. The majority of businesses in the area are up to ADA standards (except some historic inns and restaurants), and you'll find plenty of people who are more than happy to help you get around.

LODGING

Most hotels in western Massachusetts comply with the Americans with Disabilities Act. Despite the Americans with Disabilities Act, the definition of accessibility seems to differ from hotel to hotel. Some properties may be accessible by ADA standards for people with mobility problems but not for people with hearing or vision impairments, for example.

If you have mobility problems, ask for the lowest floor on which accessible services are offered. If you have a hearing impairment, check whether the hotel has devices to alert you visually to the ring of the telephone, a knock at the door, and a fire/emergency alarm. Some hotels provide these devices without charge. Discuss your needs with hotel personnel if this equipment isn't available, so that a staff member can personally alert you in the event of an emergency.

If you're bringing a guide dog, get authorization ahead of time and write down the name of the person with whom you spoke.

RESERVATIONS
When discussing accessibility with an operator or reservations agent, ask hard questions. Are there any stairs, inside or out? Are there grab bars next to the toilet and in the shower/tub? How wide is the doorway to the room? To the bathroom? For the most extensive facilities meeting the latest legal specifications, opt for newer accommodations. If you reserve through a toll-free number, consider also calling the hotel's local number to confirm the information from the central reservations office. Get confirmation in writing when you can.

SIGHTS & ATTRACTIONS
Most public facilities in western Massachusetts, whether museums, parks, or theaters, are wheelchair-accessible. Some attractions have tours or programs for people with mobility, sight, or hearing impairments.

TRANSPORTATION
Throughout the region, drivers with disabilities may use windshield cards from their own state or Canadian province to park in designated handicapped spaces.
🄵 Complaints Aviation Consumer Protection Division (⇨ Air Travel) for airline-related problems. Departmental Office of Civil Rights ✉ For general inquiries, U.S. Department of Transportation, S-30, 400 7th St. SW, Room 10215, Washington, DC 20590

☎ 202/366-4648 🖷 202/366-9371 ⊕ www.dot. gov/ost/docr/index.htm. Disability Rights Section ✉ NYAV, U.S. Department of Justice, Civil Rights Division, 950 Pennsylvania Ave. NW, Washington, DC 20530 🖷 ADA information line 202/514-0301, 800/ 514-0301, 202/514-0383 TTY, 800/514-0383 TTY ⊕ www.ada.gov. U.S. Department of Transportation Hotline 🖷 For disability-related air-travel problems, 800/778-4838 or 800/455-9880 TTY.

TRAVEL AGENCIES
In the United States, the Americans with Disabilities Act requires that travel firms serve the needs of all travelers. Some agencies specialize in working with people with disabilities.
🄵 Travelers with Mobility Problems Access Adventures/B. Roberts Travel ✉ 206 Chestnut Ridge Rd., Scottsville, NY 14624 ☎ 585/889-9096 ⊕ www.brobertstravel.com ✎ dltravel@prodigy. net, run by a former physical-rehabilitation counselor. Accessible Vans of America ✉ 9 Spielman Rd., Fairfield, NJ 07004 ☎ 877/282-8267, 888/282-8267, 973/808-9709 reservations 🖷 973/808-9713 ⊕ www.accessiblevans.com. CareVacations ✉ No. 5, 5110-50 Ave., Leduc, Alberta, Canada, T9E 6V4 ☎ 780/986-6404 or 877/478-7827 🖷 780/986-8332 ⊕ www.carevacations.com, for group tours and cruise vacations. Flying Wheels Travel ✉ 143 W. Bridge St., Box 382, Owatonna, MN 55060 ☎ 507/451-5005 🖷 507/451-1685 ⊕ www. flyingwheelstravel.com.
🄵 Travelers with Developmental Disabilities Sprout ✉ 893 Amsterdam Ave., New York, NY 10025 ☎ 212/222-9575 or 888/222-9575 🖷 212/222-9768 ⊕ www.gosprout.org.

DISCOUNTS & DEALS
Be a smart shopper and compare all your options before making decisions. A plane ticket bought with a promotional coupon from travel clubs, coupon books, and direct-mail offers or purchased on the Internet may not be cheaper than the least expensive fare from a discount ticket agency. And always keep in mind that what you get is just as important as what you save.

DISCOUNT RESERVATIONS
To save money, look into discount reservations services with Web sites and toll-free numbers, which use their buying power to get a better price on hotels, air-

line tickets (⇨ Air Travel), even car rentals. When booking a room, always **call the hotel's local toll-free number** (if one is available) rather than the central reservations number—you'll often get a better price. Always ask about special packages or corporate rates.

🛈 Airline Tickets Air 4 Less ☎ 800/AIR4LESS; low-fare specialist.

🛈 Hotel Rooms Accommodations Express ☎ 800/444-7666 or 800/277-1064 ⊕ www.acex. net. **Central Reservation Service (CRS)** ☎ 800/ 555-7555 or 800/548-3311 ⊕ www.crshotels.com. **Hotels.com** ☎ 800/246-8357 ⊕ www.hotels.com. **Quikbook** ☎ 800/789-9887 ⊕ www.quikbook.com. **Steigenberger Reservation Service** ☎ 800/223-5652 ⊕ www.srs-worldhotels.com. **Turbotrip.com** ☎ 800/473-7829 ⊕ www.turbotrip.com.

PACKAGE DEALS

Don't confuse packages and guided tours. When you buy a package, you travel on your own, just as though you had planned the trip yourself. Fly/drive packages, which combine airfare and car rental, are often a good deal. In cities, ask the local visitors bureau about hotel and local transportation packages that include tickets to major museum exhibits or other special events.

EATING & DRINKING

Although certain ingredients and preparations are common in cooking of the northeastern United States, the genre as a whole varies greatly throughout the Berkshires and Pioneer Valley, which have developed an impressive reputation in recent years for creative, if occasionally daring, cuisine. Especially in the tony Berkshires, you can expect to find stellar restaurants, many of them helmed by culinary luminaries. Outside the fancier and more urbane communities in the region, restaurant food tends more toward simple, traditional, and conservative.

Collegiate and urban communities such as Springfield, Northampton, and Amherst have a great variety of ethnic restaurants, and the Berkshires has seen an influx of these sorts of establishments in recent years, too. The region excels particularly when it comes to Italian, French, Japanese, Indian, and Thai cuisine. As is the case

throughout the northeastern United States, western Massachusetts also has quite a few diners, a few of them open into the wee hours, which typically present patrons with page after page of inexpensive, short-order cooking; these down-home, locals' favorites make great alternatives to fast-food chain restaurants when road-tripping around the region. The relatively close proximity to the ocean accounts for a number of restaurants serving fresh seafood, and many chefs use fine ingredients from the slew of boutique dairy, meat, and vegetable suppliers that have sprung up throughout the Northeast in the past couple of decades. Menus throughout the Berkshires and, to an increasing extent, in the Pioneer Valley often note which Hudson River dairy or Berkshires produce farm a particular goat cheese or heirloom tomato came from.

The restaurants we list are the cream of the crop in each price category. Properties indicated by an ✕🏠 are lodging establishments whose restaurant warrants a special trip.

MEALTIMES

Unless otherwise noted, the restaurants listed in this guide are open daily for lunch and dinner.

RESERVATIONS & DRESS

Reservations are always a good idea; we mention them only when they're essential or not accepted. Book as far ahead as you can, and reconfirm as soon as you arrive. (Large parties should always call ahead to check the reservations policy.) We mention dress only when men are required to wear a jacket or a jacket and tie.

EMERGENCIES

🛈 Hospitals Berkshire Medical Center ✉ 725 North St., Pittsfield ☎ 413/447-2000. **Fairview Hospital** ✉ 29 Lewis Ave., Great Barrington ☎ 413/ 528-8600. **North Adams Regional Hospital** ✉ 71 Hospital Ave., North Adams ☎ 413/663-3701.

GAY & LESBIAN TRAVEL

Attitudes toward same-sex couples are very tolerant throughout Massachusetts, which became the first state to legalize same-sex marriages in spring 2004. The

Berkshires and much of the Pioneer Valley rank among the most gay-friendly areas in the nation, especially the college town of Northampton. Both Northampton and Springfield have gay-oriented nightclubs, and you'll find gay-friendly inns, bed-and-breakfasts, and hotels throughout western Massachusetts.

For details about the gay and lesbian scene in the Berkshires and Pioneer Valley, consult *Fodor's Gay Guide to the USA* (available in bookstores everywhere).

🔳 **Gay- & Lesbian-Friendly Travel Agencies Different Roads Travel** ✉ 8383 Wilshire Blvd., Suite 520, Beverly Hills, CA 90211 ☎ 323/651-5557 or 800/429-8747 (Ext. 14 for both) 🖷 323/651-5454 ✉ lgernert@tzell.com. **Kennedy Travel** ✉ 130 W. 42nd St., Suite 401, New York, NY 10036 ☎ 212/840-8659, 800/237-7433 🖷 212/730-2269 ⊕ www.kennedytravel.com. **Now, Voyager** ✉ 4406 18th St., San Francisco, CA 94114 ☎ 415/626-1169 or 800/255-6951 🖷 415/626-8626 ⊕ www.nowvoyager.com. **Skylink Travel and Tour/Flying Dutchmen Travel** ✉ 1455 N. Dutton Ave., Suite A, Santa Rosa, CA 95401 ☎ 707/546-9888 or 800/225-5759 🖷 707/636-0951; serving lesbian travelers.

HEALTH
There are relatively few health issues specific to the Massachusetts. Hospitals are as common and medical care as proficient as elsewhere in the United States.

PESTS & OTHER HAZARDS
Mosquitoes, seasonal black flies, and just about every other flitting and annoying insect known to North America proliferates in humid and often lush western Massachusetts. Exercise common precautions and wear lotions or sprays that keep away such pests.

Lyme disease, which was first documented in neighboring Connecticut, is relatively common and potentially dangerous throughout the region, especially where you find significant deer populations. Lyme disease is spread by bites from infinitesimal deer ticks. Symptoms, unfortunately, vary considerably from victim to victim, and one common problem is delayed diagnosis—the longer you go without treating this problem, the more severe its effects.

Most victims show a red-ring-shape rash around the bite from the deer tick, somewhat resembling a little bull's eye and appearing from a week to many weeks after the incident. Flulike symptoms often follow—fever, achy joints, swelling, and if left untreated for more than a couple months, chronic arthritis may set in.

Unfortunately, testing for Lyme disease is a sketchy business at best, as no definitive method has yet been developed. Doctors typically rely on a series of blood tests and even more often on observation of various symptoms.

When spending time in areas **where tick infestation is a problem, wear long-sleeve clothing** and slacks, tuck your pant legs into your boots and/or socks, **apply tick and insect repellent generously,** and check yourself carefully for signs of ticks or bites. It's a good idea to wear light-color clothing, as you'll have an easier time sighting ticks, which are dark. Remember that the more commonly found wood ticks do not carry the disease, and that deer ticks are extremely small—about the size of a pinhead.

HOLIDAYS
Major national holidays are New Year's Day (Jan. 1); Martin Luther King Day (3rd Mon. in Jan.); Presidents' Day (3rd Mon. in Feb.); Memorial Day (last Mon. in May); Independence Day (July 4); Labor Day (1st Mon. in Sept.); Columbus Day (2nd Mon. in Oct.); Thanksgiving Day (4th Thurs. in Nov.); Christmas Eve and Christmas Day (Dec. 24 and 25); and New Year's Eve (Dec. 31).

INSURANCE
The most useful travel-insurance plan is a comprehensive policy that includes coverage for trip cancellation and interruption, default, trip delay, and medical expenses (with a waiver for preexisting conditions).

Without insurance you'll lose all or most of your money if you cancel your trip, regardless of the reason. Default insurance covers you if your tour operator, airline, or cruise line goes out of business—the chances of which have been increasing. Trip-delay covers expenses that arise because of bad weather or mechanical delays. Study the fine print when comparing policies.

Always **buy travel policies directly from the insurance company**; if you buy them from a cruise line, airline, or tour operator that goes out of business you probably won't be covered for the agency or operator's default, a major risk. Before making any purchase, review your existing health and home-owner's policies to find what they cover away from home.

🖸 Travel Insurers In the U.S.: **Access America** ✉ 2805 N. Parham Rd., Richmond, VA 23294 ☎ 800/284-8300 🖶 804/673-1491 or 800/346-9265 ⊕ www.accessamerica.com. **Travel Guard International** ✉ 1145 Clark St., Stevens Point, WI 54481 ☎ 715/345-0505 or 800/826-1300 🖶 800/955-8785 ⊕ www.travelguard.com.

FOR INTERNATIONAL TRAVELERS

For information on customs restrictions, *see* Customs & Duties.

CAR RENTAL

When picking up a rental car, non-U.S. residents need a reservation voucher for any prepaid reservations that were made in the traveler's home country, a passport, a driver's license, and a travel policy that covers each driver.

CAR TRAVEL

Gas stations are easy to find along major highways and in most communities throughout the region. The average price of a gallon of regular unleaded gas at this writing is $2 throughout the area. However, prices vary from station to station within any city. Stations are plentiful. Most stay open late (24 hours along large highways and in some larger towns), except in rural areas, where Sunday hours are limited and where you may drive long stretches without a refueling opportunity. Highways are well paved. Interstate highways—limited-access, multilane highways whose numbers are prefixed by "I–"—are the fastest routes. Interstates with three-digit numbers encircle urban areas, which may have other limited-access expressways, freeways, and parkways as well. Tolls may be levied on limited-access high-

ways. So-called U.S. highways and state highways are not necessarily limited-access but may have several lanes.

Along larger highways, roadside stops with restrooms, fast-food restaurants, and sundries stores are well spaced. State police and tow trucks patrol major highways and lend assistance. If your car breaks down on an interstate, pull onto the shoulder and wait for help, or have your passengers wait while you walk to an emergency phone (available in most states). If you carry a cell phone, dial *55, noting your location on the small green roadside mileage markers.

Driving in the United States is on the right. Do obey speed limits posted along roads and highways. Watch for lower limits in small towns and on back roads. On weekdays between 6 and 10 AM and again between 4 and 7 PM expect heavy traffic. To encourage carpooling, some freeways have special lanes for so-called high-occupancy vehicles (HOV)—cars carrying more than one passenger.

Bookstores, gas stations, convenience stores, and rest stops sell maps (about $3) and multiregion road atlases (about $10).

CONSULATES & EMBASSIES

🖸 Australia **Australian Consulate General** ✉ 150 E. 42nd St., 34th fl., between Lexington and 3rd Aves., Midtown East, New York, NY 10017 ☎ 212/351-6500 🖶 212/351-6501 ⊕ www.australianyc.org. 🖸 Canada **Consulate General of Canada** ✉ 1251 Ave. of the Americas, between W. 49th and W. 50th Sts., Midtown West, New York, NY 10020-1175 ☎ 212/596-1628 🖶 212/596-1793 ⊕ www.canada-ny.org. 🖸 New Zealand **New Zealand Consulate-General** ✉ 780 3rd Ave., 19th fl., Midtown East, New York, NY 10017-6702 ☎ 212/832-4038 🖶 212/832-7602. 🖸 United Kingdom **British Consulate-General** ✉ 845 3rd Ave., between E. 51st and E. 52nd Sts., Midtown East, New York, NY 10022 ☎ 212/745-0200 🖶 212/745-3062 ⊕ www.britainusa.com/ny.

CURRENCY

The dollar is the basic unit of U.S. currency. It has 100 cents. Coins are the copper penny (1¢); the silvery nickel (5¢), dime (10¢), quarter (25¢), and half-dollar (50¢); and the golden $1 coin, replacing a now-rare silver dollar. Bills are denominated $1, $5, $10, $20, $50, and $100, all mostly green and identical in size; designs and background tints vary. In addition, you may come across a $2 bill, but the chances are slim. The exchange rate at this writing is US$1.82 per British pound, US$0.74 per Canadian dollar, US$0.69 per Australian dollar, and US$0.64 per New Zealand dollar.

ELECTRICITY
The U.S. standard is AC, 110 volts/60 cycles. Plugs have two flat pins set parallel to each other.

EMERGENCIES
For police, fire, or ambulance, **dial 911** (0 in rural areas).

INSURANCE
Britons and Australians need extra medical coverage when traveling overseas.

F Insurance Information In the U.K.: **Association of British Insurers** ✉ 51 Gresham St., London EC2V 7HQ ☎ 020/7600-3333 🖷 020/7696-8999 ⊕ www.abi.org.uk. In Australia: **Insurance Council of Australia** ✉ Insurance Enquiries and Complaints, Level 12, Box 561, Collins St. W, Melbourne, VIC 8007 ☎ 1300/780808 or 03/9629-4109 🖷 03/9621-2060 ⊕ www.iecltd.com.au. In Canada: **RBC Insurance** ✉ 6880 Financial Dr., Mississauga, Ontario L5N 7Y5 ☎ 800/668-4342 or 905/816-2400 🖷 905/813-4704 ⊕ www.rbcinsurance.com. In New Zealand: **Insurance Council of New Zealand** ✉ Level 7, 111-115 Customhouse Quay, Box 474, Wellington ☎ 04/472-5230 🖷 04/473-3011 ⊕ www.icnz.org.nz.

MAIL & SHIPPING
You can buy stamps and aerograms and send letters and parcels at post offices. Stamp-dispensing machines can occasionally be found in airports, bus and train stations, office buildings, drugstores, and the like. You can also deposit mail in the stout, dark blue, steel bins at strategic locations everywhere and in the mail chutes of large buildings; pickup schedules are posted. You can deposit packages at public collection boxes as long as the parcels are affixed with proper postage and weigh less than one pound. Packages weighing one or more pounds must be taken to a post office or handed to a postal carrier.

For mail sent within the United States, you need a 37¢ stamp for first-class letters weighing up to 1 ounce (23¢ for each additional ounce) and 23¢ for postcards. You pay 80¢ for 1-ounce airmail letters and 70¢ for airmail postcards to most other countries; to Canada and Mexico, you need a 60¢ stamp for a 1-ounce letter and 50¢ for a postcard. An aerogram—a single sheet of lightweight blue paper that folds into its own envelope, stamped for overseas airmail—costs 70¢.

To receive mail on the road, have it sent c/o General Delivery at your destination's main post office (use the correct five-digit ZIP code). You must pick up mail in person within 30 days and show a driver's license or passport.

PASSPORTS & VISAS
When traveling internationally, carry your passport even if you don't need one (it's always the best form of ID) and **make two photocopies of the data page** (one for someone at home and another for you, carried separately from your passport). If you lose your passport, promptly call the nearest embassy or consulate and the local police.

Visitor visas aren't necessary for Canadian or European Union citizens, or for citizens of Australia who are staying fewer than 90 days.

F Australian Citizens **Passports Australia** ☎ 131-232 ⊕ www.passports.gov.au. **United States Consulate General** ✉ MLC Centre, Level 59, 19-29 Martin Pl., Sydney, NSW 2000 ☎ 02/9373-9200, 1902/941-641 fee-based visa-inquiry line ⊕ usembassy-australia.state.gov/sydney.

F Canadian Citizens **Passport Office** ✉ To mail in applications: 200 Promenade du Portage, Hull, Québec J8X 4B7 ☎ 819/994-3500, 800/567-6868, 866/255-7655 TTY ⊕ www.ppt.gc.ca.

F New Zealand Citizens **New Zealand Passports Office** ✉ For applications and information, Level 3, Boulcott House, 47 Boulcott St., Wellington ☎ 0800/22-5050 or 04/474-8100 ⊕ www.passports.govt.nz. **Embassy of the United States** ✉ 29 Fitzherbert Terr., Thorndon, Wellington ☎ 04/462-6000 ⊕ usembassy.org.nz. **U.S. Consulate General** ✉ Citibank Bldg., 3rd fl., 23 Customs St. E, Auckland ☎ 09/303-2724 ⊕ usembassy.org.nz.

U.K. Citizens U.K. Passport Service ☎ 0870/ 521–0410 ⊕ www.passport.gov.uk. **American Consulate General** ✉ Danesfort House, 223 Stranmillis Rd., Belfast, Northern Ireland BT9 5GR ☎ 028/ 9032–8239 ⊟ 028/9024–8482 ⊕ usembassy.org.uk. **American Embassy** ✉ For visa and immigration information or to submit a visa application via mail (enclose an SASE), Consular Information Unit, 24 Grosvenor Sq., London W1 1AE ☎ 09055/444–546 for visa information (per-minute charges), 0207/ 499–9000 main switchboard ⊕ usembassy.org.uk.

TELEPHONES

All U.S. telephone numbers consist of a three-digit area code and a seven-digit local number. Within many local calling areas, you dial only the seven-digit number. Within some area codes, you must dial "1" first for calls outside the local area. To call between area-code regions, dial "1" then all 10 digits; the same goes for calls to numbers prefixed by "800," "888," "866," and "877"—all toll free. For calls to numbers preceded by "900" you must pay—usually dearly.

For international calls, dial "011" followed by the country code and the local number. For help, dial "0" and ask for an overseas operator. The country code is 61 for Australia, 64 for New Zealand, 44 for the United Kingdom. Calling Canada is the same as calling within the United States. Most local phone books list country codes and U.S. area codes. The country code for the United States is 1.

For operator assistance, dial "0." To obtain someone's phone number, call directory assistance at 555–1212 or occasionally 411 (free at many public phones). To have the person you're calling foot the bill, phone collect; dial "0" instead of "1" before the 10-digit number.

At pay phones, instructions often are posted. Usually you insert coins in a slot (usually 35¢–50¢ for local calls) and wait for a steady tone before dialing. When you call long-distance, the operator tells you how much to insert; prepaid phone cards, widely available in various denominations, are easier. Call the number on the back, punch in the card's personal identification number when prompted, then dial your number.

LODGING

The Berkshires ranks among one of the more expensive areas in the country when it comes to accommodations; the Pioneer Valley is less expensive, but rates still exceed the national average. These tend to be seasonal destinations, and during the summer and fall high seasons, rates can be quite steep. Also, it can be tough to find weekend hotel rooms in summer and fall, so it's wise to book several weeks ahead. When visiting towns with a large college presence (Northampton, Amherst), be aware that rooms can be extremely tough to come by on weekends throughout the school year. Also take into consideration major cultural and sporting events, which can push up prices and greatly reduce availability in certain places.

You'll be charged a hotel tax, which varies among towns and counties, throughout Massachusetts.

Assume that hotels operate on the European Plan (EP, with no meals) unless we specify that they use either the Continental Plan (CP, with a continental breakfast), Breakfast Plan (BP, with a full breakfast), or the Modified American Plan (MAP, with breakfast and dinner) or are all-inclusive (including all meals and most activities).

APARTMENT & HOUSE RENTALS

If you want a home base that's roomy enough for a family and comes with cooking facilities, consider a furnished rental. These can save you money, especially if you're traveling with a group. Home-exchange directories sometimes list rentals as well as exchanges.

BED & BREAKFASTS

Historic bed-and-breakfasts and inns proliferate throughout western Massachusetts. In many rural or less touristy areas, B&Bs provide an affordable and homey alternative to chain properties, but in tourism-dependent communities (i.e., most of the major towns in this region), you can expect to pay about the same or more for a historic inn as for a full-service hotel.

Many of the state's finest restaurants are also found in country inns. Although many B&Bs and smaller establishments offer a low-key, homey experience without TVs or numerous amenities, the scene has changed greatly in recent years, especially in upscale resort areas, where many such properties now attempt to cater to business and luxury leisure travelers with high-speed Internet, voice mail, whirlpool tubs, and VCRs. Quite a few inns and B&Bs serve substantial full breakfasts—the kind that may keep your appetite in check for the better part of the day.

▪ Reservation Services **American Country Collection** ☎ 518/370-4948 or 800/810-4948 ⊕ www. bandbreservations.com serves western Massachusetts (as well as eastern upstate New York and much of Vermont).

CAMPING

Within Massachusetts' extensive state park system, parts of it concentrated in the Berkshires and Pioneer Valley, campgrounds offering both primitive and RV sites abound. In state parks, you can call or book online to reserve a campsite at any of the state's 28 camping parks as early as six months in advance and as late as two days before you arrive. Park campgrounds are almost all open from Memorial Day through Labor Day, but many of them also remain open throughout the year, even in winter. Some have cabin rentals, too. Based on availability, state parks also accept walk-ins without reservations, but it's best to call ahead to avoid disappointment.

Massachusetts also has dozens of private commercial RV and tent-camp parks.

▪ **Mass Parks (Massachusetts State Park's camping reservations service)** ☎ 877/422-6762. **Massachusetts Campground Owners Association** ☎ 781/544-3475 ⊕ www.campmass.com.

HOME EXCHANGES

If you would like to exchange your home for someone else's, join a home-exchange organization, which will send you its updated listings of available exchanges for a year and will include your own listing in at least one of them. It's up to you to make specific arrangements.

▪ Exchange Clubs **HomeLink International** ☎ Box 47747, Tampa, FL 33647 ☎ 813/975-9825 or 800/638-3841 ☎ 813/910-8144 ⊕ www.homelink. org; $110 yearly for a listing, online access, and catalog; $70 without catalog. **Intervac U.S.** ☒ 30 Corte San Fernando, Tiburon, CA 94920 ☎ 800/756-4663 ☎ 415/435-7440 ⊕ www.intervacus.com; $125 yearly for a listing, online access, and a catalog; $65 without catalog.

HOTELS

All hotels listed have private bath unless otherwise noted.

▪ Toll-Free Numbers **Best Western** ☎ 800/528-1234 ⊕ www.bestwestern.com. **Choice** ☎ 800/424-6423 ⊕ www.choicehotels.com. **Clarion** ☎ 800/424-6423 ⊕ www.choicehotels.com. **Comfort Inn** ☎ 800/424-6423 ⊕ www.choicehotels.com. **Days Inn** ☎ 800/325-2525 ⊕ www.daysinn.com. **Doubletree Hotels** ☎ 800/222-8733 ⊕ www.doubletree.com. **Embassy Suites** ☎ 800/362-2779 ⊕ www.embassysuites.com. **Fairfield Inn** ☎ 800/228-2800 ⊕ www.marriott.com. **Four Seasons** ☎ 800/332-3442 ⊕ www.fourseasons.com. **Hilton** ☎ 800/445-8667 ⊕ www.hilton.com. **Holiday Inn** ☎ 800/465-4329 ⊕ www.ichotelsgroup.com. **Howard Johnson** ☎ 800/446-4656 ⊕ www.hojo.com. **Hyatt Hotels & Resorts** ☎ 800/233-1234 ⊕ www.hyatt.com. **Inter-Continental** ☎ 800/327-0200 ⊕ www.ichotelsgroup.com. **La Quinta** ☎ 800/531-5900 ⊕ www.lq.com. **Marriott** ☎ 800/228-9290 ⊕ www.marriott.com. **Le Meridien** ☎ 800/543-4300 ⊕ www.lemeridien.com. **Omni** ☎ 800/843-6664 ⊕ www.omnihotels.com. **Quality Inn** ☎ 800/424-6423 ⊕ www.choicehotels.com. **Radisson** ☎ 800/333-3333 ⊕ www.radisson.com. **Ramada** ☎ 800/228-2828, 800/854-7854 international reservations ⊕ www.ramada.com or www.ramadahotels.com. **Renaissance Hotels & Resorts** ☎ 800/468-3571 ⊕ www.renaissancehotels.com/. **Ritz-Carlton** ☎ 800/241-3333 ⊕ www.ritzcarlton.com. **Sheraton** ☎ 800/325-3535 ⊕ www.starwood.com/sheraton. **Sleep Inn** ☎ 800/424-6423 ⊕ www.choicehotels.com. **Westin Hotels & Resorts** ☎ 800/228-3000 ⊕ www.starwood.com/westin.

MEDIA

NEWSPAPERS & MAGAZINES

The most prominent newspapers in Massachusetts are based in Boston: the *Boston Globe* and *Boston Herald*, especially. It's also fairly easy to find *The New York Times* throughout the region. Local daily papers serving the region include *The Recorder* (in Greenfield), *The Daily Hampshire Gazette* (in Northampton), *The Berkshire Eagle* (in Pittsfield), and the *Union News & Sunday Republican* (in Springfield).

The free alternative newsweekly *The Valley Advocate,* distributed throughout the Pioneer Valley, can be a great source of news on dining, arts, culture, and sightseeing.

RADIO & TELEVISION

Western Massachusetts is served by all the major television networks, whose affiliates are mostly in Springfield and Albany. There are also dozens of radio stations throughout the region.

MONEY MATTERS

Prices for services and travel vary a bit throughout the state. Generally, in western Massachusetts, prices for dining, hotels, and entertainment tend to be consistent with national averages, although some of the more posh towns in the Berkshires tend to have somewhat high restaurant and hotel prices. One good thing about the area is that there's a fairly wide variety of options; you can spend in some areas and save in others. Within the region, a cup of coffee can cost from 50¢ to $4, a pint of beer from $4 to $7, and a sandwich from $4 to $10.

Prices throughout this guide are given for adults. Substantially reduced fees are almost always available for children, students, and senior citizens. For information on taxes, *see* Taxes.

ATMS

Cash machines are abundant throughout western Massachusetts and are found not only in banks but in many grocery stores, Laundromats, delis, and hotels. But beware, many bank ATMs charge users a fee of up to $2, and the commercial ATMs in retail establishments can charge even more.

CREDIT CARDS

Throughout this guide, the following abbreviations are used: **AE,** American Express; **D,** Discover; **DC,** Diners Club; **MC,** MasterCard; and **V,** Visa.

🔂 Reporting Lost Cards **American Express** ☎ 800/992-3404. **Diners Club** ☎ 800/234-6377. **Discover** ☎ 800/347-2683. **MasterCard** ☎ 800/622-7747. **Visa** ☎ 800/847-2911.

PACKING

In western Massachusetts, jackets and ties are rarely expected for men at restaurants. In general, New Englanders tend to dress slightly more formally than their Midwest or West Coast counterparts for special events. Jeans and sneakers are acceptable for casual dining and sightseeing just about anywhere in the area. Always **come with sneakers or other flat-heeled walking shoes** for pounding the pavement in urban areas, and with good shoes or boots for hitting the area's many hiking trails.

In spring and fall, pack at least one warm jacket and sweater, since moderate daytime temperatures can drop after nightfall. Bring shorts for summer, which can be quite humid. You need a warm coat, hat, scarf, and gloves in winter; boots for often slushy streets are also a good idea. Western Massachusetts has among the coldest and snowiest weather in the Eastern United States, so pack particularly warm gear if spending much time here.

In your carry-on luggage, pack an extra pair of eyeglasses or contact lenses and enough of any medication you take to last a few days longer than the entire trip. You may also ask your doctor to write a spare prescription using the drug's generic name, as brand names may vary from country to country. In luggage to be checked, **never pack prescription drugs, valuables, or undeveloped film.** And don't forget to carry with you the addresses of offices that handle refunds of lost traveler's checks. Check *Fodor's How to Pack* (available at online retailers and bookstores everywhere) for more tips.

To avoid customs and security delays, carry medications in their original packaging. Don't pack any sharp objects in your carry-on luggage, including knives of any size or material, scissors, nail clippers, and corkscrews, or anything else that might arouse suspicion.

To avoid having your checked luggage chosen for hand inspection, don't cram bags full. The U.S. Transportation Security Administration suggests packing shoes on top and placing personal items you don't want touched in clear plastic bags.

CHECKING LUGGAGE

You're allowed to carry aboard one bag and one personal article, such as a purse or a laptop computer. Make sure what you carry on fits under your seat or in the overhead bin. Get to the gate early, so you can board as soon as possible, before the overhead bins fill up.

Baggage allowances vary by carrier, destination, and ticket class. On international flights, you're usually allowed to check two bags weighing up to 70 pounds (32 kilograms) each, although a few airlines allow checked bags of up to 88 pounds (40 kilograms) in first class. Some international carriers don't allow more than 66 pounds (30 kilograms) per bag in business class and 44 pounds (20 kilograms) in economy. On domestic flights, the limit is usually 50 to 70 pounds (23 to 32 kilograms) per bag. In general, carry-on bags shouldn't exceed 40 pounds (18 kilograms). Most airlines won't accept bags that weigh more than 100 pounds (45 kilograms) on domestic or international flights. Expect to pay a fee for baggage that exceeds weight limits. Check baggage restrictions with your carrier before you pack.

Airline liability for baggage is limited to $2,500 per person on flights within the United States. On international flights it amounts to $9.07 per pound or $20 per kilogram for checked baggage (roughly $640 per 70-pound bag), with a maximum of $634.90 per piece, and $400 per passenger for unchecked baggage. You can buy additional coverage at check-in for about $10 per $1,000 of coverage, but it often excludes a rather extensive list of items, shown on your airline ticket.

Before departure, itemize your bags' contents and their worth, and label the bags with your name, address, and phone number. (If you use your home address, cover it so potential thieves can't see it readily.)

Include a label inside each bag and **pack a copy of your itinerary.** At check-in, make sure each bag is correctly tagged with the destination airport's three-letter code. Because some checked bags will be opened for hand inspection, the U.S. Transportation Security Administration recommends that you leave luggage unlocked or use the plastic locks offered at check-in. TSA screeners place an inspection notice inside searched bags, which are resealed with a special lock.

If your bag has been searched and contents are missing or damaged, file a claim with the TSA Consumer Response Center as soon as possible. If your bags arrive damaged or fail to arrive at all, file a written report with the airline before leaving the airport.

🚩 Complaints **U.S. Transportation Security Administration Contact Center** ☎ 866/289-9673 ⊕ www.tsa.gov.

SAFETY

Most of western Massachusetts is comparable in safety and crime to the rest of the country. And although the area's cities, especially Springfield, do have some crime problems, they are—in fact—quite safe. However, do not let yourself be lulled into a false sense of security. Urban areas still have significantly higher rates of crime—both violent and nonviolent—than suburban and especially rural areas. Tourists can, unfortunately, be relatively easy targets for pickpocket and theft in any popular vacation destination. Your wisest approach in urban and touristy areas is to lock your car and never leave valuables unattended.

In cities, keep jewelry out of sight on the street; better yet, **leave valuables at home.** Don't wear gold chains or gaudy jewelry, even if it's fake. Men should **carry their wallets in their front pants pocket** rather than in their back pockets. When in bars or restaurants, never hang your purse or bag on the back of a chair or put it underneath the table.

Avoid deserted blocks in unfamiliar neighborhoods. A brisk, purposeful pace helps deter trouble wherever you go.

SENIOR-CITIZEN TRAVEL

To qualify for age-related discounts, mention your senior-citizen status up front when booking hotel reservations (not when checking out) and before you're seated in restaurants (not when paying the bill). Be sure to have identification on hand. When renting a car, ask about promotional car-rental discounts, which can be cheaper than senior-citizen rates.

⚑ Educational Programs Elderhostel ✉ 11 Ave. de Lafayette, Boston, MA 02111-1746 ☎ 877/426-8056, 978/323-4141 international callers, 877/426-2167 TTY ☎ 877/426-2166 ⊕ www.elderhostel.org. **Interhostel** ✉ University of New Hampshire, 6 Garrison Ave., Durham, NH 03824 ☎ 603/862-1147 or 800/733-9753 ☎ 603/862-1113 ⊕ www.learn.unh. edu. **Folkways Institute** ✉ 14600 S.E. Aldridge Rd., Portland, OR 97236-6518 ☎ 503/658-6600 ☎ 503/658-8672.

SPORTS & THE OUTDOORS

BICYCLING

The region's terrain is tremendously varied, and it tends to be hilly. However, the Pioneer Valley and the Berkshires are relatively uncongested and extremely popular for biking, affording cycling enthusiasts of all abilities miles of great riding. It's an especially appealing area for mountain biking.

The Ashuwillticook Rail Trail runs from the Pittsfield-Cheshire town line north up through Adams. Part of the trail is paved. It traces the old rail line and passes through rugged woodland and Cheshire Lake. The Berkshire Visitors Bureau (⇨ Visitor Information) distributes a free Berkshire Bike Touring Route, which is a series of relatively short excursions along area roads.

The Massachusetts Bicycle Coalition, an advocacy group that works to improve conditions for area cyclists, has information on organized rides and sells good bike maps of Boston and the state.

⚑ The Massachusetts Bicycle Coalition ✉ 44 Bromfield St., Boston 02178 ☎ 617/542-2453 ⊕ www.massbike.org.

BOATING & SAILING

With numerous lakes, rivers, and ponds throughout western Massachusetts, the region is rife with opportunities for sailing, canoeing, kayaking, rafting, and boating. The Connecticut River is a favorite spot for this activity.

⚑ Mass Outdoors ☎ 617/626-1600 ⊕ www.sport. state.ma.us.

FISHING

Much of western Massachusetts, with its dozens of small ponds and lakes, is renowned for its outstanding lake (lake trout, walleye, bass, perch) and river fishing (coho and chinook salmon, brown and rainbow trout).

If you're age 15 or over, you're required to obtain a fishing license for all freshwater fishing in Massachusetts. Contact Mass Outdoors, part of the Massachusetts Department of Fish and Game, for details on licenses, limits, and other fishing regulations.

⚑ Mass Outdoors ☎ 617/626-1600 ⊕ www.sport. state.ma.us.

GOLF

Western Massachusetts has several fine golf courses. Some of the top courses are private, but you can often arrange visits in advance if you're a member of a private club back home.

⚑ Massachusetts Golf Association ⌖ 300 Arnold Palmer Blvd., Norton 02766 ☎ 774/430-9100 or 800/356-2201 ⊕ www.mgalinks.org.

HIKING

The Berkshires and Pioneer Valley are rife with great hiking areas, including a 90-mi swath of the Appalachian Trail that cuts through the Berkshires. You'll also find hundreds of miles of trails elsewhere throughout the area's forests and parks.

Never drink from any stream, no matter how clear it may be. Giardia organisms can turn your stomach inside out. The easiest way to purify water is to dissolve a water purification tablet in it. Camping-equipment stores also carry purification pumps and tablets. Boil water for 15 minutes, a reliable method, though time- and fuel-consuming.

⚑ Appalachian National Scenic Trail ✉ NPS Park Office, Harpers Ferry Center, Harpers Ferry, WV 25425 ☎ 304/535-6331 or 304/535-6278 ⊕ www. nps.gov/appa.

SKIING

Although not as famous for skiing as Vermont and New Hampshire, Massachusetts does have several downhill and cross-country ski areas, most of them concentrated in the Berkshires and Pioneer Valley; see the individual chapters of this book for specifics.

STUDENTS IN THE BERKSHIRES & PIONEER VALLEY

Western Massachusetts is home to such prominent schools as Amherst College, Smith College, Mount Holyoke College, Williams College, Hampshire College, and the main campus of the University of Massachusetts, in Amherst. It's no wonder the area, especially in the Pioneer Valley, is rife with student discounts. Wherever you go, especially museums, sightseeing attractions, and performances, identify yourself as a student up front and ask if a discount is available. However, **be prepared to show your ID** as proof of enrollment and/or age.

⚡ IDs & Services STA Travel ✉ 10 Downing St., New York, NY 10014 ☎ 212/627-3111, 800/777-0112 24-hr service center 🖨 212/627-3387 ⊕ www.sta.com. **Travel Cuts** ✉ 187 College St., Toronto, Ontario M5T 1P7, Canada ☎ 800/592-2887 in U.S., 416/979-2406 or 866/246-9762 in Canada 🖨 416/979-8167 ⊕ www.travelcuts.com.

TAXES

Municipalities throughout the state charge a variety of taxes on hotel rooms, car rentals, and parking in commercial lots or garages. These range typically from 10% to 14% for hotels and rental cars, and from 10% to 19% for parking.

SALES TAX

Massachusetts' sales tax of 5% applies to almost everything you can buy retail, including restaurant meals. Prescription drugs and nonprepared food bought in grocery stores are tax exempt.

TAXIS

Abbott's Limousine and Livery Service in Lee provides transportation to and from airports throughout the region, including New York, Boston, and Hartford. In Great Barrington, Taxico provides local service and transportation to airports in Hartford, Boston and New York. Long distance transportation requires 24-hour notice.
⚡ Abbott's Limousine and Livery Service ☎ 413/243-1645 **Taxico** ☎ 413/528-0911

TIME

New York operates on Eastern Standard Time. When it is noon in New York it is 9 AM in Los Angeles, 11 AM in Chicago, 5 PM in London, and 3 AM the following day in Sydney.

TIPPING

The customary tipping rate for taxi drivers is 15%–20%, with a minimum of $2; bellhops are usually given $2 per bag in luxury hotels, $1 per bag elsewhere. Hotel maids should be tipped $2 per day of your stay. A doorman who hails or helps you into a cab can be tipped $1–$2. You should also tip your hotel concierge for services rendered; the size of the tip depends on the difficulty of your request, as well as the quality of the concierge's work. For an ordinary dinner reservation or tour arrangements, $3–$5 should do; if the concierge scores seats at a popular restaurant or show or performs unusual services (getting your laptop repaired, finding a good pet-sitter, etc.), $10 or more is appropriate.

Waiters should be tipped 15%–20%, though at higher-end restaurants, a solid 20% is more the norm. Many restaurants add a gratuity to the bill for parties of six or more. Ask what the percentage is if the menu or bill doesn't state it. Tip $1 per drink you order at the bar, though if at an upscale establishment, those $15 martinis might warrant a $2 tip.

TOURS & PACKAGES

Because everything is prearranged on a prepackaged tour or independent vacation, you spend less time planning—and often get it all at a good price.

BOOKING WITH AN AGENT

Travel agents are excellent resources. But it's a good idea to collect brochures from several agencies, as some agents' suggestions may be influenced by relationships with tour and package firms that reward them for volume sales. If you have a special interest, find an agent with expertise in that area; the American Society of Travel Agents (ASTA; ⇨ Travel Agencies) has a database of specialists worldwide. You can log on to the group's Web site to find an ASTA travel agent in your neighborhood.

Make sure your travel agent knows the accommodations and other services of the place being recommended. Ask about the hotel's location, room size, beds, and whether it has a pool, room service, or programs for children, if you care about these. Has your agent been there in person or sent others whom you can contact?

Do some homework on your own, too: local tourism boards can provide information about lesser-known and small-niche operators, some of which may sell only direct.

BUYER BEWARE

Each year consumers are stranded or lose their money when tour operators—even large ones with excellent reputations—go out of business. So check out the operator. Ask several travel agents about its reputation, and try to **book with a company that has a consumer-protection program.** (Look for information in the company's brochure.) In the United States, members of the United States Tour Operators Association are required to set aside funds ($1 million) to help eligible customers cover payments and travel arrangements in the event that the company defaults. It's also a good idea to choose a company that participates in the American Society of Travel Agents' Tour Operator Program; ASTA will act as mediator in any disputes between you and your tour operator.

Remember that the more your package or tour includes, the better you can predict the ultimate cost of your vacation. Make sure you know exactly what is covered, and beware of hidden costs. Are taxes, tips, and transfers included? Entertainment and excursions? These can add up.

⚁ Tour-Operator Recommendations American Society of Travel Agents (⇨ Travel Agencies). **National Tour Association** (NTA) ✉ 546 E. Main St., Lexington, KY 40508 ☎ 859/226-4444 or 800/682-8886 🖷 859/226-4404 ⊕ www.ntaonline.com. **United States Tour Operators Association** (USTOA)

✉ 275 Madison Ave., Suite 2014, New York, NY 10016 ☎ 212/599-6599 🖷 212/599-6744 ⊕ www.ustoa.com.

TRAIN TRAVEL

Two Amtrak routes traverse western Massachusetts, providing access from all over the Northeast to both the Berkshires and the Pioneer Valley; these are the *Lake Shore Limited,* which runs from Chicago to Boston and has stops in Pittsfield and Springfield, and the *Vermonter,* which runs from Washington, D.C. to St. Albans, Vermont, with stops in Springfield and Amherst.

CUTTING COSTS

Amtrak offers a **North America rail pass,** available to both U.S. and Canadian residents, that gives you unlimited travel within the United States and Canada within any 30-day period ($699 peak, $495 off-peak), and several kinds of **USA Rail passes** (for non-U.S. residents only) offering unlimited travel for 15 to 30 days. Amtrak also has senior-citizen, children's, disability, and student discounts, as well as occasional deals that allow a second or third accompanying passenger to travel for half price or even free. The **Amtrak Vacations** program customizes entire vacations, including hotels, car rentals, and tours.

FARES & SCHEDULES

Approximate standard sample one-way fares (based on 7-day advance purchase—prices can be 10% to 50% higher otherwise), times, and routes (note that times vary greatly depending on the number of stops) on major carriers to Springfield from: Boston, 2 hours, $28; New York City, 3½ hours, $45; Philadelphia, 5 hours, $60; and Cleveland, 12 hours, $90.

Approximate standard sample one-way fares (based on 7-day advance purchase—prices can be 10% to 50% higher otherwise), times, and routes (note that times vary greatly depending on the number of stops) on major carriers to Pittsfield from: Boston, 4 hours, $20; New York City, 6½ hours, $52; and Cleveland, 11 hours, $82.

⚁ Train Information Amtrak ☎ 800/872-7245 ⊕ www.amtrak.com.

TRANSPORTATION AROUND THE BERKSHIRES & PIONEER VALLEY

The most practical way to get around western Massachusetts is by car, which you really need to move easily among attractions, explore different towns, get from where you're staying to restaurants and shops. In rural areas, outside all but a few small cities or larger towns in the region, a car is an absolute necessity. With several regional airports served by major airlines situated throughout the area, as well as train and bus service from major nearby cities, you can generally count on traveling to the Berkshires and Pioneer Valley by plane, train, or bus and then renting a car once you arrive.

TRAVEL AGENCIES

A good travel agent puts your needs first. Look for an agency that has been in business at least five years, emphasizes customer service, and has someone on staff who specializes in your destination. In addition, **make sure the agency belongs to a professional trade organization.** The American Society of Travel Agents (ASTA)—the largest and most influential in the field with more than 20,000 members in some 140 countries—maintains and enforces a strict code of ethics and will step in to help mediate any agent-client disputes involving ASTA members if necessary. ASTA (whose motto is "Without a travel agent, you're on your own") also maintains a Web site that includes a directory of agents. (If a travel agency is also acting as your tour operator, *see* Buyer Beware *in* Tours & Packages.)

🛈 Local Agent Referrals **American Society of Travel Agents** (ASTA) ✉ 1101 King St., Suite 200, Alexandria, VA 22314 ☎ 703/739-2782 or 800/965-2782 24-hr hotline 🖷 703/684-8319 ⊕ www. astanet.com. **Association of British Travel Agents** ✉ 68-71 Newman St., London W1T 3AH 🖷 020/7637-2444 🖷 020/7637-0713 ⊕ www.abta.com. **Association of Canadian Travel Agencies** ✉ 130 Albert St., Suite 1705, Ottawa, Ontario K1P 5G4 ☎ 613/237-3657 🖷 613/237-7052 ⊕ www.acta.ca. **Australian Federation of Travel Agents** ✉ Level 3, 309 Pitt St., Sydney, NSW 2000 ☎ 02/9264-3299 or 1300/363-416 🖷 02/9264-1085 ⊕ www.afta.com. au. **Travel Agents' Association of New Zealand**

✉ Level 5, Tourism and Travel House, 79 Boulcott St., Box 1888, Wellington 6001 ☎ 04/499-0104 🖷 04/499-0786 ⊕ www.taanz.org.nz.

VISITOR INFORMATION

🛈 Tourist Information **Berkshires Visitors Bureau** ✉ 3 Hoosac St., Adams 01220 ☎ 413/743-4500 or 800/237-5747 ⊕ www.berkshires.org. **Massachusetts Office of Travel and Tourism** ✉ 10 Park Plaza, Suite 4510, Boston 02116 ☎ 617/973-8500, 800/447-6277 for brochures ⊕ www.massvacation. com. The **Greater Springfield Convention and Visitors Bureau** ✉ 1441 Main St., Springfield 01103 ☎ 413/787-1548 or 800/723-1548 ⊕ www. valleyvisitor.com; Riverfront Visitor Information Center ✉ 1200 W. Columbus Ave.

🛈 Local Information **Mohawk Trail Association** 🖅 Box 1044, North Adams 01247 ☎ 413/743-8127 ⊕ www.mohawktrail.com. **Stockbridge Chamber of Commerce** ✉ Elm St., Stockbridge ☎ 413/298-5200 or 866/626-5327 ⊕ www.stockbridgechamber. org.**South County Chamber of Commerce** ✉ 362 Main St., Great Barrington ☎ 413/528-1510 ⊕ www.southernberkshires.com. **Lee Chamber of Commerce** ✉ 3 Park St., Lee ☎ 413/243-0852.

🛈 Government Advisories **U.S. Department of State** ✉ Overseas Citizens Services Office, 2100 Pennsylvania Ave. NW, 4th fl., Washington, DC 20520 ☎ 202/647-5225 interactive hotline, 888/407-4747 ⊕ www.travel.state.gov. **Consular Affairs Bureau of Canada** ☎ 800/267-6788 or 613/944-6788 ⊕ www.voyage.gc.ca. **U.K. Foreign and Commonwealth Office** ✉ Travel Advice Unit, Consular Division, Old Admiralty Bldg., London SW1A 2PA ☎ 0870/606-0290 or 020/7008-1500 ⊕ www.fco. gov.uk/travel. **Australian Department of Foreign Affairs and Trade** ☎ 300/139-281 travel advice, 02/6261-1299 Consular Travel Advice Faxback Service ⊕ www.dfat.gov.au. **New Zealand Ministry of Foreign Affairs and Trade** ☎ 04/439-8000 ⊕ www. mft.govt.nz.

WEB SITES

Do check out the World Wide Web when planning your trip. You'll find everything from weather forecasts to virtual tours of famous cities. Be sure to visit Fodors.com (⊕ www.fodors.com), a complete travel-planning site. You can research prices and book plane tickets, hotel rooms, rental cars, vacation packages, and more. In addition, you can post your pressing questions in the Travel Talk section. Other planning tools include a currency converter and weather reports, and there are loads of links to travel resources.

Check out the Massachusetts State Home page (⊕ www.mass.gov) for information on state government, and for links to state agencies on doing business, working, learning, living, and visiting in the Empire State. Gorp.com is a terrific general resource for just about every kind of recreational activity; just click on the Massachusetts link under "Destinations," and you'll be flooded with links to myriad topics, from wildlife refuges to ski trips to backpacking advice. Citysearch.com and Digitalcity.com both offer a wide range reviews and links to dining, culture, and services in major cities and destinations throughout the state.

SOUTH COUNTY

1

By Carole
Owens

Surrounded by the rolling Berkshire Hills, the beauty of South County is enhanced by the Housatonic River winding through it. The banks of the Housatonic are puncuated by 13 communities that vary in size from the tiny villages of Tyringham and Mount Washington, with populations of 350 and 167 respectively, to the towns of Lee and Great Barrington, each with approximately 6000 citizens.

Earlier traders and Dutch settlers described South County as wild country, destitute of roads, only Indian trails, and so heavily wooded that it was forbidding. But the English settlers looked upon the Housatonic Valley and the Berkshire Hills and saw opportunity. The fertile banks of the Housatonic River provided rich soil for farming and the flowing waters provided power for mills, tanneries, and blacksmiths. The woodland provided lumber for building and pulp for the paper mills. The Indian trails became a New England pathway because South County sat at the nexus of New York, Connecticut, and Massachusetts, and its roads were the shortest, most direct connection between Hartford, Albany, Boston and Springfield.

Along these roads in the 18th cenutry, inns sprang up in Sheffield, Great Barrington, New Marlborough, and Stockbridge to welcome guests, and South County found an economic base. Since then Benedict Arnold, Aaron Burr, Daniel Webster, Ralph Waldo Emerson, Henry Wadsworth Longfellow, Edith Wharton, Nathaniel Hawthorne, Herman Melville, Presidents Cleveland, Taft, Arthur, Theodore and Franklin Roosevelts, the Vanderbilts, Astors, and Mellons all slept here.

Today, South County still attracts the rich and famous because it maintains its rural charm while providing fine museums, theaters, classical music festivals, and glamorous inns. Carol Channing, Carol Burnett, Julia Roberts, John Travolta, Henry Williamsm and Steven Spielberg all have spent time in South County. Because of the unique combination of natural beauty and commercial sophistication, South County is the embodiment of rural chic. Yet South County is not uniformly a cultural mecca. Small villages like Otis, Alford, and Sandisfield offer city dwellers an escape from elaborate entertainments, fancy dining, and crowds by providing simple rural charm and natural beauty.

High season in South County is still Memorial Day to Labor Day, when the area is lush with greenery and loud with enthusiastic crowds. Many cultural attractions are only open during this season. The month of October is called the "late season." People travel from as far away as England and Japan to see the vibrant colors of the area's fall foliage. From Thanksgiving through April is ski season, and Great Barrington and Otis offer superb downhill and cross-country skiing. Winter is also time for special events like "Christmas on Main Street" in Stockbridge. Norman Rockwell's quintessential American small town is decked out and ready for company. You can shop for gifts, attend stage and choral productions, meet Santa Claus, and ride in a horse drawn sleigh over the hills. In all the villages across South County, you can find old fashion Christmas cheer: caroling on Main street, burning yule logs, and drinking mulled cider through the month of December.

EXPLORING SOUTH COUNTY

South County probably has thousands more trees than people. This portion of the Berkshires consists of 13 incorporated entities, but only Great Barrington and Lee are actual towns; the other eleven are villages. It is well worth the drive to visit these villages, but don't expect to find a restaurant, drug store, or even a gas station in every one. A car is essential in South County, as no train service exists and there's only limited bus and taxi service. Roads are clearly marked, however. U.S. 7 and Routes 71, 23, and 102 are the main roads in South County.

About the Restaurants

Country ambience meets urban sophistication in South County. Clever chefs and restaurateurs have adapted 18th-century stagecoach inns, 19th-century Berkshire cottages, and 20th-century storefronts into reputable dining establishments. Contemporary American, Vietnamese, sushi, and British afternoon tea sit comfortably alongside little country cafés, where owners behind the counter squeeze fresh orange juice and serve homemade sausage, farm-fresh eggs, and hot apple pie.

But what sets this region apart from its city cousins are the fruits, vegetables, and dairy that are minutes away from farm to table. South County is proud of its local produce and many restaurants display a logo at the bottom of their menus, "We serve Berkshire Grown."

About the Hotels

In South County, you can choose from large inns with more than 100 rooms, chain motels, and exclusive hostelries. Yet, the most authentic Berkshire experience is a stay at one of the small bed-and-breakfasts that abound throughout the area. From the time in 1781 when the widow Anna Bingham requested a license to operate "a large and elegant house" as a tavern and inn, the most common lodging here has been a room in a private house. All are smoke-free and few accept pets. Most accommodations in the region require a three-night minimum on summer and holiday weekends.

WHAT IT COSTS				
$$$$	**$$$**	**$$**	**$**	**¢**
RESTAURANTS over $28	$20–$28	$12–$20	$8–$12	under $8
HOTELS over $220	$170–$220	$120–$170	$80–$120	under $80

Restaurant prices are for a main course at dinner, excluding sales tax of 5%. Hotel prices are for two people in a standard double room in high season, excluding service charges and 9.7% tax.

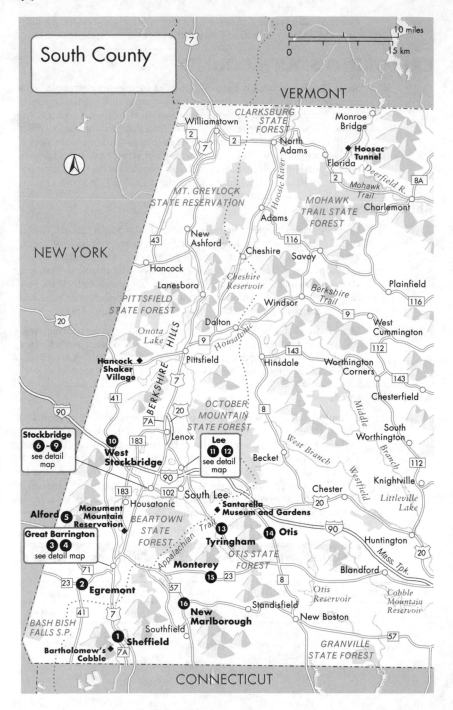

South County

0 ————— 10 miles
0 ————— 15 km

VERMONT

CLARKSBURG STATE FOREST

Williamstown

Monroe Bridge

North Adams

◆ **Hoosac Tunnel**

Florida

Deerfield R.

8A

2

Mohawk Trail

MOHAWK TRAIL STATE FOREST

Charlemont

NEW YORK

MT. GREYLOCK STATE RESERVATION

New Ashford

Adams

116

Cheshire

Savay

Hancock

Cheshire Reservoir

Plainfield

Lanesboro

Berkshire Trail

116

PITTSFIELD STATE FOREST

Windsor

9

West Cummington

Onota Lake

Dalton

112

Hancock Shaker Village ◆

Pittsfield

Hinsdale

143

Worthington Corners

143

Chesterfield

BERKSHIRE HILLS

9

Housatonic

41

OCTOBER MOUNTAIN STATE FOREST

8

South Worthington

7

7A

20

Stockbridge
6-**9**
see detail map

183

10

Lenox

Lee
11 **12**
see detail map

West Branch

Becket

112

West Stockbridge

90

Knightville

Littleville Lake

183

102

South Lee

Chester

20

Alford **5**

Monument Mountain Reservation

Housatonic

BEARTOWN STATE FOREST

Appalachian Trail

Santarella ◆ Museum and Gardens

90

Huntington

Great Barrington
3 **4**
see detail map

13

14 **Otis**

20

Tyringham

23 **2**

71

OTIS STATE FOREST

Mass. Tpk.

23

Egremont

57

Monterey

15 23

8

Blandford

BASH BISH FALLS S.P.

41

7

16 **New Marlborough**

Standisfield

New Boston

Otis Reservoir

Cobble Mountain Reservoir

57

Southfield

GRANVILLE STATE FOREST

1 **Sheffield**

Bartholomew's Cobble ◆

7A

CONNECTICUT

SHEFFIELD

❶ *142 mi west of Boston; 6 mi north of Canaan, Connecticut.*

Sheffield likes its "firsts." The first permanent Berkshire settler came to Sheffield in 1725. It was the first town established, in 1733. Sheffield built the region's first meeting house and Congregational Church, in 1735. The town proprietors tempted the local manpower to build the church with a carrot and a stick, that is, a measure of rum for working or a fine for shirking. Thirty-six years after the first settler arrived, in 1761, Berkshire County was established and Sheffield declared itself the first shiretown, or county seat. Its courthouse was only two months old when the land underneath the building was declared to be within the borders of Great Barrington.

Nonetheless, Sheffield maintains a proud history. To preserve this history, the Sheffield Historical Society has purchased and preserved seven key buildings on its historic **Main Street.** A stroll down the historic street will take you past the 1774 Dan Raymond House, the 1820 Parker Hall, the Carriage House and Tool exhibit, an 1876 house, an 1830s smoke-house, and an 1834 stone store. Many houses have their construction date written above the door. Continuing the historic theme, Sheffield has more antiques stores than any other town in the Berkshires, and the several inns either incorporate the date built in their name or have available written histories about the structure. In Sheffield you not only know where you are but when you are.

Outside of town, on Route 41, drive past the Berkshire School and look on the right for a trail marker to **Race Brook Falls.** The falls have a satisfying drop, and the brook lives up to its name, racing along with a loud splashy noise. The trail is part of the Appalachian Trail.

Bartholomew's Cobble is a natural rock garden beside the Housatonic River (the Native American name means "river beyond the mountains"). The 277-acre site is filled with trees, ferns, wildflowers, and 5 mi of hiking trails. The visitor center has a museum. ⊠ *Weatogue Rd., Rte. 7A* ☎ *413/229–8600* 🖃 *$5* ⊙ *Daily dawn–dusk.*

Where to Eat

$–$$$ ✕ **Limey's.** A casual roadhouse with an English pub flare, Limey's is part bar, part dining room. You have two menus to choose from: the lighter menu includes such staples as burgers, potato skins, and grilled sandwiches; the dinner menu nods to the British owners with fish-and-chips and steak-and-kidney pie as well as chops, steak, chicken, and fish. ⊠ *650 N. Main St.* ☎ *413/229–9000* 🖃 *MC, V* ⊙ *No lunch.*

$ ✕ **Village on the Green Restaurant and Pizzeria.** This little establishment is friendly, generous with portions, and serves casual American fare and pizza. ⊠ *113 Main St.* ☎ *413/229–7500* 🖃 *MC, V.*

Where to Stay

$$–$$$$ 🏨 **Race Brook Lodge.** This brook-side compound of former haylofts, ice-houses, and hoop sheds proudly promotes itself as a "chintz-free" lodging alternative. Indeed, the lodge and its several outbuildings have cozy and rustic rooms with plush touches and inviting designs, including hand-hewn beams, wide-plank floors, country quilts, eclectic art, pitched ceilings, skylights, and hand-stenciling. Several of the buildings contain just three or four guest rooms and kitchens, making them ideal for families or friends traveling together. With a brief interruption, the Stagecoach Tavern has served travelers since 1829. It is now reopening as part of Race Brook Lodge. ⊠ *864 S. Undermountain Rd., Rte. 41, Sheffield 01257* ☎ *413/229–2916 or 888/725–6343* 🖶 *413/229–6629* ⊕ *www. rblodge.com* 🛏 *30 rooms, 28 with bath, 2 suites* ♿ *Dining room, some kitchens, Internet, meeting room, no-smoking rooms; no room phones, no room TVs* ▤ *AE, MC, V* ⫪⊙⫪ *BP.*

$$–$$$ ⊞ **Birch Hill Bed & Breakfast.** High on a hill, this 1780s house overlooks lakes and meadows. Set on 20 acres, it has the feel of a country manor. The rooms are finished with some antiques and thoughtful touches like robes. ⊠ *254 S. Undermountain Rd., 01257* ☎ *413/229–2143 or 800/ 359–3969* 🖶 *413/229–3405* ⊕ *www.birchhillbb.com* 🛏 *7 rooms, 5 with bath* ▤ *No credit cards* ⫪⊙⫪ *BP.*

$$–$$$ ⊞ **Broken Hill Manor.** Although this inn is 4 mi from Sheffield, it's well worth the trip. The house was built for the Worthington family in 1900, and their collection of Egyptian pieces graces the common rooms and bedrooms, including reproductions of the royal chair and Nubian guard from King Tut's tomb and a brass bed. For breakfast, such specialties of the house as cinnamon pancakes are served in either the dining room or on the patio. Complimentary afternoon tea or wine is served upon request. Bedrooms are spacious and each is named for a heroine of opera. ⊠ *771 West Rd., 01257* ☎ *413/528–6159 or 877/535–6159* ⊕ *www. brokenhillmanor.com* 🛏 *8 rooms* ▤ *AE, D, MC, V* ⫪⊙⫪ *BP.*

$$ ⊞ **The Sheffield Inn.** A seat in the shade on the wraparound porch of this buttery-white house evokes a bygone era. Indeed, the house opened as an inn shortly after it was built in 1848. Inside, large common rooms are appointed with antiques and Oriental rugs. Bedrooms have a country feel, some with brass beds, and patchwork quilts. The house is on 10 acres, which you are encouraged to roam about. ⊠ *84 Maple St., 01257* ☎ *413/229–9992* ⊕ *www.sheffieldinn.com* 🛏 *6 rooms* ♿ *No room TVs* ▤ *AE, D, MC, V* ⫪⊙⫪ *BP.*

$–$$ ⊞ **Berkshire 1802 House.** Set on 2 acres, this Victorian house provides a warm New England ambience, from its colorful and bold antique interior appointments to its homemade breakfast. The rooms have a rainbow of patchwork quilts and hand-painted furniture. The two rooms with shared bath work well as a suite for a family or friends traveling together. ⊠ *48 S. Main St., 01257* ☎ *413/229–2612* ⊕ *www. berkshire1802.com* 🛏 *7 rooms, 5 with bath* ♿ *No room TVs* ▤ *AE, D, MC, V* ⫪⊙⫪ *BP.*

$–$$ ⊞ **Staveleigh House.** In this charming 1817 colonial, innkeeper Ali Winston serves a memorable breakfast that might include apple-cheddar quiche, Belgian waffles, pumpkin bread, or baked rhubarb jam. Tea and cookies or cakes are served in the afternoons in the common room or outside under the trees. Rooms are appointed with period furnishings, and come with a twin, queen, or king-size bed. ⊠ *59 Main St., 01257*

☎ *413/229–2129* ⊕ *www.staveleigh.com* ⇆ *7 rooms, 5 with bath* ♿ *No TV in some rooms* ☰ *AE, D, MC, V* ❢❢ *BP.*

The Arts

The **Barrington Stage Company** (☎ 413/528–8806, box office 413/528–8888 ⊕ www.barringtonstageco.org) delights audiences with dramatic plays, comedies, and musicals. In season, performances such as *Sweet Charity* are presented on the main stage at the Consolati Performing Arts Center on the Southern Berkshire Regional School campus. A second stage is devoted to new plays and experimental works. Ticket prices range from $15 to $48 for the main stage, $12 to $32 for the second stage. Call and ask about dates and performers scheduled for the BSC night-time cabarets. Off-season there are productions and other events at the BSC StudioSpace on Main Street.

The **Berkshire Choral Festival** (✉ 245 N. Undermountain Rd. ☎ 413/229–8526 ⊕ www.chorus.org), at the Berkshire School, is a five-week summer study program for young singers. At the end of each week, the school hosts a performance; tickets range from $25 to $40. Performances begin at 8 PM, but attendees are invited to come any time after 5 to picnic and stroll the grounds. There is a preperformance talk by a musicologist followed by a concert, which has featured the music of Brahms, Beethoven, and Haydn.

Shopping

Antiques

Antiques stores line U.S. 7, from the Great Barrington border through Sheffield to the Connecticut border. All are open on weekends, some on weekdays.

Bradford Auction Galleries (✉ 725 N. Main St. ☎ 413/229–6667) holds monthly auctions of furniture, paintings and prints, china, glass, silver, and Oriental rugs. A tag sale of household items occurs daily.

At **Bruce Sikora Antiquarian** (✉ 549 Rte. 7 ☎ 413/229–6049), you'll find fine arts and decorative accessories.

Centuryhurst Antiques (✉ 173 S. Main St. ☎ 413229–8131) specializes in clocks.

Stop in at **Corner House Antiques** (✉ Rte. 7 ☎ 413/229–6627) for 19th- and 20th-century wicker and bamboo.

Cupboard and Roses Antiques (✉ 296 S. Main St. ☎ 413/229–3070) has a large collection of 18th- and 19th-century painted furniture from Scandinavia.

Dovetail Antiques (✉ Rte. 7 ☎ 413/229–2628) specializes in 18th-, 19th-, and 20th-century clocks, stoneware, and spongeware.

Good & Hutchinson (✉ 749 N. Main St. ☎ 413/229–8832) sells American and European furniture, paintings, and decorative accessories. They also do appraisals.

At the end of Berkshire School Road, follow the sign to **Hill House Antiques** (✉ 276 S. Undermountain Rd. ☎ 413/229–2374) for Arts and Crafts pieces, mission furniture, and some reproductions.

Le Trianon Fine Antiques (✉ 1854 N. Main St. ☎ 413/528–0775) specializes in 18th- and 19th-century continental formal and country furniture.

At **May's Everything Shop** (✉ 779 N. Main St. ☎ 413/229–2037) small items, collectibles, toys, and dolls are the specialty.

Painted Porch Antiques (✉ 102 S. Main St. ☎ 413/229–2700) sells French and English country furniture.

Twin Fire Antiques (✉ 1350 Berkshire School Rd. ☎ 413/229–8899) carries in country pine furniture.

EGREMONT

❷ *8 mi northwest of Sheffield.*

Egremont is made up of two village centers, North Egremont and South Egremont, separated by Baldwin Hill. North Egremont, on Route 71, has a country store, two bed-and-breakfasts, and an old coach inn converted into the Elm Court restaurant. South Egremont, on Routes 23 and 41, has the historic Egremont Inn, the Old Mill restaurant, and many antiques shops.

Egremont was incorporated in 1760 and named after the Earl of Egremont (many Berkshire towns incorporated before the Revolutionary War were named after towns or people in England). At that time, it consisted of grist- and sawmills, farms, and a tavern. The village sprang to life when the stagecoach came down the Albany to Hartford Turnpike, which stopped in Egremont en route.

Egremont provides an alluring combination of outdoor activities, good food, and antiques shops. It has some of the highest hills in the Berkshires, perfect for skiing, hiking, and soaking up the panoramic views. Egremont is not a walking town. The village centers are heavily trafficked, and there are no sidewalks. However you can still get outside, walk the back roads, ski Catamount, and golf at Egremont Country Club.

About 4 mi outside of town, **Prospect Lake** is an ideal spot for walking, boating, picnicking, and swimming. Although most of the lake is bordered by private homes, here you can find a beach, picnic tables, a snack bar and boats for rent. Anglers can purchase a 3-day fishing license at the park. ✉ *50 Prospect Lake Rd., Route 41, Egremont* ☎ *413/528–4158* 💲 *$5* ⊙ *June–Oct.*

> off the
> beaten
> path

BASH BISH FALLS – If you have the time to wind your way to this far corner of South County, don't miss Bash Bish Falls. To get here, head south on Route 41, and then make an immediate right onto Mount Washington Road, which leads to Bash Bish State Park and the falls. The falls drop 200 feet into a pool. If you think you see a reflection in the water below, it may be the face of White Swan.

White Swan was an Indian maiden, and the legend is that she stared into the water when she was grieving over a lost love. She had married a brave she loved but could not give him children. He had deserted her and took another wife who did conceive. She stared into the water, feeling abandoned and forlorn, when she thought she heard the voice of her dead Mother call to her from beneath the water. Just as she rose to leap into the pool, her former lover approached. He tried to save her but failed, and they fell the 200 feet together. His body was recovered, but hers was never found. The legend continues that in certain light you can see her smiling up at you from below the water.

Where to Eat

$$–$$$ ✕ **Elm Court Inn.** Inside this 1791 former stagecoach inn, chef-owner Urs Bieri has created a choice of continental dishes with Swiss accents. You can choose from three menus: the chef's choice prix-fixe dinner, the seasonal menu, and the menu of classics. The seasonal menu might include grilled loin of New Zealand venison with polenta or roasted cod with fennel and an "Atkins Diet" side selection. Among the classics are Wiener schnitzel and rack of lamb. The atmosphere is warm and welcoming, both in the large dining room and the tavern area. ⊠ *227 Rte. 71, North Egremont* ☎ *413/528–0325* ▤ *AE, D, MC, V* ☉ *Closed Tues. and Wed.*

$$–$$$ ✕ **John Andrew's Restaurant.** Housed in an 1890 farmhouse on the edge of town, this restaurant brings its pastoral warmth into its kitchen. Such entrees as organic salmon, Stone Church Farm roasted chicken, and double-cut pork chops with potato and apple wood smoked bacon cake highlight the menu. There are also appetizers, salads, and pasta dishes. You can dine inside, where coral washed walls and hardwood floors lend a cozy ambience, or outside in the garden. A bar menu of lighter fare, such as grilled lobster sandwich with shoe string potatoes, is offered every night but Saturday. ⊠ *Rte. 23, South Egremont* ☎ *413/528–3469* ▤ *MC, V* ☉ *Closed Wed., Nov.–June. No lunch.*

$$ ✕ **Old Mill.** This rambling restaurant fashioned out of a 1797 gristmill and blacksmith's shop has wide-plank floors and large windows overlooking the river below. With such a charmed setting, the kitchen could get away with serving old-hat American standbys, but the food here is at least as appealing as the space in which it is served. The menu lists a mix of regional New England and Southern dishes, including a succulent oven-roasted poussin with garlic. A lighter menu is served in the cozy bar. ⊠ *Rte. 23, South Egremont* ☎ *413/528–1421* ▤ *AE, DC, MC, V* ☉ *Closed Mon. No lunch.*

¢–$ ✕ **Mom's.** You can order breakfast until 3 PM and lunch until 4 PM inside this roadside diner, complete with a screen door that slams, a high counter, and bare-wood tables. From omelets, eggs, sausage, bacon to burgers, wraps, soups, and salads, the food is hearty and cooked-to-order. If the sun is shining and the weather is warm, grab a seat on the rear deck. Your toes can almost reach the mill stream. ⊠ *Rte. 23, South Egremont* ☎ *413/528–2414* ▤ *MC, V* ☉ *No dinner.*

Where to Stay

$$–$$$$ ✕🏠 **Egremont Inn.** The public rooms in this 1780 stagecoach inn are enormous, and each has a fireplace. Bedrooms are on the small side but have four-poster beds (some have claw-foot baths) and, like the rest of the inn, unpretentious furnishings. On summer weekends, in July and August, you can book only three-night packages. They range in price from $490 to $730, and include breakfast daily and one dinner during your stay. Windows sweep around two sides of the stylish restaurant ($$–$$$), where flames flicker in a huge fireplace. The menu changes frequently but might include pan-seared Chilean sea bass with shiitakes and leeks or filet mignon with mashed potato and a caramelized-onion sauce. There's live jazz twice weekly. ✉ *10 Old Sheffield Rd., South Egremont 01258* ☎ *413/528–2111 or 800/859–1780* 🖷 *413/528–3284* ⊕ *www. egremontinn.com* ⇙ *19 rooms, 1 suite* ⏥ *Restaurant, tennis court, pool, bar, meeting rooms; no room phones, no room TVs, no smoking* ☰ *AE, D, MC, V* ¶☉ *CP, MAP.*

$$–$$$$ 🏠 **Weathervane Inn.** Originally a farmhouse built in 1785, this inn is set on 10 landscaped acres. In the 1835 Greek Revival addition are period-appointed guest rooms and comfortable sitting rooms. Home-baked cookies and cakes are served daily at afternoon tea, and the owners will prepare boxed picnics and formal dinners for groups of 10 or more upon request. Spa services including yoga and massage are available. Golf courses and tennis courts are nearby. ✉ *Rte. 23* ⏎ *Box 388, South Egremont 01258* ☎ *413/528–9580 or 800/528–9580* 🖷 *413/528–1713* ⊕ *www.weathervaneinn.com* ⇙ *8 rooms, 2 suites* ⏥ *Pool, bar, meeting rooms; no TV in some rooms, no smoking* ☰ *AE, MC, V* ¶☉ *BP.*

$$–$$$ 🏠 **Swiss Hutte.** You're only a few steps from the room to the slopes at this hotel, set in its own private valley at Catamount. In summer you can relax on either a patio or a balcony to enjoy the view. The grounds have walking paths and a pond, and like so many places in the Berkshires, it is not easy to know where you are: if you walk from your room to the dining room, you are crossing the state line from Massachusetts to New York. The large dining room, surrounded by lace-curtained windows, is bright and formal. Chef and owner Gert Alper creates continental cuisine using Berkshire Grown products. ✉ *Rte. 23, South Egremont 01258* ☎ *413/528–6200* ⊕ *www.swisshutte.com* ⇙ *12 rooms* ⏥ *Restaurant, outdoor pool* ☰ *MC, V* ¶☉ *MAP.*

$–$$ 🏠 **Baldwin Hill Farm Bed-and-Breakfast.** This 19th-century farmhouse sits on a hilltop surrounded by 450 acres. From the front porch you can see mountains, and with a turn of the head, you can gaze out over the well-tended farmland. The front parlor, furnished with antiques, has a fieldstone fireplace and a piano. A full breakfast is served in the dining room each morning; you make your selections the night before. Outside you have acres to hike and, in winter, to cross-country ski. ✉ *121 Baldwin Hill Rd., South Egremont 01258* ☎ *413/528–4092 or 888/528–4092* 🖷 *413/528–6365* ⊕ *www.baldwinhillfarm.com* ⇙ *6 rooms, 4 with bath* ⏥ *Outdoor pool; no room TVs, no smoking* ☰ *AE, MC, V* ¶☉ *BP.*

Sports & the Outdoors

Golf

If you would like to hit a little white ball at the same time that you walk, call **Egremont Country Club** (⊠ 685 S. Egremont Rd., Rte. 23 ☎ 413/528–4222) and ask for a tee time. Greens fees are $22 on weekdays and $36 on the weekends. There is a clubhouse, tennis courts, and pro shop. It is a challenging and scenic course. The first nine holes, you are in Great Barrington; the back nine you're in Egremont.

Horseback Riding

At **Blue Riding Stables** (⊠ 15 Farm La. ☎ 413/528–5299) lessons focus on the walk, trot, and canter with an emphasis on balance. Ponies, donkeys, goats, cats, bunnies, and chickens are also here to visit with. Note, though, that all riding is bareback, and trail riding is not available. There are indoor and outdoor riding areas.

Skiing

CATAMOUNT SKI AREA With a 1,000-foot vertical drop and 100% snowmaking capacity, this scenic slope on the New York state border is ideal for family skiing, with its slow and even grades. Nevertheless, the most varied terrain in the Berkshires is here, meaning that skiers of all abilities and tastes can find something to keep them happy. ⊠ *Rte. 23, South Egremont, 01258* ☎*413/528–1262, 800/342–1840 snow conditions* ⊕ *www.catamountski.com.*

Child care. Skiing and snowboarding programs are held for kids 4–12 and 7–12, respectively; a playroom caters to children ages 2–6.

Downhill. There are 28 trails, served by seven lifts, plus a snowboard area called Megaplex Terrain Park, which is separated from the downhill area and has its own lift and a 400-foot halfpipe. A 2002 addition is the Sidewinder, an intermediate cruising trail, more than 1 mi from top to bottom. There's also lighted nighttime boarding and skiing.

Shopping

Kenver Ltd. (⊠ 39 Main St., South Egremont ☎ 413/528–2330) carries elegant sports- and outdoors-wear, plus snowshoes, skis, skates, and other top-of-the-line equipment.

The pieces at **Geffner-Schatzky Antiques** (⊠ 40 Main St., Rte. 23, South Egremont ☎ 413/528–0057) were collected by the owners during their trips to Europe. The shop is full of unusual and beautiful items, with and emphasis on 19th- and 20th-century French furnishing and lighting. The jewelry case has the just-for-fun to the fairly fabulous.

Inside **Red Barn Antiques** (⊠ 72 Main St., South Egremont ☎ 413/528–3230) is an assortment on antique furniture, accessories, and glass, but the real emphasis here is on lighting. On display are kerosene lights and early electric light fixtures. You can also get fine metals polished and old light fixtures restored.

The Splendid Pheasant (⊠ Rte. 23, South Egremont ☎ 413/528–5755) divides its collection into two buildings. In one is American folk art, game boards, weather vanes, and country furniture, and the other houses 18th-

and 19th-century furniture and decorative accessories. The store is open daily June through September and by appointment the rest of the year.

GREAT BARRINGTON

③-④ *4 mi east of Egremont.*

As in Stockbridge and many Berkshire towns, Main Street in Great Barrington lies at the bottom of a bowl, with mountains rising all around. The Housatonic River runs through town, crossed by many bridges.

Great Barrington was the first place in the nation to free slaves under due process of law; it was also the birthplace of W. E. B. DuBois, the civil rights leader, author, and educator. Great Barrington was also the first town in the world to have a system of electric lights in commercial use provided by alternating current. Franklin L. Pope, who was born here, was a partner of Thomas Edison. Pope invented the first system for transmission of Wall Street quotes over telegraph lines. With Edison he invented the electrical-signal system for railroads. Another resident, William Stanley, invented a multiple system of alternating current. He lit the streets here in 1886 before they had electric street lights in New York City or Washington, D.C. Another town notable was William Cullen Bryant, who left Great Barrington for New York, where he founded the *New York Review* and was editor of the *New York Evening Post*. He loved the work but missed the Berkshires. "There is no tonic," he wrote, "like the Housatonic."

Today Franklin L. Pope's former home is the Wainwright Inn; William Cullen Bryant's former home is the Finnerty-Stevens Funeral Home (the front section, not the side and rear additions), and Stanley's former home is Eisner Camp and Conference Center. The largest town in South County, Great Barrington has great restaurants and is a favorite of antiques hunters.

The **Housatonic River Walk** is well worth a step off the pavement. You enter through the gate on the left of Brooks Pharmacy (197 Main St.) and take the stairs down to the riverbank, where you can stroll along a short path. The sound of rushing water,a bench to sit and rest, and the natural setting are welcome changes from concrete and traffic noise above, especially on a hot summer day. This is the Berkshire version of the pause that refreshes.

Three miles north of Great Barrington, en route to Stockbridge, you can leave your car in a parking lot beside U.S. 7 and climb Squaw Peak in **③ Monument Mountain Reservation** (☎ 413/298–3239). The 3-mi circular hike (a trail map is displayed in the parking lot) takes you from 1,000 to 1,640 feet. There's a turnoff where you can choose a less steep or a steeper ascent. Early in his career, William Cullen Bryant wrote a story about Monument Mountain. It was the Berkshire version of *Romeo and Juliet*. A squaw, forbidden by the Mohican Indian tribe to marry her beloved, leaped from the top of the mountain. When the tribe saw what their stubbornness had wrought they regretted their decision. It became a tradition that as any tribe member passed the spot from which she

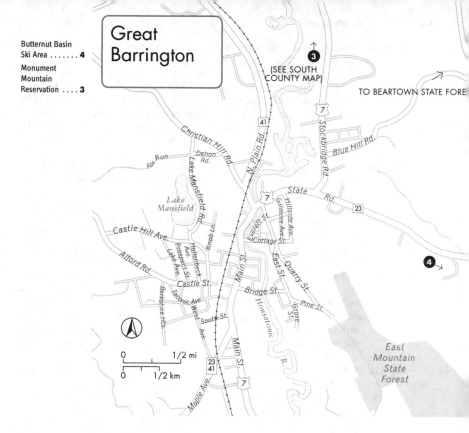

Great Barrington

(SEE SOUTH COUNTY MAP)

TO BEARTOWN STATE FORE[ST]

leaped, they would place a stone, mourn the loss, and remember their own stony hearts. The pile of stone grew, formed the top of the mountain, and gave it its name. When you reach the top there is a 15-foot-high outcropping said to be the collection of stones. In the 1850, a party of guests of David Dudley Field climbed this mountain; caught in a rain storm, they spent many hours and formed a friendship. Among the many guests were Nathaniel Hawthorne and Herman Melville. From the top of the surrounding mountains on a clear day you can see all the way to Mt. Greylock and down into the nearby towns.

Where to Eat

$$–$$$$ ✕ **Bizen.** Diners seeking authentic Japanese fare need look no farther than this sushi bar–cum–restaurant. A corridor edged with river rocks and carpeted with bamboo leads to individual dining areas, which typically bustle with patrons. In Japanese fashion, you remove your shoes and sit on cushions at low tables; you can also order from the sushi bar or sake lounge. Sushi, sashimi, hand rolls, soups, and a variety of grilled and cooked dishes fill out the menu. Prix-fixe meals are also offered, prices of which vary depending on the number of appetizers, entrées, and sakes. ✉ *17 Railroad St.* ☎ *413/528–4343* ✍ *Reservations essential* ▱ *AE, D, MC, V.*

$$–$$$$ ✕ **Pearl's.** Run by the same owners as Lenox's trendy Bistro Zinc, Pearl's adds a dash of big-city atmosphere to the Berkshires with its pressed-tin ceilings, tall booths, exposed-brick walls, and well-coiffured crowd. The menu updates the old bigger-is-better steak-house tradition by serving thick-and-tender chops, prime rib, wild game, raw oysters, and fresh lobsters with innovative ingredients. Call ahead for a table on weekends, or simply hobnob and sip well-chosen wines and creative drinks at the elegant bar. ✉ 47 Railroad St. ☎ 413/528–7767 ⊟ AE, MC, V ⊗ No lunch.

$$–$$$ ✕ **Castle Street Cafe.** Chef-owner Michael Ballon's approach to food is to stress the freshest locally grown produce in simple, elegant recipes. Warm duck salad, wild king salmon with saffron, and portobello mushroom ravioli with wild mushroom sauce are some of the highlights. Hardwood floors and sleek furnishings, accented by rotating original local art, create a pleasing ambience and complement the eclectic fare. If you choose to sit at the bar, you can order from a menu of lighter fare. ✉ 10 Castle St. ☎ 413/528–5244 ⊟ AE, D, MC, V ⊗ Closed Tues.

★ **$$–$$$** ✕ **Due.** Next door to Verdura is what appears to be a separate restaurant; not quite. The cuisine is Spanish, not Italian, and the interior is less tony urban and more European bistro, but inside the two are connected. Both restaurants share the same kitchen and same friendly and enthusiastic staff. The genius of the cooking is in the blending of herbs and seasonings. Mediterranean fare rarely tastes better. ✉ 44 Railroad St. ☎ 413/528–8969 ⊟ AE, MC, V.

$$–$$$
Fodor'sChoice
★ ✕ **Shiro.** Sushi and other Japanese fare have become increasingly popular in Great Barrington in recent years, helping solidify the town's reputation as the Berkshires' most sophisticated restaurant town. Shiro is a warmly lit, art-filled space that serves superb sushi but also such delicious hot entrées as lightly battered and fried wasabi shrimp over wilted spinach, and tempura tuna and crab in seaweed roll served with a spicy aioli and caviar. A full range of sakes is available. ✉ 105 Stockbridge Rd. ☎ 413/528–1898 ⊟ AE, D, MC, V.

★ **$$–$$$** ✕ **Verdura.** With all the fancy culinary hot spots that have opened in Great Barrington in the past few years, this restaurant stands out. The understated and classy decor, youthful and friendly staff, and superbly executed Tuscan cooking make for a satisfying experience. In a handsome storefront space with sponge-dappled ocher and pale green walls, you can try saffron-lobster risotto with mascarpone or wood-grilled prosciutto-wrapped brook trout with lentils, roasted fennel, and sage-brown butter. The wild-mushroom pizza with leeks, chèvre, and white-truffle oil is another favorite. ✉ 44 Railroad St. ☎ 413/528–8969 ⊟ AE, MC, V.

$–$$ ✕ **Helsinki Tea Company.** The emphasis is on Finnish, Russian, and Jewish cuisines, prepared with lots of spices and served in big portions, at this restaurant that suggests a lost world of Old European elegance. A hodgepodge of colorful cushions, fringed draperies, and objets d'art creates the feeling of an intimate café. It doesn't get much cozier than sitting by a roaring fire, tucking into an order of Midnight Train to Moscow (chicken-apple bratwurst, hot cabbage slaw, and potato latkes), and then lingering over one of the numerous tea choices (or something stronger—the restaurant has a full liquor license) and live music at the attached Club Helsinki. Sunday brunch is a popular affair. ⊠ *284 Main St.* ☎ *413/528–3394* ☰ *MC, V.*

¢–$ ✕ **Baba Louie's.** This intimate and always-crowded pizza spot with a rustic ambience serves delicious thin-crust pies with a riot of exotic ingredients. The pomodoro bianco comes topped with roasted portobellos, roasted garlic, tomatoes, and chèvre; and the Isabella is covered with roasted sweet potatoes, roasted parsnips, caramelized onions, shaved fennel, and balsamic vinegar. The tasty panini sandwiches, bruschetta, or Gorgonzola-pear salad are also worth a try. ⊠ *286 Main St.* ☎ *413/ 528–8100* ☰ *D, MC, V.*

¢ ✕ **Martin's Restaurant.** Snag a window table for breakfast as this family-run diner, which looks out onto a busy street, and watch Great Barrington life unfold. Nothing comes from a can or freezer here. Martin's makes its own turkey, corned beef, and granola. Breakfast is served all day, and the burgers are good. Crayons are at every table for kids of all ages. ⊠ *40 Railroad St.* ☎ *413/528–5455* ☰ *No credit cards* ☽ *No dinner.*

Where to Stay

$$$–$$$$ ▦ **Wainright Inn.** Built in 1766 as the Troy Tavern & Inn, this hostelry had one brief period as a private home, when it was inhabited by Franklin L. Pope. The portraits of the electrical innovator and his wife are displayed on the mantel in the front room. You enter the inn via the large wraparound porch into an antiques-filled parlor and dining room. The tables and sideboards are filled with fresh flowers and objets d'art. The rooms, many of which have fireplaces and four-poster beds, are appointed with a mix of modern and period furnishings. ⊠ *518 S. Main St., 01230* ☎ *413/528–2062* ⊕ *www.wainwrightinn.com* ↩ *8 rooms* ♨ *Internet; no smoking, no room phones, no room TVs* ☰*MC, V* ⦿*BP.*

$$–$$$ ▦ **Seekonk Pines Inn.** With so many charming and homey touches, it is hard to pick one room in this 1832 inn. Possibly it is the trundle beds, or the doll and old game collections displayed in the parlor, or the stenciling on the walls. Perhaps it is that each room is named for one of the home's former owners. Each room is appointed with antiques and curios. Outside, you can while away the late afternoon on the wraparound porch or take a stroll around the grounds. There are plenty of great places nearby for hiking, biking, and cross-country skiing. In the morning, sculptor and owner Bruce Lefkowitz cooks breakfast. A two-bedroom cabin with a kitchen, ideal for families or friends traveling together, is also available. ⊠ *142 Seekonk Cross Rd., 01230* ☎ *413/528–4192 or 800/292–4192* ⊕ *www.seekonkpines.com* ↩ *6 rooms, 1 cabin* ♨ *Pool; no room phones, no room TVs, no smoking,* ☰ *MC, V* ⦿ *BP.*

$–$$$ ▦ **Windflower.** When you enter this late 19th-century white clapboard house, a broad staircase and gracious rooms invite you into warm, period surroundings. Fresh flowers, a piano, and game boards complement the common rooms. The period decor extends into the bedrooms, some of which have fireplaces and canopied beds; three rooms have the added amenity of opening onto the screened porch overlooking a stream. In the morning, you're treated to a full breakfast, and afternoon tea is served with home-baked goods. And before dinner, take a walk along the water or a stroll through the perennial gardens. ⊠ *684 S. Egremont Rd., 01230* ☎ *413/528–2720 or 800/992–1993* ⊕ *www.windflowerinn. com* ⋑ *13 rooms* ⚹ *Pool* ▤ *MC, V* ⦿ *BP.*

$–$$ ⌑ **The Turning Point.** This building has been doing service as an inn since 1802, when the stagecoach came through. The well-appointed common rooms and bedrooms are cozy and comfortable. As this inn is owned by a chef, breakfast is one of the attractions. Chef Rachel O'Rourke bakes daily hot and savory treats such as chocolate zucchini bread, lemon scones, or pumpkin waffles to accompany a smoked salmon omelet with cavier garnish. The two-bedroom cottage in the rear of the property is perfect for a family or a group of friends traveling together. The inn is only minutes away from Butternut ski area. ⊠ *3 Lake Buel Rd., 01230* ☎ *413/ 528–4777* ⊕ *www.turningpointinn.com* ⋑ *6 rooms, 2 with bath, 1 cottage* ⚹ *No room TVs* ▤ *No credit cards* ⦿ *BP.*

Nightlife & the Arts

Nightlife

From 4 PM to midnight on weekdays and 5 PM to midnight on weekends, head to **Armi** (⊠ 485 S. Main St. ☎ 413/528–3296) for live music, an open mike, an occasional poetry reading, drinks, and comfort food from around the world. **Club Helsinki** (⊠ 284 Main St. ☎ 413/528–3394) draws some of the region's top jazz, blues, soul, and folk acts in the region; it's open-mike on Sunday.

The Arts

The **Dorian Young Gallery** at Simon's Rock (⊠ 84 Alford Rd. ☎ 413/ 528–0771) hosts art and photography shows and a film festival. Call for dates and details. A variety of high-energy performances by **Mixed Company** (⊠ Rosseter St. ☎ 413/528–2320) is performed in a jewel box theater. When they bid you goodnight after the show, you will leave smiling. In the center of Great Barrington, the **Triplex** (⊠ 70 Railroad St. ☎ 413/ 528–8886) screens first-run films and has a café on the balcony in the lobby. It is the only movie house in South County.

Sports & the Outdoors

Canoeing

You can launch a canoe on the Housatonic River off Bridge Street; a canoe launch is part of the Housatonic River Walk. **Housatonic River Outfitters** (⊠ 684 S. Main St. ☎ 413/528–8811) rents canoes and sells fishing gear, hiking shoes, and maps. They have guide services and give good advice about enjoying the river and the outdoors.

Hiking

On Route 23, about 4 mi east of where U.S. 7 and Route 23 intersect is a sign for the **Appalachian Trail** and a parking lot. Enter the trail for a moderately stenuous 45 minute hike. About 5 minutes in you can see the devastation form the Force 4 tornado that struck Great Barrington on Memorial Day 1995. Shortly after, you will cross a stream. At the top of the trail is Ice Gulch, a gorge so deep and cold that there is often ice in it even in summer. Follow the Ice Gulch ridge to the shelter and a large flat rock from which you can see a wide panorama of valley.

Scenic Flights

Take off in a private plane with **Berkshire Aviation** (✉ Great Barrington Airport, 70 Egremont Plain Rd. ☎ 413/528–1010) and tour the Berkshires. Scenic flights accommodate up to three passengers and cost $90 per hour. In an hour, you can fly the length of the county from north to south, or you can plot your own course and fly over the attractions of your choice.

Skiing

❹ **Butternut Basin Ski Area** has good base facilities, pleasant skiing, 100% snowmaking capabilities, and the longest quad lift in the Berkshires. Two top-to-bottom terrain parks are for snowboarders. Ski and snowboard lessons are available. Kids six and under ski free midweek on nonholidays if accompanied by a paying adult. Usually in the summer Butternut hosts a crafts show and children's activities. Call for details. ✉ *Rte. 23* ☎ *413/528–2000 Ext. 112, 413/528–4433 ski school, 800/438–7669 snow conditions* ⊕ *www.skibutternut.com.*

Child care. The nursery takes children ages 6 months–6 years. The ski school has programs for kids ages 4–12.

Cross-country. Butternut Basin has 8 km (6 mi) of groomed cross-country trails.

Downhill. Only a steep chute or two interrupt the mellow terrain on 22 trails, most of them intermediate. Eight lifts keep skier traffic spread out.

Shopping

Most of the shops in Great Barrington are clustered on Main Street, Railroad Street, and White House Square.

Antiques

South County has the greatest concentration of antiques stores in the Berkshires. Most are on U.S. 7, which is known in Great Barrington as South Main Street, Main Street (in the town center), and Stockbridge Road (north of town).

If you would like to see jewels last worn by your favorite star at an awards ceremony, go to **Bella Collections** (✉ 152 Main St. ☎ 413/528–3936) and look at the Erica Courtney and Sandra Goodkind jewelry. You can ask to have a piece specially designed, or select a one-of-kind ring or necklace. This eclectic store also sells garden furnishings, paintings, and boutique items.

The country folk art merchandise at **Birdhouse Gallery** (✉ 280 Main St., U.S. 7 ☎ 413/528–0984) is always fun and unusual. Selection changes often.

At the **Country Dining Room** (✉ 178 Main St., U.S. 7 ☎ 413/528–5050) you can find elegant antique furniture, glass, and china.

Elise Abrams Antiques (✉ 11 Stockbridge Rd., U.S. 7 ☎ 413/528–3201) sells fine antique china, glassware, and furniture. It's across the street from Jennifer House Commons.

Emporium (✉ 319 Main St., U.S. 7 ☎ 413/528–1660) specializes in art glass, sterling, and fine decorative arts. Peruse the Kahn's Jewelers case for estate and antique jewelry.

Evergreen Contemporary Crafts (✉ 291 Main St., U.S. 7 ☎ 413/528–0511) is the place to go for hand-crafted jewelry, Painted Pony jackets, polished-wood jewel boxes, wind chimes, menorahs, and handbags.

At the **Great Barrington Antiques Center** (✉ 964 S. Main St., U.S. 7 ☎ 413/644–8848) 50 dealers crowd onto one floor, selling Oriental rugs, furniture, and smaller decorative pieces.

The 200 dealers at **Jennifer House Commons** (✉ 420 Stockbridge Rd., U.S. 7) include **Carriage House Antiques,** owned by cabinet maker Erik Schultz, which sells restored late 19th-century tables, chairs, and sideboards; **Coffman's,** which sells furniture, rugs, and accessories from all periods prior to 1950; **Olde Antiques,** which sells smaller collectibles from decanters to chandeliers; and **Wingate Limited,** an interior design showroom with flooring, lighting, linens, furnishings, and some antiques and reproductions. For a respite, stop at the Brewery Restaurant, where you can order burgers, salads, and other pub fare as well as sample house-made beer. The restaurant also serves the heftiest desserts in South County.

For high-end and imported linens and bedding, stop at **La Pace** (✉ 313 Main St., U.S. 7 ☎ 413/528–1888). This small store is packed with everything you need to make your bed and bath luxurious.

Arts & Crafts
Geoffrey Young Gallery (✉ 40 Railroad St. ☎ 413/528–2552) displays contemporary art with an emphasis on up-and-coming artists. Every three weeks, the works change and highlight a different artist.

Owned by photographer Fred Collins, the **Iris Gallery for Fine Art Images** (✉ 47 Railroad St. ☎ 413/644–0045) displays work from a variety of photographers. Past exhibits included the landscapes and conceptual work of the owner.

Stop at **Out of Hand** (✉ 81 Main St., U.S. 7 ☎ 413/528–3791) for a variety of crafts from Berkshire and international artisans. The store also sells women's clothes, textiles, glassware, and baskets.

Beauty
Body and Soul (✉ 40 Railroad St. ☎ 413/528–6465) gives refreshing half-hour and one-hour massages and facials. Special services include a "hot rocks" massage and aromatherapy. Waxing, manicures, and parafin treatments are also available.

For body care, consult **Sappa** (✉ 308 Main St., U.S. 7 ☎ 413/528–6098), where you can find oils, lotions, soaps, and more.

Clothing
Women have been going to **Byzantium** (✉ 32 Railroad St. ☎ 413/528–9496) since 1978. This perennial favorite sells clothes for all occasions at affordable prices.

M. Lacey (⊠ 325 Stockbridge Rd., U.S. 7 ☎ 413/528–5991) sells European clothing for infants and children, as well as cribs, furniture, and nursery accessories.

Food
Satisfy your sophisticated palate at **Bizalion** (⊠ 684 Main St. ☎ 413/644–9988), a French specialty food shop and café, where you can find imported cheeses, 10 different olive oils, cured meats, and brick-oven baked baguettes and pastries. The café serves wine, coffee, charcuterie plates, quiche, and sandwiches.

The **Chef Shop** (⊠ 31 Railroad St., Great Barrington ☎ 413/528–0135) is the place for cookware, bake ware, and much more. If you want to test your skills as a chef, the shop conducts cooking classes and product demonstrations.

A mecca for the health-conscious, the **Co-op Market** (⊠ 42 Bridge St. ☎ 413/528–7547) carries organic fruits and vegetables, multigrain breads, and homeopathic supplements. A small café serves soup, sandwiches, and salads.

Rubiner's Cheesemongers and Grocers (⊠ 264 Main St., Great Barrington ☎ 413/528–0488) sells cheeses, cured meats, fish, and other imported foods. In the front, the mahogany shelves and copper-clad counters display rare and exotic items as well as simple fare. In the back, is a small cafe where you can order coffee and sandwiches to stay or to go.

Home Furnishings
Barbara Boughton Interiors (⊠ 40 Railroad St. ☎ 413/644–9288) integrates art and antiques into interior design.

The specialty of the house at **Mistral's** (⊠ 7 Railroad St. ☎ 413/528–1618) is *accessoir à Provençal*. On the main floor are decorative accessories for the kitchen and dining room, table linens, ceramics, and china. Upstairs is dedicated to soaps and oils, towels, bathrobes, and linens.

From the varied collection of housewares and accessories available at **Seeds & Co.** (⊠ 34 Railroad St. ☎ 413/528–8122), you can find that special something to keep or give as a gift. The look is modern, eye-catching, and different from the ordinary.

ALFORD

❺ *5 mi northwest of Great Barrington.*

Alford village center is a time capsule. Like many early New England villages, the center of town consisted of three buildings—a church, a town hall, and a schoolhouse. Embodied in those three buildings was the soul of the village—religion, government, and education. But where other South County village centers have grown to include more buildings, in Alford no building obscures the past, and it subsequently looks as if time passed it by.

The first Alford settlers arrived in 1740 to what was then the north corner of Great Barrington. In 1756, when the town was incorporated, the

BEST PICKINS'

NATHANIAL HAWTHORNE WROTE *TANGLEWOOD TALES* while living in the little red house in Stockbridge (1850–1852). The story begins as the children are gathered together to go berry and nut picking. Today the pickins' are still good in South County. Here's where to go to find the best.

At **Taft Farm** (✉ 21 Division St., Great Barrington ☎ 413/528-1015) you can buy fruits, vegetables, and berries at the stall, or you can pick your own. The farm also sells free range chickens and fresh eggs. If you arrive at **Rawson Brook Farm** (✉ 185 New Marlboro Rd. Monterey) at 5 PM, you can see goats being milked. If not, you can shop for cheese. You can pick blueberries at **Blueberry Hill Farm** (✉ East St. Mount Washington ☎ 413/528-1479). In fall, the best apple picking is at **Windy Hill Nursery** (✉ Rte. 7 Stockbridge ☎ 413/298-3217). You can pick your own at **Gould Farm** (✉ Gould Rd. Monterey ☎ 413/528-1804) or you go across the street and just eat the farm fresh produce at Gould Farm's Roadside Cafe. On the five weekends prior to Halloween, Howden Farm (✉ Rannapo Rd. Sheffield ☎ 413/229-8481) you can take a hayride and pick your own pumpkin to carve. The Howden pumkin and the Howden "biggie" are the standards for the pumpkin industry nationwide.

citizens of Alford had high hopes for the future. They made their living on farms and in the marble quarries, and that marble was highly prized and used in major civic buildings in New York City and Albany. Buoyed by initial success, Alford incorporated as a separate village, and it seemed the community had as much potential for prosperity and growth as any place in Berkshire County.

Yet Alford has remained a sleepy village. Fortune and growth followed the railroad tracks, and Alford was bypassed. What may have seemed misfortune then has become an advantage now. More than half the houses in Alford are inhabited by second-home owners—people from the city seeking a rural setting and a New England village untouched by time.

Alford Road takes you to the village center. The library, occupying the former town hall, is across the road from the new town hall. The church and the cemetery are on either side of the new town hall. Of note is the cemetery, where you can find the names of the founding fathers of Alford and some of the oldest names in Berkshire County history. You can read the inscriptions or step back and look at the cemetery as a whole: the tombstones are chess pieces.

en route Leaving Alford on Alford Road, turn onto Seekonk Road and then up Round Hill. At the crest of Round Hill is an idyllic rural scene: sheep grazing on the hillside, a well-tended farm, and distant views of the Berkshire Hills. Turn around, go back to Seekonk, and continue to Egremont via Baldwin Hill. At the top of Baldwin Hill, you will find a 360 degree panorama of mountains and rolling fields that glisten with snow in the winter, brightly colored leaves in fall, and acres of wild flowers in summer. It is one of the most beautiful views in Berkshire County, and in an area where every turn affords a pleasant aspect, that is saying something. At the bottom of Baldwin Hill Road, enter Egremont on Routes 23 and 41.

STOCKBRIDGE

6–**9** *10 mi northeast of Alford.*

Stockbridge is the quintessence of small-town New England charm—untainted by industry or large-scale development. It is also the blueprint for small-town America as represented picture-perfectly on the covers of the *Saturday Evening Post* by painter Norman Rockwell. From 1953 until his death in 1978, Rockwell lived in Stockbridge and painted its buildings and its residents, inspired by their simple charm. More than one hundred years earlier, Henry Sedgwick, reflecting on its ability to inspire artists and writers, called Stockbridge the poet's hearth and home.

The town has been home to and the inspiration for Poet Laureate Billy Collins; writers Owen Wister, Rachel Field, Catharine Sedgwick, Nathaniel Hawthorne, and William Shirer; playwrights Bill Gibson and Robert Sherwood; *Vanity Fair* editor Frank Crowninshield; sculptor Daniel Chester French; psychological theorist Eric Erickson; and painters Frederic Church and George Inness; songwriters James Taylor and Arlo Guthrie. Just as Rockwells illustrations of Stockbridge captured the nation, so Guthrie's song about Thanksgiving dinner in Stockbridge, "Alice's Restaurant", became an anthem for a generation.

Indeed, Stockbridge is the stuff of story and legend. Travelers have been checking into the Red Lion Inn on Main Street since the 18th century, and Stockbridge remains only slightly altered in appearance since that time. In 18th- and 19th- century buildings surrounding the inn, you'll find a handful of engaging shops and eateries. The rest of Stockbridge is best appreciated via a country drive or bike ride over its hilly, narrow lanes.

What to See

6 The 15-acre **Berkshire Botanical Gardens** contain greenhouses, ponds, nature trails, and perennial, rose, day lily, and herb gardens of both exotic and native plantings—some 2,500 varieties in all. ☒ *Rtes. 102 and 183, 2 mi east of downtown* ☎ *413/298-3926* ⊕ *www.berkshirebotanical. org* ☜ *$7* ☉ *May–Oct., daily 10–5.*

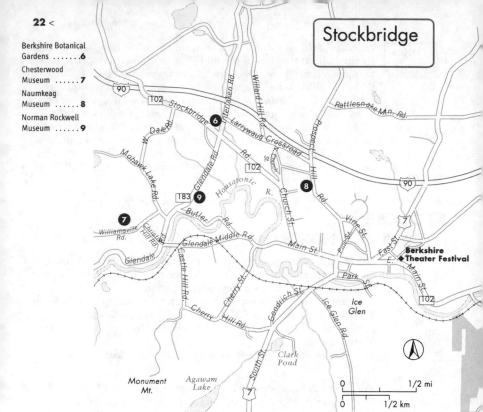

Stockbridge

⑦ Chesterwood was for 33 years the summer home of the sculptor Daniel
Fodor'sChoice Chester French (1850–1931), who created *The Minuteman* in Con-
★ cord and the Lincoln Memorial in Washington, D.C. Tours are given
of the house, which is maintained in the style of the 1920s, and of the
studio, where you can view the casts and models French used to create the Lincoln Memorial. The beautifully landscaped 122-acre grounds
also make for an enchanting stroll. ✉ *Williamsville Rd. off Rte. 183*
☎ *413/298–3579* ⊕ *www.chesterwood.org* ✍ *$10* ☉ *May–Oct.,*
daily 10–5.

Walking **Main Street** is an architectural treat. In less than ¼ mi, you
can see myriad examples of Early American architecture (such as the
1739 Mission House), early-18th-century farmhouses and inns (such
as the Red Lion), and late 18th-century Berkshire cottages built on the
grand scale (such as Taggart House and the two main buildings at Austen
Riggs Center).

★ ⑧ **Naumkeag,** a Berkshire cottage once owned by Joseph Choate, an am-
bassador during the administration of U.S. president William McKinley and a successful New York lawyer, provides a glimpse into the gracious

living of the gilded era of the Berkshires. The 26-room gabled mansion, designed by Stanford White in 1886, sits atop Prospect Hill. It is decorated with many original furnishings and art that spans three centuries; the collection of Chinese porcelain is also noteworthy. The meticulously kept 8 acres of formal gardens designed by Fletcher Steele are themselves worth a visit. ⊠ *5 Prospect Hill Rd.* ☎ *413/298–3239* ⊕ *www.thetrustees.org* ⊠ *$10* ☉ *Memorial Day–Columbus Day, daily 10–5.*

❾ The **Norman Rockwell Museum** traces the career of one of America's most beloved illustrators, beginning with his first *Saturday Evening Post* cover in 1916. In addition to the collection of 570 Rockwell illustrations, the museum also mounts exhibits by other artists. Rockwell's studio was moved to the museum grounds and is complete in every detail. Stroll the 36-acre site, picnic on the grounds, or relax at the outdoor café. ⊠ *Rte. 183, 2 mi from Stockbridge* ☎ *413/298–4100* ⊕ *www.nrm.org* ⊠ *$12* ☉ *Weekdays 10–5, weekends 10–4.*

need a break? The tiny **Stockbridge Coffee House** (⊠ 6 Elm St. ☎ 413/298-3169) serves up fresh brewed coffee, biscotti, muffins, and scones. In summer you can order ice cream.

Where to Eat

$$–$$$ ✗ **Once Upon a Table.** The atmosphere is casual yet vaguely romantic at this little restaurant-in-the-mews off Stockbridge's Main Street. The continental and contemporary American cuisine includes seasonal dishes, with appetizers such as potpie of escargots, and entrées that include seared crab cakes with horseradish-cream sauce as well as rack of lamb with garlic-mashed potatoes. At lunch try the Caesar salad or the wicked Rueben sandwich. ⊠ *36 Main St.* ☎ *413/298–3870* ⊛ *Reservations essential* ⊟ *AE, MC, V.*

¢–$ ✗ **Theresa's Stockbridge Cafe & Main Street Market.** Down the alley off Main Street is Theresa's, formerly Alice's Restaurant, right where Arlo Guthrie said it was in his famous song. The menu offers an eclectic mix of Greek and Italian fare. Homemade muffins are baked fresh daily, you can order hand-dipped ice-cream cones in the afternoon, and dinner entrées include spicy chicken and great pizza. You can sit down or get your food to go. Sharing the same kitchen with Theresa's, Main Street Market in the storefront serves hearty breakfasts and soups and sandwiches for lunch. ⊠ *40 Main St.* ☎ *413/298–3060* ⊟ *MC, V.*

Where to Stay

$–$$$$ ✗🏨 **Red Lion Inn.** An inn since 1773, the Red Lion has hosted presidents, **Fodor's Choice** senators, and celebrities. It consists of a large main building and seven ★ annexes, each of which is different (one is a converted fire station). If you like historic buildings filled with antiques, request a room in the main building: many of these units are small, and the furnishings are a tad worn in places, but this is the authentic inn. If you want more space and more modern furnishings, request a room in one of the annex buildings. The venerable old inn has a brand new chef, and Brian Alberg is infusing new life and tastes. A James Beard Society member, he emphasizes seasonal ingredients and locally grown produce. His menu includes roasted root vegetable hash with apple cider served with grilled pork tenderloin and a spinach and carmelized onion and goat cheese quiche. The main dining room ($$–$$$$) has a somewhat formal ambience; Widow Bingham's Tavern is cozier and less formal; for pub fare and live music, head to the Lion's Den. ⊠ *30 Main St., 02162* ☎ *413/298–5545 or 413/298–1690* 🖷 *413/298–5130* ⊕ *www.redlioninn.com* ↩ *84 rooms, 71 with bath, 24 suites* ♿ *3 restaurants, cable TV, some in-room VCRs, pool, gym, massage, bar, meeting rooms* ☰ *AE, D, DC, MC, V* ❘⊙❘ *CP.*

$$$$ ⊞ **Elm Court.** Built in 1886 for Emily Thorne Vanderbilt Sloane, this Berkshire cottage is one of grand proportion and luxury. The rooms are large, appointed with elegant window treatments, and furnished with antiques, some original to the house. Complimentary breakfast and afternoon tea are served daily in the dining room or in your room. You can request catered dinners and private yoga sessions. There is a full bar in the Library and in-room spa services available including manicure, pedicure and massage. You can tour the greenhouses, roam grounds originally designed by Frederick Law Olmsted, and sit in the room where the "1919 Elm Court Talks" led to the League of Nations. ⊠ *310 Old Stockbridge Road, 01240* ☎ *413/637–1556* ⊕ *www.elmcourt.com* ↩ *3 rooms, 2 suites* ♿ *In-room data ports, some in-room hot tubs, room service, massage, meeting rooms* ☰ *AE, D, DC, MC, V* ❘⊙❘ *BP.*

$$$$ ⊞ **Wheatleigh.** Gilded Age grandeur meets 21st-century comfort at this 1893 Italianate mansion. Henry H. Cook, railroad and real-estate tycoon, presented Wheatleigh to his daughter, Georgie, as a wedding gift when she married Count Carlos de Heredia. Rooms are large and beautifully appointed with no detail overlooked. Some rooms have fireplaces and private patios. The luxury of tumbled marble bathrooms, some with the original deep soaking tubs, is matched by a full complement of Bulgari toiletries. For dinner you can choose from a formal prix-fixe menu in the dining room or order à la carte in the library. ⊠ *Hawthorne Rd., 02140* ☎ *413/637–0610* 🖷 *413/637–4507* ⊕ *www.wheatleigh.com* ↩ *10 rooms, 9 suites* ♿ *2 restaurants, room service, tennis court, outdoor pool, exercise equipment, massage, meeting rooms; no room TVs* ☰ *AE, D, DC, MC, V.*

$$$$ ⊞ **Taggart House.** Originally built as a guesthouse for the prestigious Sedgwick family, the Taggart is a true Berkshire cottage. From its elegant billiard room and library to its dining rooms and antique appointments, the house evokes opulence. Upstairs, the bedrooms are furnished with antique beds and armoires, some with fireplaces. Some of the bathrooms have such special features as heated towel bars, step-down baths, large soaking tubs, and antique light fixtures. ⊠ *18 Main St., 01262* ☎ *413/298–5152 or 800/918–2680* ⊕ *www.taggarthouse.com* ↩ *4 rooms* ☰ *MC, V* ❘⊙❘ *BP.*

$$–$$$$ 🏨 **Inn at Stockbridge.** Antiques and feather comforters are among the
Fodor'sChoice   accents in the rooms of this 1906 Georgian Revival inn run by the at-
★   tentive Alice and Len Schiller. The two serve breakfast in their elegant
dining room, and every evening they provide wine and cheese. Each of
the rooms in the adjacent "cottage" building has a decorative theme such
as Kashmir, St. Andrews, or Provence; the junior suites in the new "car-
riage" building have Berkshire themes. The airy and posh rooms have
CD players, irons and ironing boards, hair dryers, and in some cases
gas fireplaces. ⊠ *U.S. 7* ✆ *Box 618, 02162* ☎ *413/298–3337 or 888/
466–7865* 🖷 *413/298–3406* ⊕ *www.stockbridgeinn.com* ⇔ *8 rooms,
8 suites* ♿ *Some in-room hot tubs, some in-room VCRs, pool; no TV
in some rooms, no smoking* ⊟ *AE, D, MC, V* ⦿ *BP.*

$$–$$$$ 🏨 **Seasons on Main.** Step back in time at this 19th-century Greek Revival bed-and-breakfast, where Pat and Greg O'Neill provide all the com-
forts of home. Antiques fill the guest rooms, each of which is decorated
to represent one of the four seasons; both the Winter and Fall rooms
have fireplaces. Breakfast is served in the large dining room. The inn is
near the Berkshire Theatre Festival, Main Street shopping, and Laurel
Hill. ⊠ *47 Main St., 01262* ☎ *413/298–5419* ⊕ *www.seasonsonmain.
com* ⇔ *4 rooms* ♿ *No smoking, no kids* ⊟ *MC, V* ⦿ *BP.*

$$ 🏨 **Conroy's B & B.** Joanne and Jim Conroy's warmth and hospitality fill
the rooms of this 1828 brick farmhouse. Inside the main house, the aroma
of home baking and the sound of a crackling fire from the common room
fireplace are a familiar scene. You can choose from rooms in the house
or in the converted barn behind the house. Country antiques and re-
productions furnish the large and comfortable rooms, some of which
have fireplaces. An apartment suite in the barn, with a loft bedroom and
a kitchen, sleeps four people. ⊠ *11 East St., U.S. 7, 01262* ☎ *413/298–
4990 or 888/298–4990* ⊕ *www.conroysinn.com* ⇔ *8 rooms, 5 with bath,
1 suite* ♿ *No smoking* ⊟ *MC, V* ⦿ *BP.*

$–$$$ 🏨 **Arbor Rose.** What was once an early 19th-century farmhouse is now
a comfortable bed-and-breakfast. The four rooms in the main house have
four-poster beds with European-style quilts. Next door is a saw mill that
has been converted into a three-room apartment with kitchen, living room,
and two bedrooms each with private bath available for seasonal rental.
At the rear of the property is a mill pond with water fall and stream;
beyond is a wooded area perfect for a brief ramble. Full breakfast includes fresh baked goods and strawberries, apples, and pears grown on
the property. ⊠ *8 Yale Hill Rd., 01262* ☎ *413/298–4744* ⊕ *www.
arborrose.com* ⇔ *4 rooms, 1 apartment* ♿ *No smoking* ⊟ *AC, MC,
V* ⦿ *BP.*

Nightlife & the Arts

Nightlife
Step into **The Lions Den** (⊠ Main St. ☎ 413/298–5545), downstairs at
the Red Lion Inn, for live music nightly, from 8 to midnight in the summer months and most weekends year-round. You can also order from
a menu of pub fare.

The Arts

Since 1929, the **Berkshire Theatre Festival** (✉ 6 Main St. ☎ 413/298–5536, 413/298–5576 box office ⊕ www.berkshiretheatre.org) has presented plays nightly in the summer months. BTF has two theaters: the Main Stage and the Unicorn. The four plays presented each summer on the Main Stage tend to be of better-known vehicles with established actors. The Unicorn, a smaller theater, mounts experimental plays and new works. Check with the theater for special events such as play readings, talk-backs (where you can discuss a play with the author and actors), and concerts.

Shopping

Most of the stores in Stockbridge are clustered on Elm and Main streets. If that isn't enough, visit during August, October, and December, when crafts fairs and country markets are held.

The **American Cafe and Gallery** (✉ 7–9 South St., U.S. 7 ☎ 413/298–0250) is filled with a bounty of attractive and useful crafts. In the café, which serves lunch and dinner Monday through Saturday, all the items are handcrafted and for sale. The chair you sit on, the table you eat at, the decoration on the walls, every glass and dish, even the salt and pepper shakers are for sale.

Inside **American Craftsman** (✉ 36 Main St. ☎ 413/298–0175) you can find a varied selection of crafts fashioned from wood, metal, and glass, from miniature water fountains and puzzle boxes to paper weights and jewelry.

Heirloom Jewelry (✉ 36 Main St. ☎ 413/298–4436) has a jewel for every pocketbook from rare and expensive to fun and affordable. There are antique pieces, some using old jewels, and jewelry in new settings.

The dynamic **Holsten Galleries** (✉ 3 Elm St. ☎ 413/298–3044) shows wares of top contemporary glass sculptors of the Northeast.

In the back of a mews in the center of Main Street is **Origins Gallery** (✉ 36 Main St. ☎ 413/298–0002), where you can browse colorful carved animals, baskets, stone sculpture from Zimbabwe, and other works from Africa.

At the end of Main Street is **Seven Arts** (✉ 7 Main St. ☎ 413/298–5101), which stocks Rockwell prints and plates, souvenirs and gifts.

The **Stockbridge Wine Cellar and Cheese Shop** (✉ 3 Elm St. ☎ 413/298–3454) sells imported and domestic wines, cheeses, and specialty foods. In summer you can order a picnic basket filled with smoked salmon, fresh country bread, pâté, salad, or hummus with beer, soda, or wine. Stop in on Saturday from noon to 5 for a wine-and-cheese tasting.

Vlada Boutique (✉ Elm St. ☎ 413/298–3656) sells comfortable, affordable clothes and accessories for women.

PERMANENT ADDRESSES

VISITING HOUSE MUSEUMS, *such as the homes of Edith Wharton, William Cullen Bryant or Herman Melville, is a popular pasttime throughout the country. For many others, however, graveyards are rich sources of art, history, and even humor. With some of the oldest cemetaries in the country, South County towns provide some of the most interesting "permanent addresses."*

In the center of the Stockbridge cemetary is the Sedgwick Pie, a circular plot reserved for Sedgwick family graves. The tallest and most prominent marker belongs to family patriarch, Judge Theodore Sedgwick. The graves of generations of Sedwicks radiate around him. The story goes that the Sedgwicks are buried in The Pie feet inward, and therefore, on Judgment Day the Sedgwicks can rise up in perfect order, facing their patriarch.

Graveyards tell more than the stories of a family; they are sometimes rich repositories of the history of a whole town. Just down the road from Stockbridge Cemetery are the ancient burial grounds of the Stockbridge Indians. The inscription on the marker reads: "Friends of our Fathers." The marker was placed there by the white settlers of Stockbridge so that future generations would not forget that Chief Konkapot and the Stockbridge Indians helped settle and defend the land. Chief Konkapot wrote to the Massachuisetts legislature: "Only show us where your enemies are. That is all we need to know. (to fight with you)." On his tombstone, Chief Konkapot had the following enscribed: "Here lies John Konkapot. God be as good to him as he would be to you if he were God and you were John Konkapot."

Graveyards are rich sources of history, but there is also the possibility of finding a laugh or at least a chuckle even in a graveyard. Take for example a headstone in Lee: "Here lies Highfield Colantha Mooie." Never heard of her? Underneath this stone, according to its inscription, lies "A Holstein Cow Who held the world record for lifetime milk production. Born, lived and died right here. 1919–1937." In Mill River, the tombstone of a woman reads "Being the wife of five husbands." The first three husbands are listed by name followed by an "etc." In Alford a tomb stone reads: "To Cognac and Old Rye Et Hoc Genus Omne (And Everything of the kind)." But the last word goes to the inscription over the entrance to the Great Barrington cemetery:"Hark from the tombs a doleful sound, my ears attend the cry. Ye living men come view the ground where you must shortly lie."

At **Williams & Sons Country Store** (⊠ 38 Main St. ☎ 413/298–3016) it's all nostalgia, from penny candy, candles, and jams to jellies, tea, toys, and candlesticks.

At the corner of Main Street and the mews, in what once was the Stockbridge town hall, is **Yankee Candle** (⊠ 34 Main St. ☎ 413/298–3004) where you can find candles and candle holders of every description.

en route   The common route from Stockbridge to West Stockbridge is Route 102. But if you drive down Prospect Hill to Rte. 183, take a right and then a left onto Lenox Road you'll find **Yokun Ridge** and one of the most coveted views in the Berkshires. As the mountains rise on all sides of Lake Mahkeenak, you'll see why locals call it Stockbridge Bowl. A trail on the right leads along the ridge to Route 102 and back in a 2-mi walk. Walk all or part of it, return to your car, and continue on Lenox Road to the sign for West Stockbridge.

WEST STOCKBRIDGE

❿ *5 mi northwest of Stockbridge.*

The Williams River winds through this pretty little town. It was here, in 1838, when the first railroad chugged into Berkshire County. The train station now houses an art gallery. You can still stop by an old mill along the river, which was once used to cut the marble into slabs, and shop for antiques. The city itself makes for a pleasant stop, as its streets are dotted with galleries, specialty shops, and restaurants.

At the **Berkshire Center for Contemporary Glass** you can watch glassblowers create magnificent pieces. This handsome gallery displays and sells the works of some of the country's foremost artists working in this medium. ⊠ *6 Harris St.* ☎ *413/232–4666* ⊕ *www.berkshireweb.com/bcfcg* ▣ *Free* ☉ *Daily 10–6.*

Where to Eat

$$–$$$ ✕ **Rouge.** From the gray-green shingles of this little house and the illu-
Fodor'sChoice   minated small red sign to the simple and comfortable interior, every-
★   thing about Rouge reminds you of a restaurant in the French countryside. Owner–chef William Merelle is indeed from Provence, where he met his American wife (and co-owner) Maggie. They intend that the food, wine, and surroundings evoke pleasure. Try the sesame-crusted salmon served with a honey-soy-sake glaze; papparadelle with roasted garlic, olives, and Monterey goat cheese; or grilled steak with Old Chatham blue cheese. ⊠ *3 Center St.* ☎ *413/232–4111* ▤ *AE, D, MC, V* ☉ *Closed Mon. and Tues. No lunch.*

★ $–$$ ✕ **Truc Orient Express.** Happy Pancake, Shaking Beef, and beef on rice noodles are just a few of the well-prepared Vietnamese specialties at this restaurant across from the Berkshire Center for Contemporary Glass.

Plenty of wood, windows, and artwork create a lovely setting. Portions tend to be on the small side but are beautifully presented. There's an extensive gift shop on premises. ⊠ *3 Harris St.* ☎ *413/232–4204* ☐ *AE, D, MC, V* ☉ *No lunch.*

★ ¢-$ ✕ **Caffe Pomo de'Oro.** A floor-to-ceiling window and skylights dominate the main room in this café, where the sun washes the scrubbed Mexican tiles. Along the walls are food items for sale, such as homemade jellies, jams, and tomato sauce, and bins of fresh bread. You can order scones and stuffed croissant with coffee and tea or Brie with cucumber, red onion, and tomatoes on peasant bread with a coffee drink, or a simple turkey sandwich; breakfast or lunch, it is all good. ⊠ *6 Depot St.* ☎ *413/232–4616* ☐ *AE, D, MC, V* ☉ *No dinner.*

Where to Stay

$$$-$$$$ ⊞ **Shaker Mill Inn.** This early-19th-century former stagecoach stop contains large rooms and suites, all with private entrances. Bright, contemporary appointments flavor each room, all of which have decks or balconies; some have fireplaces. The rooms are connected by an attractive wooden walkway, edged with garden beds. If you want more space, the one- and two-bedroom suites are ideal. ⊠ *2 Oak St., 01266* ☎ *413/232–4600 or 800/958–9942* 🖷 *413/232–4601* ⊕ *www.shakermillinn.com* ⟿ *7 rooms, 2 suites* ⚖ *Kitchenettes, some microwaves, refrigerators, cable TV, hot tub* ☐ *AE, D, MC, V* |⊚| *BP.*

$$-$$$$ ⊞ **The Williamsville Inn.** Since 1797, this renovated country inn has provided a pleasant respite for Berkshire visitors. Set on 10 acres, enhanced with flower and herb gardens, the property comprises a main house and a historic barn, both of which have rooms. The fine linens, duvets, and gas fireplaces or woodstoves lend old-world charm to the rooms. The inn also has an indoor playroom and outdoor play yard for kids. The dining room has a bank of windows on one wall for a sunny breakfast, and the fireplace, oil lamps, and candlelight adds to charm of dinners. German entrées are highlighted on the menu. ⊠ *286 Great Barrington Rd., Rte. 41, 01266* ☎ *413/274–6118* 🖷 *413/274–3539* ⊕ *www.williamsvilleinn. com* ⟿ *15 rooms, 1 suite* ⚖ *Restaurant, tennis court, pool, playground; no smoking* ☐ *AE, D, MC, V* |⊚| *BP.*

Shopping

At **Antiqualia** (⊠ 2 Main St. ☎ 413/232–0400) you can peruse the largest collection of old and antique quilts. You can also find rugs, jewelry, and other accessories.

Since 1888, **Charles H. Baldwin & Sons** (⊠ 1 Center St. ☎ 413/232–7785) has sold vanilla and other extracts for baking as well as maple syrup and imported licorice.

On Route 41 in the direction of Great Barrington look for the brightly colored flags and giant flower vase marking the entrance to **Hoffman Pottery** (⊠ 103 Great Barrington Rd. ☎ 413/232–4646), where you can shop for functional pieces, garden accessories (including decorative birds and masks), and pots of all sizes. The pottery is highly glazed, brightly colored, and wonderfully fun.

Hotchkiss Galleries (⌂ 8 Center St. ☎ 413/232–0200) sells mobiles and more mobiles. The gallery also carries some jewelry, furniture, and contemporary art.

In the big old mill building by the river, **Sawyer Antiques** (⌂ 1 Depot St. ☎ 413/232–7062) specializes in Early American furniture and accessories.

At the **Train Station Gallery** (⌂ 6 Depot St. ☎ 413/232–7930), Elaine Ranney sells her own paintings as well as the paintings, sculptures, and etchings of other contemporary artists.

LEE

⑪–⑫ *10 mi east of West Stockbridge.*

Lee was incorporated after the Revolutionary War but began as a farming community. Though the land was fertile, it was burdened with too many large stones, which turned out to be marble.

Lee marble was one of the hardest marbles, making it perfect for public buildings, and soon quarries sprang up. Lee quarries produced the marble used for 900 tombstones in Arlington Cemetery as well as for public buildings in New York City and Albany. Closer to home, Lee marble was used as foundation stone for the 19th-century Berkshire cottages of the Vanderbilts and Westinghouses. The Housatonic River supplied the waterpower for the next successful industry in Lee, paper, but it was the surrounding forest that supplied the necessary pulp.

In 1867 Lee was the site of the first demonstration for making paper from wood pulp rather than rags. It was an immediate success and so were Lee paper mills. Water, wood, and the railroad station made Lee ideal for paper mills during the 19th century. Lee never became a major mill town, however. With the construction of the Massachusetts Turnpike right through the heart of town, it turned instead into a retail and services hub for Berkshires vacationers. The bustling downtown contains a mix of touristy and workaday shops, leafy streets with bed-and-breakfasts, restaurants, and an outlet shopping center that sits just off the turnpike.

⑪ You can see October Mountain, part of **October Mountain State Forest** from almost any point in Lee. To find the entrance drive down Main Street to Center Street, turn right and travel 2 miles to the electric plant and look for the entrance on your right. October Mountain is the largest state forest in Massachusetts with 11,000 acres and 50 campsites each with its own table and fireplace. There are two modern comfort stations with hot showers, a picnic area, campground, loop trail, and a trail to the ridge. ⌂ *Woodland Road* ☎ *413/243-1778.*

⑫ **Laurel Lake** is on Route 20 north of town. There is a pull off, and the lake is small but lovely. People fish off the pier or just sit by the water. ⌂ *Laurel Street.*

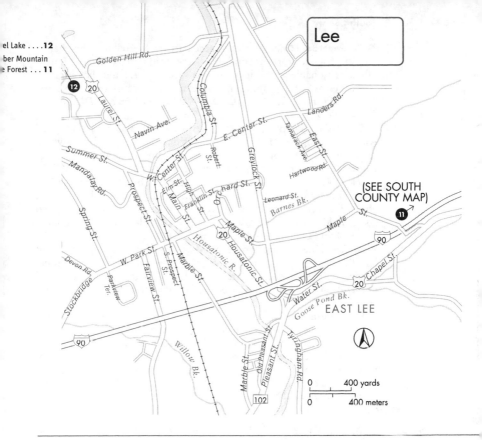

Lee

(SEE SOUTH
COUNTY MAP)

EAST LEE

0	400 yards
0	400 meters

Where to Eat

$–$$$ ✕ **Bombay Bar & Grill.** As you enter this restaurant, you'll most likely encounter Indian music softly playing in the background. This is an authentic Indian restaurant, where such signature dishes as chicken *malai* kebab, chicken *tikka masala*, and lamb *kashmiri* fill out the menu. Set inside the Black Swan Inn, the restaurant overlooks Laurel Lake. ✉ *445 Laurel St.* ☎ *413/243–6731* ▭ *AE, D, MC, V* ☯ *Closed Mon.*

$–$$$ ▦ **From Ketchup to Cavier.** Creating a seasonally changing menu, chef–owner Christian Urbain strives to serve everything from ketchup to caviar, hence this restaurant's name. Menu samplings have included Long Island duck with apples and mushrooms served with cherry demiglace, crisp-skin salmon over asparagus with onion bread pudding, and a Black Angus burger served with sweet-potato fries. The restaurant, inside an early-19th-century house, is divided into intimate dining rooms with period accents and a pervasive European charm. ✉ *150 Main St.* ☎ *413/243–6397* ▭ *AE, MC, V* ☯ *Closed Tues. No lunch.*

$$ ✕ **The Sweet Basil Grille.** Steps from the Historic Merrell Inn, this charming, laid-back trattoria in South Lee serves traditional red-sauce Italian fare at reasonable prices, including its specialty veal and such vegetarian dishes as pasta primavera. You can dine upstairs or downstairs. ⊠ *1575 Pleasant St., Rte. 102* 🕾 *413/243–1114* 🖃 *AE, DC, MC, V* ⊘ *No lunch.*

$–$$ ✕ **Cactus Cafe.** Burritos, tacos, sautéed calamari, and tostados topped with sole highlight the menu at this storefront café. The black-and-white-tile floor and multicolor table tops bring a touch of South of the Border to old New England. ⊠ *54 Main St.* 🕾 *413/243–4300* 🖃 *MC, V.*

$–$$ ✕ **Salmon Run.** This casual fish house serves salads, beef and poultry dishes, and lots of seafood. Salmon is the specialty, and you can order it grilled, charred, poached with dill sauce, Cajun-style, baked, or stuffed. Two rooms hold a mix of booths and tables; you can also dine at the counter. ⊠ *78 Main St.* 🕾 *413/243–3900* 🖃 *AE, MC, V.*

¢–$ ✕ **Arizona Pizza.** A large house fitted as a comfortable restaurant and bar, this casual local favorite not only serves pizza but also calzone, stromboli, pasta dishes, salads, and burgers. The staff is young and cheerful and the portions large. ⊠ *51 Park St.* 🕾 *413/243–3900* 🖃 *AE, D, MC, V.*

¢ ✕ **Rose's Restaurant.** Inside this brightly colored café, the rose motif is evident: roses are on the menus, the wallpaper and the china. Take a seat at the counter or a table and try the corned beef hash, eggs, or omelets with fresh baked muffins for breakfast; for lunch, consider a sandwich, wrap, or salad and finish with Rose's own apple pie or carrot cake. ⊠ *160 Housatonic St., Lee* 🕾 *413/243–3333* 🖃 *MC, V* ⊘ *No dinner.*

Where to Stay

★ $$$–$$$$ 🏠 **Applegate Inn.** This 1925 Georgian Revival mansion sits at the end of a regal circular drive, overlooking 6 acres of lush lawns and apple trees. The Greenock Golf course is across the road. The inn has been exquisitely decorated: one room has a spacious steam shower and a fireplace, and another contains a French reproduction sleigh bed with fireplace and stunning views over the grounds to the mountains beyond. A carriage house contains two plush suites with stereos and wet bars; chocolates and crystal decanters filled with brandy and liqueurs add a touch of class. Owners Len and Gloria Friedman have attended to every detail in the house for a touch of elegance in the country. ⊠ *279 W. Park St., 01238* 🕾 *413/243–4451* 🌐 *www.applegateinn.com* �� *6 rooms, 2 suites* ⚭ *Some in-room data ports, some in-room hot tubs, some in-room VCRs, pool; no kids under 12, no smoking, no room TVs* 🖃 *MC, V* ⚐ *BP.*

$$$–$$$$

Fodor'sChoice

★ 🏠 **Devonfield Inn.** This grand, pale yellow-and-cream Federal house sits atop a birch-shaded hillside dotted with a few quaint outbuildings and 29 acres of rolling meadows. The nine guest rooms have colonial-style furnishings—many have Oriental rugs, lace-canopy four-poster beds, and working fireplaces. An immense penthouse suite is a favorite for special occasions, and a separate, contemporary cottage has its own kitchen with a pitched cathedral ceiling and private deck. A gracious pool and lanai sit behind the house. Owner Pam Loring serves such toothsome fare as vanilla-cinnamon French toast or baked pear pancakes at breakfast and attends to every detail, including chocolates and spring water in each room, a video library, and a butler's pantry with cookies, popcorn, and beverages. ⊠ *85 Stockbridge Rd., 01238* ☎ *413/243–3298 or 800/664–0880* 🖷 *413/243–1360* ⊕ *www.devonfield.com* ⟳ *6 rooms, 3 suites, 1 cottage* ⚐ *Some in-room hot tubs, some in-room VCRs, tennis court, pool, bicycles, cross-country skiing; no TV in some rooms, no kids under 12* ⊟ *AE, MC, V* ⦿ *BP.*

$$–$$$$ 🎴 **Chambery Inn.** A former 19th-century French country school houses this exceptional place in downtown Lee. The rooms are quite large, some enough for two queen beds, with 13-foot-high embossed ceilings and state-of-the-art baths. Amish-style furniture fits nicely with the architecture and is attractive and comfortable. There are no common rooms; you choose breakfast from a breakfast card, and it's delivered to your room each morning in a basket. ⊠ *199 Main St., 01238* ☎ *413/243–2221 or 800/537–4321* 🖷 *413/243–1828* ⊕ *www. berkshireinns.com* ⟳ *3 rooms, 6 suites* ⚐ *No kids under 12, no smoking* ⊟ *AE, D, MC, V* ⦿ *BP.*

$–$$$$ 🎴 **Historic Merrell Inn.** Built in the 1780s as a private residence (and converted to a stagecoach stop), this inn has good-size rooms, several with working fireplaces. Meticulously maintained, the inn has an unfussy authentic style, with polished wide-board floors, painted walls, and antiques. The sitting room has an open fireplace and contains the only intact "birdcage" bar—a semicircular bar surrounded by wooden slats—in the country. The purpose of a birdcage bar was to prevent thirsty Colonials from reaching across and helping themselves. Breakfast is cooked to order and served in the keeping room, where travelers have dined since 1786. ⊠ *1565 Pleasant St., Rte. 102, 01260* ☎ *413/243–1794 or 800/243– 1794* 🖷 *413/243–2669* ⊕ *www.merrell-inn.com* ⟳ *9 rooms, 1 suite* ⊟ *MC, V* ⦿ *BP.*

Sports & the Outdoors

Golf

Mountains provide the backdrop for the 18-hole golf course at **Greenock Country Club** (⊠ W. Park St. ☎ 413/243–3323). Greens fees are $20 for 9 holes, $30 for 18 holes. A pro shop and bar are on the premises.

Shopping

At **Highlawn Farm** (⊠ 535 Summer St. ☎ 413/243–0672) you can visit the cows, watch the milking, and buy fresh milk, cream, butter, and blue cheese. **Lee Five and Ten** (⊠ 50 Main St. ☎ 413/243–6000) is a real old-time five and dime with candy, cosmetics, toys, household goods, and those hard to find items that nobody else seems to carry anymore.

Prime Outlets at Lee (⊠ U.S. 20, at I–90 Exit 2 ☎ 413/243–8186) contains 65 shops, among them Geoffrey Beene, Coach, J. Crew, Polo, Harry and David's, and Anne Klein. **Pamela Loring Gifts and Interiors** (⊠ 151 Main St. ☎ 413/243–2689) carries a wide selection of decorative pieces, fine toiletries, pictures, and frames. **Zabian's** (⊠ 15 Main St. ☎ 413/243– 0508) sells jewelry, watches, clocks, and gifts.

TYRINGHAM

⑬ *4 mi southeast of Lee.*

Tyringham is walled off by mountains but also perhaps by choice. No major roads, railroads, or buses traverse the town. In the mid-19th century, the town had a mill wheel on every inch of waterway, but when the railroad went to Lee rather than Tyringham, the mills followed. During its next phase of growth, Richard W. Gilder, editor of *Scribner's* (later *Century Magazine*) built a summer house. A power in the literary world, Gilder invited Frances Folsom to visit, and she later returned with her husband, President Grover Cleveland.

Edith Wharton visited and wrote a poem "Moonlight over Tyringham." Mark Twain sat in the only store in Tyringham, called Tinker's, feet propped on the pot-bellied stove, and swapped tales with the locals. He gave the library a set of his books as a parting gift. The Shakers, under the leadership of Ann Lee, began their Berkshire sojourn in Tyringham, religiously trudging to the "shaking ground" to shake off their sins. Egyptologist Robb de Peyster Tytus built his 1,000-acre estate, Ashintully (Gaelic for "brow of the hill"), and Henry Hudson Kitson, sculptor, built a whimsical house here, where he sculpted the *Pilgrim Maiden* and the *John and Priscilla Alden Memorial.*

All that is left of Robb de Peyster Tytus' 1910 Georgian mansion are the columns and the **Ashintully Gardens.** The house burned to the ground, but the gardens are worth the trip. At the center of the formal garden is a fountain, and the whole is surrounded by hills and forest. A stream runs through it, traversed by walking bridges. A ½-mi trail leads to the ruins. ⊠ *Sodem and Main Rds.* ☎ *413/298–3239* ⊕ *www.thetrustees. org* ⊠ *Free* ⊙ *June–Oct., Wed.–Sat. 1–5.*

OTIS

⑭ *13 mi southeast of Lee.*

A more rustic alternative to the polish of Stockbridge and Lenox, Otis has a ski area and 20 lakes and ponds, supplying plenty of what made the Berkshires desirable in the first place—access to the great outdoors. The dining options here are slim; your best bet is to pack a picnic lunch from Lenox. Nearby Becket (⇨ Chapter 2) hosts the outstanding Jacob's Pillow Dance Festival in summer, and entering from Becket, a sign says, "Welcome to Otis where nature smiles."

Where to Eat

$ ✕ **Katie's.** People go out of their way to get to Katie's, an old drive-in that locals claim serves the best fried chicken anywhere. And like a drive-in, you park and walk to the window to order. Burgers, shakes, curly fries, and salads round out the menu. ⊠ *1922 E. Otis Rd.* ☎ *413/229–7485* ⊟ *No credit cards* ⊙ *Closed Oct.–May.*

Where to Stay

$–$$$ ⊞ **Lakeside Estates.** Overlooking the Otis Reservoir and surrounded by 8 acres, this New England–style farmhouse has stellar views in all directions. Country furniture fills the common rooms and bedrooms, which are adorned with stenciled walls and patchwork quilts. There's a woodsy play area for children, garden areas, and a "buggy shed" with buggies. On warm mornings breakfast is served on the wraparound porch, which also serves as a perfect spot to while away the afternoon. ⊠ *99 Kibbe Rd., 01029* ☎ *413/269–9900* 🖷 *413/229–8935* ⊕ *www. lakesideestatesbnb.com* ➥ *3 rooms, 1 suite* ⊟ *No credit cards* ¶◯¶ *BP.*

$$ ⊞ **The New Boston Inn.** The antique billiard table fits well in this historic treasure. Surrounded by woods and ponds, it has served travelers as an inn since 1737. You can still get a drink in the pub or duck with a peach and brandy reduction, scampi, and other fine fare in the restaurant. ⊠ *101 N. Main St., Sandisfield 01255* ☎ *413/258–4477* ⊕ *www.newbostoninn. com* ➥ *7 rooms* ⚲ *Restaurant; no smoking* ⊟ *AE, MC, V* ¶◯¶ *BP.*

Sports & the Outdoors

Deer Run Maples (⊠ 135 Ed Jones Rd. ☎ 413/269–7588) is one of several sugarhouses where you can spend the morning tasting freshly tapped maple syrup that's been drizzled onto a dish of snow. Sugaring season varies with the weather; it can be anytime between late February and early April.

You can hike, bike, or cross-country ski at the 3,800-acre **Otis State Forest** (⊠ Rte. 23 ☎ 413/269–6002). The 8,000-acre **Tolland State Forest** (⊠ Rte. 8 ☎ 413/269–6002) allows swimming in the Otis Reservoir and camping.

Skiing

OTIS RIDGE The least expensive ski area in New England, Otis Ridge has long been a haven for beginners and families, but experts will find slopes here, too. The remote location is quite stunning, the buildings historic. For downhill skiers, there are six trails serviced by a pair of lifts. Otis Ridge is home to the oldest operating ski camp in the country, having taught boys and girls ages 8–15 for more than 50 years. The camp also has a snowboarding program. ⊠ *Rte. 23, 01253* ☎ *413/269–4444* ⊕ *www.otisridge.com.*

MONTEREY

❶❺ *7 mi west of Otis.*

Monterey is the little village with the unexpected (for New England) name. Once it was part of Tyringham and called Greenwood. In 1847 it separated from Tyringham and selected the name to commemorate General (later President) Zachary Taylor's victory in the Mexican War. Monterey was bypassed by the train, the highway department, and the growth of neighboring towns.

A story is told in town that a man from the city said, "without better roads, and a plan to attract business, I promise you, your village will stagnate." The local replied, "Praise God." Today Monterey is no more than a widening in the road where the clapboard buildings that typify New England are slightly closer together. Surrounded by woods and lakes, Greenwood might have been the most appropriate name after all.

At **Bidwell House** you can tour 196 acres of fields, woodlands, and gardens. At the center is the 1750 saltbox, a wooden house with a short pitched roof in front and long pitch to the rear. The house, built originally as a parsonage, has been restored and filled with period antiques. On the grounds are dry-laid walls, barn foundations, and heirloom vegetable garden. ⊠ *Art School Rd.* ☎ *413/528-6888* ⊕ *www.bidwellhousemuseum. org* ⊠ *$6* ⊙ *Memorial Day–mid-Oct., Tues.–Sun. 11–4.*

Northwest of Monterey is **Beartown State Forest,** which has miles of hiking trails and a small campground where the fee for a site is $4 a night (first come, first served). Enter the park from Tyringham Road in the town of Monterey, and you'll immediately find Benedict Pond, a perfect spot for picnicking and boating. Around the Pond is a 2-mi "loop trail" It is a favorite for sheer beauty and a moderately challenging walk. If you enter from Lee, you will find great swimming at a secluded beach. ⊠ *69 Blue Hill Rd.* ☎ *413/528–0904.*

Where to Eat

¢ ✕ **Roadside Store and Cafe.** Part of Gould Farm, this store and café sells healthy organic foods made with their own produce, house-made sausage, milk from Highlawn Farm, bread from Berkshire Mountain Bakery, and goat cheese from Rawson Brook Farm. Bon appétit, Berkshire-style. ⊠ *Rte. 23* ☎ *413/528–2633* ▭ *No credit cards* ⊙ *No dinner.*

Shopping

To find a treasure or just to browse, go to **Grenadier Pottery** (⊠ 12 Tyringham Rd. ☎ 413/528–9973), where potter Ellen Grenadier will invite you in to watch her work. In the showroom, you can shop for custom tiles and tableware.

Looking for the charm of old New England, stop by the **Monterey General Store** (⊠ Rte. 23 at Tyringham Rd. ☎ 413/528–4437), where the sign out front advertises awls, bees wax, lamp oil, hand-wrought nails, gum boots, and rock candy. Although the store no longer carries most of these items, you can shop for more modern grocery items, sandwiches, and baked goods.

NEW MARLBOROUGH

⑯ *5 mi south of Monterey; 9 mi east of Sheffield.*

New Marlborough was incorporated in 1759. It is an area of low rolling hills traversed by the Konkapot River and its tributaries. Like many of the South County villages, it has a long history and a short Main Street. However, it continues to attract visitors and second-home owners.

From the village center, head 5 mi south on Mill River/Southfield Road to **Umpachene Falls.** At Umpachene Falls Road, turn left at the parking lot. Umpachene has a choice of trails plus a picnic area and cascading falls.

The village center at nearby **Mill River** is on the National Register of Historic Places. A side trip to this attractive area, and a walkabout is fun for history buffs and students of architecture. The village center of this once bustling mill town is a mixture of carefully preserved 18th and 19th century buildings.

Where to Stay

$$$–$$$$ ✕🏠 **The Old Inn on the Green.** A distinctive inn and restaurant make up this property in tranquil New Marlborough. The 1760 Old Inn has five authentically restored, antiques-filled guest rooms. The ultradeluxe Thayer House includes six elegantly appointed rooms and a courtyard terrace with a pool. The four-bedroom Colonial Hannah Stebbins House is also on the Green. Owner/chef Peter Platt continues the tradition of fine dining in the restaurant ($$$–$$$$) dining rooms, which lit entirely by candlelight and warmed by fireplaces. It's worth the trip here to sample such splendid regional American creations as pan-seared yellowtail, snapper, garlic polenta, chorizo, and tomato-fennel ragout. ✉ *Rte. 57, New Marlboro 01230* ☎ *413/229–3131* ⊕ *www.oldinn.com* ↝ *9 rooms* ♨ *Restaurant, some in-room hot tubs, pool, meeting rooms* ☰ *AE, MC, V* 🍽 *CP.*

$$$–$$$$ 🏠 **Red Bird Inn.** Built in 1791, this house has provided comfort to guests since it opened in 1829 as a coach inn. Owner Doug Newman presides over this colorful inn, as well as the buffet breakfast. Common rooms and guest rooms are adorned with a mix of antiques and objets d'art. Outside, you can ramble the 10 acres or take advantage of the proximity to biking, hiking alongside Umpachene River, and boating on Lake Buel. ✉ *15 Adsit Crosby Rd., at Rte. 57, 01230* ☎ *413/229–2349* 📠 *413/229–2433* ↝ *6 rooms* ☰ *AE, MC, V* 🍽 *BP.*

Shopping

At the **Buggy Whip** (✉ Main St., Southfield ☎ 413/229–3576), 95 antique dealers sell a variety of furniture, architectural pieces, china, glass, and books.

David M. Weiss Antiques (✉ 15 Mill River Rd., Mill River ☎ 413/229–2716) specializes in landscape paintings, portraits, furniture, and accessories.

At **Kettering Antiques** (✉ 135 Main St. ☎ 413/229–6647) you can shop for formal 18th- and 19th-century English and American furniture and accessories. They also do restoration work.

CENTRAL COUNTY

2

BITE INTO FRENCH CLASSICS
at Bistro Zinc in Lenox ⇨*p.44*

PAMPER YOURSELF
on a spa weekend at Canyon Ranch ⇨*p.47*

TAKE IN THE SYMPHONY
on the lawn at Tanglewood ⇨*p.51*

WATCH BALLET DANCERS
twirl under the stars
at Jacob's Pillow Dance Festival ⇨*p.56*

HIKE TO THE CASCADING FALLS
at Windsor Jamb ⇨*p.58*

By Eileen
Pierce

More than merely the geographic hub of the Berkshires, Central County also acts as something of a social and economic anchor. It's home to the dapper village of Lenox, where captains of industry built their Gilded Age summer "cottages," as well as to the Berkshires' county seat and only city, Pittsfield, a faded industrial powerhouse that today shows signs of an urban renaissance.

Surrounding Lenox and Pittsfield—which border each other along the county's main north–south thoroughfare, U.S. 7—you'll discover a network of quiet hilltowns, some of whose "downtowns" consist of little more than a shady village green, prim Congregational church and neighboring meeting house, and a general store. Among these smaller towns, Dalton has a bit more going on than the rest, and it's noted as the home of paper manufacturer Crane and Co., which supplies the U.S. Mint with the cotton-fiber paper used in currency. Tiny Hancock is home to one of the best-preserved Shaker communities in the country, Lanesborough offers myriad sports and outdoorsy diversions (from go-karts to Mt. Greylock's craggy hiking trails), and sleepy Becket hosts the prestigious Jacob's Pillow Dance Festival for nine weeks each summer.

Indeed, arts venues are a vital draw in Central County, the most famous being Lenox's Tanglewood Festival, a pastoral country compound that hosts the Boston Symphony Orchestra all summer. Lenox has long been a community of summer ritual, from the grand parties of the Gilded Age to today's Tanglewood concerts, which gets the whole region buzzing with activity from mid-June to Labor Day. Concertgoers traditionally arrive well before performance time—blankets and lawn chairs in hand—for preprandial hobnobbing followed by often lavish picnic dinners. It's quite a spectacle.

Also during summer season, you can attend a performance of the tongue-in-cheek News in Revue satire troupe or of the Shakespeare and Company theatrical group, both of which are based in Lenox, whose downtown of galleries, fine boutiques, and snazzy restaurants makes for hours' of pleasurable strolling. Lenox also contains a vast cache of stellar, albeit pricey, country inns, some of them occupying the Leviathan cottages once owned by America's wealthiest families. You can tour some of them, such as Ventfort Hall and Edith Wharton's former stomping grounds, The Mount.

Despite its dignified demeanor and decidedly upscale vibe, Lenox still maintains a relatively easygoing personality; this is Old Money New England, largely absent of affectation and snobbery. Nevertheless, if you're seeking a quieter—and less expensive—base for your Central County explorations, it's worth staying in one of the smaller satellite communities or even in Pittsfield. This city of 45,000 looks a bit chipped and frayed in places, but its downtown has been discovered by entrepreneurial-minded sorts in recent years, and a handful of noteworthy cafés and shops have opened. It's also home to the largest hotel in the region, the Crowne Plaza Pittsfield, which is right in the heart of downtown, steps from kid-popular Berkshire Museum, a repository of fine art, historical documents, and natural-history artifacts.

Because of the summertime festivals of Lenox, Central County draws the bulk of its visitors from around Memorial Day through Columbus Day; this is true here even more than in North County and South County. It's for this reason that you can find some excellent values and enjoy relatively few crowds if you plan your visit during the off-season, when most attractions, inns, and restaurants still open (at least on weekends). In winter, you can enjoy snowmobile tours in Lanesborough and skiing and snowboarding in the county's only full-service winter resort, Jiminy Peak, which is in Hancock. Whatever the time of year, you're sure to find a great variety of things to see and do in this bustling, culturally rich swath of the verdant Berkshires towns and villages.

EXPLORING CENTRAL COUNTY

Central County is easily accessed from Albany and the west via U.S. 20 and from the Pioneer Valley and the east via Route 9. From farther east, such as Boston, it's best just to come by way of the Mass Pike and then shoot up U.S. 7 toward Lenox and Pittsfield, which are the two best bases for exploring the region. These two communities contain most of Central County's restaurants and accommodations as well as the bulk of attractions, performing and fine arts venues, and shops.

In addition to U.S. 7, which leads south Great Barrington and north to Williamstown, Route 8 is Central County's other major north-south route. Take it south from Pittsfield to reach Becket and U.S. 20 en route to Westfield and Springfield; take it north to reach Adams and North Adams. As is the case throughout the Berkshires, driving is as much a pastime in these parts as it is a means of getting around—Central County offers some of the most beautiful country lanes in the state.

About the Restaurants

Central County offers a fine selection of ethnic cuisine, from Indian, Chinese, Italian, and French to Mediterranean, South American, and Mexican. And though you'll find this variety of cuisine served in myriad restaurants, from cafés and country restaurants to pubs and steak houses, most places generally stop serving after 10 PM.

About the Hotels

Besides the Crowne Plaza in Pittsfield and the Yankee Motor Inn in Lenox, most of the lodgings in the area are bed-and-breakfasts and inns of all shapes and sizes, plus four resorts that differ in atmosphere, service, and price. In summer and fall, however, don't plan on a last-minute weekend getaway, as the best lodgings all demand three- or four-night minimums on weekends and holidays.

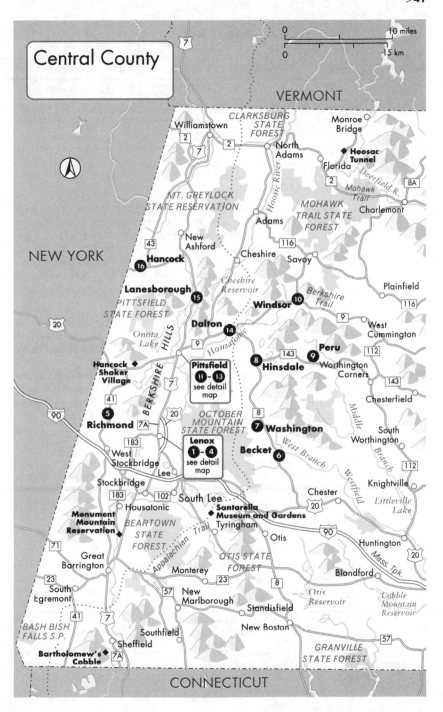

Central County

0 _____ 10 miles
0 _____ 15 km

VERMONT

Williamstown

CLARKSBURG STATE FOREST

Monroe Bridge

◆ **Hoosac Tunnel**

North Adams

Florida

2

Deerfield R.

8A

Mohawk Trail

MT. GREYLOCK STATE RESERVATION

Hoosic River

MOHAWK TRAIL STATE FOREST

Charlemont

NEW YORK

New Ashford

Adams

116

Cheshire

Savoy

43

16 **Hancock**

Cheshire Reservoir

Berkshire Trail

Plainfield

116

Lanesborough

PITTSFIELD STATE FOREST

15

10 **Windsor**

9

West Cummington

20

Onota Lake

BERKSHIRE HILLS

Dalton

14

Housatonic

143

Peru

9

112

8 **Hinsdale**

Worthington Corners

143

Hancock ◆ Shaker Village

9

Pittsfield
11 - 13
see detail map

7

Chesterfield

41

5

90

OCTOBER MOUNTAIN STATE FOREST

8

South Worthington

Richmond

7A

20

7 **Washington**

West Branch

Middle Branch

Becket

6

Lenox
1 - 4
see detail map

Westfield

112

183

West Stockbridge

Lee

Chester

20

Knightville

Littleville Lake

Stockbridge

183

102

South Lee

◆ **Santarella Museum and Gardens**

Housatonic

Tyringham

Otis

90

Huntington

20

Mass. Tpk.

Monument Mountain Reservation

BEARTOWN STATE FOREST

Appalachian Trail

71

Great Barrington

OTIS STATE FOREST

Monterey

23

Blandford

Otis Reservoir

Cobble Mountain Reservoir

23

South Egremont

57

New Marlborough

8

Standisfield

41

7

New Boston

57

BASH BISH FALLS S.P.

Southfield

Sheffield

GRANVILLE STATE FOREST

Bartholomew's Cobble

7A

CONNECTICUT

	WHAT IT COSTS				
	$$$$	**$$$**	**$$**	**$**	**¢**
RESTAURANTS	over $28	$20–$28	$12–$20	$8–$12	under $8
HOTELS	over $220	$170–$220	$120–$170	$80–$120	under $80

Restaurant prices are for a main course at dinner, excluding sales tax of 5%. Hotel prices are for two people in a standard double room in high season, excluding service charges and 9.7%–10% tax.

LENOX

❶–❹ *5 mi north of Lee.*

Long a bastion of privilege and immense wealth, Lenox is a small New England hamlet with a big reputation for even bigger mansions. Wealthy sorts from New York, Pennsylvania, and southern New England began building "summer cottages" here in the late 19th century. These lavish and majestic buildings often contained 20, 30, or even 40 rooms. Over the years some of the estates have burned, others have been razed, and still several more have been subdivided, but a decent number of them are now inns or B&Bs.

The famed Tanglewood music festival has been a fixture in Lenox for decades, and it's a part of the reason the town remains fiercely popular during the summer months. Booking a room here or in any of the nearby communities can set you back dearly when music or theatrical events are in town. Many of the town's most impressive homes are downtown; others you can only see by taking to the curving, tortuous back roads that traverse the region. In the center of the village, a few blocks of shabby-chic Colonial buildings contain shops and eateries.

What to See

🄲 **❶** The **Berkshires Scenic Railway Museum,** in a restored 1903 railroad station in central Lenox, displays antique rail equipment, vintage exhibits, and a large working model railway. It's the starting point for the diesel-hauled **Berkshire Scenic Railway,** a 2½-hour narrated round-trip train ride between Lenox and Stockbridge. ✉ *Willow Creek Rd.* ☎ *413/637–2210* ⊕ *www.berkshirescenicrailroad.org* 🎫 *Train $13, museum free* ⊙ *May–Oct., weekends 10–4.*

❷ The sleek, modernist **Frelinghuysen Morris House & Studio** occupies a verdant 46-acre property and exhibits the works of American abstract artists Suzy Frelinghuysen and George L. K. Morris as well as those of contemporaries including Picasso, Braque, and Gris. ✉ *92 Hawthorne St.* ☎ *413/637–0166* ⊕ *www.frelinghuysen.org* 🎫 *$10* ⊙ *Mid-June–early Sept., Thurs.–Sun. 10–4; early Sept.–mid-Oct., Thurs.–Sat. 10–4.*

❸ **The Mount,** a mansion built in 1902 with myriad classical influences, was
Fodor'sChoice the former summer home of novelist Edith Wharton. The house and
★ grounds were designed by Wharton, who is considered by many to have set the standard for 20th-century interior decoration. In designing

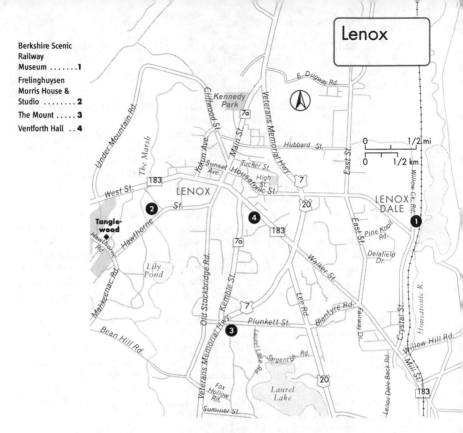

Lenox

Kennedy Park

E. Dugway Rd.

Hubbard St.

Cliffwood St.

Under Mountain Rd.

Veterans Memorial Hwy.

East St.

Willow Ck. Rd.

The Marsh

Yokun Ave.

Main St.

7a

Sunset Ave.

Tucker St.

High St.

Housatonic St.

183

West St.

LENOX

St.

7

20

LENOX DALE

2

Tangle-
wood

Hawthorne

Hawthorne Rd.

Mahkeenac Rd.

Lily Pond

Old Stockbridge Rd.

Kemble St.

4

183

7a

Walker St.

Pine Knoll Rd.

Delafield Dr.

East St.

Crystal St.

Housatonic R.

Willow Hill Rd.

Mill St.

183

7

Lee Rd.

Plunkett St.

3

Laurel Lake Rd.

Blantyre Rd.

Fairway Dr.

Lenox Dale Back Rd.

Bean Hill Rd.

Sargent Bk. Rd.

Fox Hollow Rd.

Laurel Lake

20

Sumner St.

0   1/2 mi
0   1/2 km

the Mount, she followed the principles set forth in her book *The Decoration of Houses* (1897), creating a calm and well-ordered home. An extensive restoration of the property began in October 2001 and will be ongoing for some time. The Mount continues to undergo and extensive restoration, and only the downstairs rooms are finished. An excellent guided tour is included in the entry fee. A "Women of Achievement" lecture series takes place here on Monday in July and August. ⊠ *2 Plunkett St.* ☎ *413/637–1899 or 888/637–1902* ⊕ *www.edithwharton.org* 🎫 *$7.50* ☉ *Late May–Oct., daily 9–5.*

④ Built in 1893, **Ventfort Hall,** was the summer "cottage" of Sarah Morgan, the sister of highfalutin financier J. P. Morgan. Inside is the **Museum of the Gilded Age,** which explores the role of Lenox and the Berkshires as the definitive mountain retreat during that fabled era. The building was in danger of being torn down when a group of preservationists formed to buy this 12-acre property in 1997. Since then a top restoration team has been hard at work repairing the elegant exterior brickwork and roofing, the ornate interior paneling and grand staircase, and the gabled carriage house. In 1998 Miramax films shot the orphanage scenes from *The Cider House Rules* movie here (other scenes were shot in Northampton). Although work continues on the building, tours are conducted. ⊠ *104 Walker St.* ☎ *413/637–3206* ⊕ *www.gildedage.org*

🚃 *$8* ⊙ *May–Oct., Mon.–Sat. tours on the hr 11:30–2:30; Nov.–Apr., Sat. tours at 10 and 11.*

Where to Eat

$$–$$$$ ✕ **Café Lucia.** *Bistecca alla fiorentina* (porterhouse steak grilled with olive oil, garlic, and rosemary) and ravioli *basilico e pomodoro* (with fresh tomatoes, garlic, and basil) are among the dishes that change seasonally at this northern Italian restaurant. The sleek decor includes track lighting and photographs of the owners' Italian ancestors. Weekend reservations are essential up to a month ahead during Tanglewood. ⊠ *80 Church St.* ☏ *413/637–2640* ▤ *AE, DC, MC, V* ⊙ *Closed Mon. and, Nov.–June, Sun. No lunch.*

$$–$$$$ ✕ **Church Street Cafe.** A little more laid-back both in style and ambience than its nearby competitors, Church Street Cafe presents a no-less ambitious and intriguing menu of creative globally inspired dishes. From the baked onion–and–St. Andre Cheese tart to the miso-citrus–glazed salmon and the New Mexican home-style tortilla stuffed with barbecued brisket, the dishes served here are an international culinary treat. In warm weather you can dine on a shaded outdoor deck. ⊠ *65 Church St.* ☏ *413/637–2745* ▤ *MC, V.*

$$–$$$ ✕ **Antonio's Ristorante.** The Gallo family, who've been operating Antonio's since 1988, use three ingredients for success: family, great food, and warm traditions. Marvelous sepia photos on the wall of Gallo family members testify to the clan's coherence along with the cuisine, which is prepared from cherished ancestral Italian recipes, including the *vitello* Di Cotoletta parmigiana and the *pollo marsala* (boneless chicken simmered in Antonio's creamy marsala sauce). When the weather's right, the outside deck is as charming a place to dine as any in the county. ⊠ *15 Franklin St.* ☏ *413/637–9894* ▤ *AE, DC, MC, V* ⊙ *No lunch weekdays.*

$$–$$$ ✕ **Bistro Zinc.** Crisp lemon-yellow walls, warm tile floors, and tall windows create a bright and inviting ambience at this stellar French bistro, which feels reminiscent of a country house in a Provence village. The kitchen turns out expertly prepared and refreshingly simple classics like steak frites, saddle of rabbit, and spinach lasagna. Zinc's long, wood bar, always full and determinedly sophisticated, is the best Lenox can offer for nightlife. If you can overlook the occasionally self-important attitudes of the staff, Zinc is top-notch. ⊠ *56 Church St.* ☏ *413/637– 8800* ▤ *MC, V* ⊙ *Closed Tues.*

$$–$$$ ✕ **Dish Café Bistro.** Tiny would be an understatement for describing this recent arrival to the Lenox restaurant scene. But what it lacks in space, it more than makes up for in its eclectic cuisine. From the exquisite breakfast frittata with asparagus, leeks, and shiitake mushrooms to the lunch salad of dried cranberries, apples, pecans, and chèvre to the superb grilled salmon with lobster risotto, Dish proves that some of the best food continues to be found in some of the most unassuming places. ⊠ *37 Church St.* ☏ *413/637–1800* ▤ *D, DC, MC, V* ⊙ *No dinner Mon. and Tues.*

$$–$$$ ✕ **Spigalina.** In an unprepossessing pale-green house in downtown
Fodor'sChoice   Lenox, Spigalina serves high-quality cuisine, reflecting the flavors of Spain,
★   Southern France, Greece, and Morocco. The wild mushroom risotto is

quite simply extraordinary, and the Greek-style spaghetti with sautéed shrimp and scallops as well as the rack of lamb are other standouts. ⊠ *80 Main St.* ☎ *413/637–4455* ▤ *AE, D, MC, V* ⊘ *No lunch.*

$$–$$$ ✕ **Trattoria Il Vesuvio.** *Proprietaria* Anna Arace, a native of Pompeii, is on hand nightly to assure that every dish meets her exacting standards. Among the house specialties are *arrosto di vitello* (roast breast of veal stuffed with sliced prosciutto and spinach, cooked in a brick oven and served with red wine sauce), and linguine with baby clams. Save room for Anna's homemade tiramisu. It's a short drive north of downtown, on the main road to Pittsfield. ⊠ *242 Pittsfield-Lenox Rd., U.S. 7/20* ☎ *413/637–4904* ▤ *AE, D, MC, V* ⊘ *Closed Sun. Sept.–June. No lunch.*

$–$$$ ✕ **Firefly.** The lounge with its elegantly sculpted bar is as inviting as the sophisticated dining room inside this relatively new addition to the Lenox restaurant scene. Although the charcoal-grilled butterflied Cornish hen and the Moroccan roasted-vegetable tagine are popular, it's the farfalle made with locally foraged mushrooms, sweet peas, roasted shallots, and mascarpone that is nearly impossible to resist. ⊠ *71 Church St.* ☎ *413/637–2700* ▤ *AE, D, DC, MC, V* ⊘ *No lunch.*

$–$$ ✕ **Love Dog Café & Herbal Apothecary.** The Southwestern motif of this café is carried out in a soothing color scheme, which complements the organic cuisine. Unless you're on a strict tofu diet, try the BLT with vegetarian "fakin' " bacon or the organic sourdough sunny flax-seed bread smothered in vegan pesto. You can also order a variety of wraps and salads, as well as burritos, quesadillas, and panini. Plus, it's the only restaurant in the Berkshires that serves a macro bowl of organic pressure-cooked brown rice, grilled tamari-ginger tofu, and steamed veggies. ⊠ *The Lenox Shops, 55 Pittsfield-Lenox Rd., U.S. 7/20* ☎ *413/637–8022* ▤ *MC, V* ⌂ *BYOB* ⊘ *Closed Mon. No dinner Sun.*

¢–$$ ✕ **Panda House.** The Panda focuses on food over decor, as you won't find this Chinese restaurant decked out with golden dragons; it's unadorned and well lit. The menu is long and dependable with all the usual suspects. Many of the dishes are named after A. Michael DeSisto, the founder of a private school for troubled teenagers of the rich and famous, who dined here frequently. ⊠ *506 Pittsfield-Lenox Rd.* ☎ *413/ 499–0660* ▤ *AE, D, MC, V.*

¢–$ ✕ **Carol's Restaurant.** If energy and enthusiasm mean anything, this busy spot represents its owner's relentless pursuit of all things New Age and spiritually daring. For breakfast, try "James Taylor's favorite & coffee" (a feta, tomato, and spinach omelet), named after the town's most famous resident; for lunch, try one of dozens of delicious salads and sandwiches. On weekends you can have a tarot card reading with your meal. ⊠ *8 Franklin St.* ☎ *413/637–8948* ▤ *No credit cards* ⊘ *No dinner.*

¢–$ ✕ **What's The Scoop.** A family restaurant and ice-cream shop serving breakfast all day and homemade soups, this tucked-away café has deep inviting booths and a shaded terrace where weary shoppers can cool down with an ice-cream soda and the county's best overstuffed BLT. A Kids World menu includes a beverage, chips, ice cream, and eight sandwich options. ⊠ *18 Franklin St.* ☎ *413/637–9933* ▤ *AE, D, MC, V* ⊘ *Closed Tues. Sept.–June.*

THE LENOX SPAS

WITH THREE WORLD-CLASS SPAS—all significantly different from each other in price, product, and appeal—Lenox is a fitness Mecca for folks looking to enhance their bodies as well as their minds.

Of the three Lenox spas, **Canyon Ranch** (⇨ Lenox, Where to Stay) is the most luxurious, a spa designed to focus on the spiritual, emotional, and physical well being of its guests. Surrounded by sweeping manicured lawns, fountains, orchards, topiary gardens, the a vast two-level, 100,000 square foot complex has five gyms, a yoga studio, gyrotonic/Pilates Studio, indoor and outdoor pools, exercise and weight training rooms, and indoor tennis, racquetball, squash and basketball courts. The myriad treatments and activities include movement therapy, spiritual awareness, fitness, therapeutic bodywork, massage, skin care, Ayurvedic and Pregnancy health, brain wellness, acupuncture, Sisley facials, Binki Shiodhara, Lymphatic massage and acupuncture. In addition to day and weekend programs, it also offers custom five- to eight-day programs. The price includes most spa treatments, gracious accommodations, and three meals a day.

On beautifully landscaped grounds, the **Kripalu Center for Yoga and Health** (⇨ Lenox, Where to Stay) takes a more ascetic approach, providing simple accommodations with striking views of the Berkshires, and a Yoga program that is internationally renowned. Healing, meditation, yoga and wellness retreats and seminars are all centered on spiritual restoration and transformation. Facials, though available, take a back seat to learning to embrace ìthe Divine Mystery.î Though Kripalu and the Ranch are both earnestly committed to assisting guests explore options for a healthier lifestyle, the former continues to adhere to the principles and practices recommended by its founder Swami Kripalu. The emphasis here is on purity of mind as well as body, and the study of self, the pursuit of non-violence, non-attachment, rigorous honesty, austerity, a commitment to loving service, self-observation and awareness are all far more important than buffing up, slimming down, or counting carbs.

Cranwell Resort, Spa & Golf Club (⇨ Lenox, Where to Stay) is far less imposing, and offers a fraction of the treatments, seminars, and health therapies offered by the Canyon Ranch and Kripalu. It also has a splendid, 18-hole, par 70, championship golf course, 58 acres of lesson tees, short-game practice areas, a large indoor practice area, four dining venues, varied accommodations, a Har-Tru tennis court complex, indoor and outdoor pools, and 10 kilometers of groomed cross-country skiing trails. Before it added its spa, Cranwell was an all-season resort, and it continues to act more like a family destination where mom can have a massage while dad hits the course and the kids are entertained by the staff. Other activities include theme dinners, casino nights, and comedy theatre. Canyon Ranch is inclusive of tax and gratuities, meals, and includes a choice of spa services. Ask about their getaway spa, golf and romance packages, as well as its highly touted Mother/Daughter Spa Getaway. Cranwell is the only spa resort that serves alcohol and allows kids.

Where to Stay

$$$-$$$$ ✕🖵 **Gateways Inn.** The 1912 summer cottage of Harley Proctor (as in
Fodor'sChoice Proctor and Gamble) has experienced some ups and downs during its
★ tenure as a country inn. But under the skillful direction of innkeepers
Fabrizio and Rosemary Chiariello, it looks better than ever. Rooms come
in a variety of configurations and styles, most with working fireplaces,
detailed moldings, and plush carpeting. In the restaurant ($$$-$$$$;
closed Mon.; no lunch weekdays) you might dine on sautéed medallions
of venison or baked acorn squash with a wild rice–cranberry stuffing
and roasted-chestnut ragout. The restaurant offers a light late-night menu
during the Tanglewood season. The inn also makes sublimely delicious
picnic lunches. You can sample dozens of rare grappas and single-malt
whiskies in the bar. ⊠ *51 Walker St., 01240* ☎ *413/637–2532* 🖷 *413/
637–1432* ⊕ *www.gatewaysinn.com* ➳ *11 rooms, 1 suite* ⚫ *Restau-
rant, in-room data ports, some in-room VCRs, bar, meeting room; no
smoking* ⊟ *AE, D, MC, V* ⦿*BP.*

$$$$ ✕🖵 **Blantyre.** Modeled after a castle in Scotland, this supremely elegant
1902 manor house sits amid nearly 100 acres of manicured lawns and
woodlands. Lavishly decorated rooms in the main house have hand-carved
four-poster beds, overstuffed chaise lounges, and Victorian bathrooms.
The rooms in the carriage house are well-appointed but can't compete
with the formal grandeur of the main house. The restaurant ($$$$; reser-
vations essential; jacket and tie) serves upscale country-house fare—no
cream or heavy sauces, light on the butter. A typical entrée might be roasted
Arctic char with fennel confit, crispy potatoes, mussels, crab, and saf-
fron. After-dinner coffee and cognac are served in the music room,
where a harpist plays. ⊠ *16 Blantyre Rd., off U.S. 20, 01240* ☎ *413/
637–3556* 🖷 *413/637–4282* ⊕ *www.blantyre.com* ➳ *17 rooms, 5
suites, 1 cottage* ⚫ *Restaurant, some in-room hot tubs, 4 tennis courts,
pool, hot tub, massage, sauna, croquet, hiking; no smoking* ⊟ *AE,
DC, MC, V* ⊘ *Closed early Nov.–early May* ⦿ *CP.*

$$$$ 🖵 **Canyon Ranch.** This world-class spa resort provides a full slate of vig-
Fodor'sChoice orous activities and beauty-and-body treatments. Colonial-style rooms
★ with floral bedspreads and light-wood furnishings are set inside a con-
temporary inn, while the ornate Bellefontaine Mansion, with its rap-
turous views, houses the dining room, library, and activity areas. In the
spa you can book everything from salt and seaweed treatments to deep-
tissue massage. Rates are all-inclusive; there's a three-night minimum.
Note that alcohol is not permitted in public areas or available anywhere
for purchase. ⊠ *165 Kemble St., 01240* ☎ *413/637–4100 or 800/742–
9000* 🖷 *413/637–0057* ⊕*www.canyonranch.com* ➳*126 rooms* ⚫ *Din-
ing room, tennis courts, 2 pools (1 indoor), aerobics, health club, hot
tub, sauna, spa, bicycles, basketball, hiking, racquetball, squash, cross-
country skiing; no kids under 14, no smoking* ⊟ *AE, D, MC, V* ⦿*FAP.*

$$$$ 🖵 **Cranwell Resort, Spa, and Golf Club.** The best rooms in this 380-acre,
five-building complex are in the century-old Tudor mansion; they're fur-
nished with antiques and have marble bathrooms. Two smaller build-
ings have 20 rooms each, and there are several small cottages, each of
which has a kitchen. Somewhat marring the property are an abundance
of tightly spaced condos behind the hotel buildings. Most of the facili-

ties are open to the public, as are the resort's restaurants, where you can dine formally or informally. There's also a full golf school. The 35,000-square-foot spa has a full complement of women's and men's treatments, plus several types of massage. ⊠ *55 Lee Rd., 02140* ☎ *413/637–1364 or 800/272–6935* 🖶 *413/637–4364* ⊕ *www.cranwell.com* 🛏 *107 rooms ⚐ 3 restaurants, driving range, 18-hole golf course, 4 tennis courts, pool, health club, spa, bicycles, hiking, cross-country skiing, concierge, meeting rooms* ⊟ *AE, D, DC, MC, V* ⍾ *CP.*

$$$$ 🖭 **Stonover Farm.** This country inn on scenic Underhill Mountain Road, less than a mile from Tanglewood's Main Gate, is what you get if you mix a successful L.A. record producer with 1890 stone farmhouse. Wickedly contemporary within, set on 10 pastoral acres and looking country-fetching and idyllic on the outside, Stonover Farm combines all the technological advances of the 21st century with the luxurious comforts of the past. Flat-screen TVs and Bose radios are in each sumptuous suite. The secluded Rock Cottage is equipped with a fireplace, a living–dining area, fully equipped kitchen, and a grand furnished deck—perfect for families. ⊠ *169 Undermountain Rd., 01240* ☎ *413/637–9100* ⊕ *www.stonoverfarm.com* 🛏 *3 suites, 1 cottage ⚐ In-room DVD players* ⊟ *AE, D, MC, V* ⍾ *BP* ⊘ *Closed Jan.–Apr.*

$$$–$$$$ 🖭 **Apple Tree Inn & Restaurant.** Overlooking the Stockbridge bowl and the Berkshire Hills, this restored 1885 farmhouse provides colorful country-theme rooms and suites, many with fireplaces. The main house is far more tempting than the attached lodge, though the latter is closer to the pool, which has one of the best views in the Berkshires. Breakfast is served in the gazebo-shape dining room, which has panoramic mountain views. The oak-beamed tavern is a great place to order a brew and mull over all the reasons you should move to the Berkshires. ⊠ *10 Richmond Mountain Rd., 01240* ☎ *413/637–1477* 🖶 *413/637–2528* ⊕ *www.appletree-inn.com* 🛏 *31 rooms, 3 suites ⚐ Restaurant, bar, cable TV, tennis court, pool; no smoking* ⊟ *AE, D, MC, V* ⍾ *CP.*

$$$–$$$$ 🖭 **Birchwood Inn.** Perched atop the hill on the north end of Main Street, this lovely 1767 mansion is remarkable for its extraordinary library and a front porch that invites whiling away a summer afternoon with a good book and a cold glass of lemonade. The period-appointed rooms are comfortable, some with fireplaces, and the full breakfast would satisfy any gourmand. Afternoon tea in the library makes this an idyllic and thoroughly delightful lodging choice. ⊠ *7 Hubbard St., 01240* ☎ *413/637–2600 or 800/524–1646* 🖶 *413/637–4604* ⊕ *www.birchwood-inn.com* 🛏 *11 rooms ⚐ Cable TV; no kids under 12, no smoking* ⊟ *AE, D, MC, V* ⍾ *CP.*

$$$–$$$$ 🖭 **The Cornell Inn.** Three guesthouses comprise this attractive late 19th-century gray-and-white Victorian. Rooms in the main house are adorned with period furnishings; the MacDonald House is appointed with Colonial pieces, and the carriage house is decorated with a country flavor. Many of the rooms have fireplaces, four-poster beds, and outdoor decks or patios. The Japanese garden, with its waterfall and pool stocked with colorful koi, is as peaceful and secluded a spot as you're likely to find within walking distance of downtown Lenox. A full breakfast is served in the dining room, but on summer mornings look for a table on the terrace, or the one in the shaded area above the waterfall. ⊠ *203 Main St., 01240* 🕾 *413/637–0562* 🖶 *413/637–0927* ⊕ *www.cornellinn.com* ↬ *28 rooms ♿ Cable TV, some in-room hot tubs, some kitchens; no kids under 13, no smoking* ⊟ *AE, D, MC, V* ⦿ *CP.*

$$$–$$$$ 🏨 **Eastover Resort & Conference Center.** Activities abound at this sprawling family resort, from badminton, horseshoes, and miniature golf to a putting green, driving range, and sand volleyball. Rooms are spartan and appointed with contemporary furnishings. Meals, all activities, and evening entertainment are included in the price. ⊠ *430 East St., 01240* 🕾 *413/637–0625 or 800/822–2386* 🖶 *413/637–4939* ⊕ *www. eastover.com* ↬ *138 rooms, 2 suites ♿ Meeting rooms, 2 pools (1 indoor), 5 tennis courts, miniature golf, putting green, driving range, gym, badminton, horseshoes, volleyball, no-smoking rooms* ⊟ *AE, D, MC, V* ⦿ *FAP.*

$$$–$$$$ 🏨 **Hampton Terrace.** A remnant of the Gilded Age and an inn since 1937, this property is notable for its charming guest rooms and its richly detailed public rooms, adorned with sconces, fireplaces, elaborate moldings, country furnishings, and a striking three-story suspended stairway. More than half its rooms have fireplaces and hot tubs. The inn is minutes away from Tanglewood. ⊠ *91 Walker St., 01240* 🕾 *413/ 637–1773 or 800/203–0656* ⊕ *www.hamptonterrace.com* ↬ *10 rooms ♿ In room VCRs; no kids under 10, no smoking* ⊟ *AE, MC, V* ⦿ *BP.*

$$$–$$$$ 🏨 **Harrison House.** An inviting white Victorian house with a sweeping wraparound porch across from Lenox's White Church on the Hill, this upscale inn is particularly notable for its attractive, mature landscaping. Rooms are lavish with decadent furnishings—every unit has a working fireplace, and a few have four-poster or canopy beds. Plush duvets, ceiling fans, and Victorian-style wallpapers add to the sense of romance. It's a bit smaller and less busy than most of the inns in Lenox, and the hosts are friendly and enthusiastic. The inn is close enough to walk into town but set nicely on a hillside away from the tourist bustle. Tea is served every afternoon. ⊠ *174 Main St., 01240* 🕾 *413/637– 1746* ⊕ *www.harrison-house.com* ↬ *6 rooms ♿ No room phones; no smoking* ⊟ *AE, D, MC, V* ⦿ *BP.*

$$–$$$$ 🏨 **Brook Farm Inn.** This 1870s Victorian and its gardens are tucked away in a beautiful wooded glen a short distance from Tanglewood. The innkeepers are music and literature aficionados and often have light opera, jazz, or Broadway tunes playing in the fireplace-lighted library, whose shelves contain copious volumes of verse. On Saturday poetry is read at afternoon tea. Rooms have antiques, light-pastel color schemes, and in many cases four-poster beds. Even the smallest units, with their eaved ceilings and cozy configurations, are highly romantic. ⊠ *15 Hawthorne St., 01240* 🕾 *413/637–3013 or 800/285–7638* ⊕ *www.brookfarm. com* ↬ *12 rooms, 1 suite ♿ In-room data ports, pool, library; no room TVs, no kids under 15, no smoking* ⊟ *MC, V* ⦿ *BP.*

$$–$$$$ 🏨 **Cliffwood Inn.** Six of the seven guest rooms in this 1889 Georgian Revival white-clapboard mansion have fireplaces, and four more fireplaces glow in the common areas, reflecting off the polished wooden floors. Many of the inn's ornate antiques come from Europe; most guest rooms have canopy beds. ⊠ *25 Cliffwood St., 01240* 🕾 *413/637–*

3330 or 800/789–3331 ☐ *413/637–0221* ⊕ *www.cliffwood.com* ↩ *6 rooms, 1 suite* ⚲ *Some in-room hot tubs, some in-room VCRs, pool, hot tub; no room phones, no TV in some rooms, no kids under 11, no smoking* ⊟ *No credit cards* ⏐◯⏐ *BP.*

$$–$$$$ ⊞ **Garden Gables.** This 1780s summer cottage on 5 acres of wooded grounds has been an inn since 1947. The three common parlors have fireplaces, and one long, narrow room has a rare five-legged Steinway piano. Rooms come in various shapes, sizes, and colors and have American country–style antiques; some have brass beds, and others have pencil four-posters. Some rooms have sloping ceilings, fireplaces, whirlpool baths, or woodland views. Three have private decks. Breakfast is served buffet-style in the airy dining room. ⊠ *135 Main St.* ⌖ *Box 52, 01240* ☎ *413/637–0193* ☐ *413/637–4554* ⊕ *www.lenoxinn. com* ↩ *19 rooms* ⚲ *Cable TV, in-room data ports, some in-room hot tubs, pool; no TV in some rooms, no kids under 12, no smoking* ⊟ *AE, D, MC, V* ⏐◯⏐ *BP.*

$$–$$$$ ⊞ **Kemble Inn.** Set on 3 acres in the center of Lenox, this 1881 Berkshire cottage, with its breathtaking mountain views from its rear windows, is one of the most impressive and graceful of the town's many inns. The rooms are named after Berkshire literary giants, and many have marble fireplaces, carved four-poster beds, and hot tubs. A cheery breakfast room and broad porch overlook the valley and hills beyond, and you cannot open the front door into the vast foyer without pausing for a moment to dream of bygone days. ⊠ *2 Kemble St., 01240* ☎ *413/ 637–4113 or 800/358–4113* ⊕ *www.kembleinn.com* ↩ *14 rooms* ⚲ *Cable TV; no kids under 12, no smoking* ⊟ *D, MC, V* ⏐◯⏐ *CP.*

$$–$$$$ ⊞ **Kripalu Center for Yoga & Health.** Originally built as a Jesuit Seminary, this vast, bulky brick building sits on 300 hilltop acres overlooking the Stockbridge Bowl, across the road from Tanglewood. In the 1970s Yoga master Swami Kripalu began this program in a determinedly Eastern direction. Today, the Swami is gone, and the Omega Institute is managing the center. The Kripalu Approach emphasizes the transformation and freeing of the self through various practices, treatments, and philosophies, particularly yoga. It offers dozens of yoga, wellness, meditation, and self-help and awareness workshops throughout the year. A stay at Kripalu includes three yoga sessions and three prepared meals daily. Accommodations or simple and modern, ranging from dormitory style rooms with bunk beds to small twin-bed rooms. The Kripalu also offers a variety of massages, rubs, masks and scrubs, as well as ayurvedic treatments derived from an ancient Indian tradition that is designed to release toxins and restore balance, calm, and harmony. ⊠ *West St., 01240* ☎ *413/ 448–3400* ⊕ *www.kripalu.org* ↩ *174 rooms, 142 with shared bath* ⚲ *Cafe, spa, hot tubs, fitness classes; no room phones, no room TVs, no smoking* ⊟ *MC, V* ⏐◯⏐ *FAP.*

★ $–$$$$ ⊞ **Whistler's Inn.** The antiques decorating the parlor of this eccentric 1820s English Tudor mansion are ornate, with a touch of the exotic. The library, formal parlor, music room (with a Steinway grand piano and Louis XVI original furniture), and gracious dining room all impress. Designer drapes and bedspreads adorn the rooms, three of which have working fireplaces. The carriage house is only open May through October; one room in it has African decor, and another is done in Southwestern style. The inn is nestled amid 7 acres of gardens and woods across from Kennedy Park. ⊠ *5 Greenwood St., 01240* ☎ *413/637–0975* ⊟ *413/637–2190* ⊕ *www.whistlersinnlenox.com* ⇱ *14 rooms* ⅏ *Badminton, croquet, library* ⊟ *AE, D, MC, V* ⦿ *BP.*

$$–$$$ ⊞ **Walker House.** With its lush gardens and deep shade, this 1804 Federal-style inn evokes the Deep South. Surrounded as it is by towering pines, the inn's interior is dim at best, though owners Peggy and Richard Houdek have used bright wallpapers and furnishing to lighten things up quite a bit. A library contains overstuffed bookshelves. ⊠ *64 Walker St., 01240* ☎ *413/637–1271 or 800/235–3098* ⊟ *413/637–2387* ⊕ *www.walkerhouse.com* ⇱ *8 rooms* ⅏ *No room phones, no room TVs, no smoking* ⊟ *No credit cards* ⦿ *CP.*

★ $–$$ ⊞ **Yankee Inn.** Custom-crafted Amish canopy beds, gas fireplaces, and high-end fabrics decorate the top rooms at this immaculately kept property, one of several modern hotels and motels along U.S. 7. The more economical units contain attractive, if nondescript, country-style furnishings and such useful amenities as coffeemakers and irons with ironing boards. The same owners run an appealing B&B in downtown Lee, the Chambéry Inn. ⊠ *461 Pittsfield-Lenox Rd., U.S. 7 and 20, 01240* ☎ *413/499–3700 or 800/835–2364* ⊟ *413/499–3634* ⊕ *www.yankeeinn. com* ⇱ *96 rooms* ⅏ *In-room data ports, refrigerators, indoor pool, gym, hot tub, meeting rooms* ⊟ *AE, D, MC, V* ⦿ *CP.*

The Arts

The Emmy–award winning satire troupe **The News in Revue** (⊠ Cranwell Resort, U.S. 20 ☎ 413/637–1364 ⊕ www.newsinrevue.com) performs every night but Wednesday at 8:30 in July and August.

Shakespeare and Company (⊠ 70 Kemble St. ☎ 413/637–1199, 413/637–3353 tickets) performs the works of Shakespeare and Edith Wharton from late May through October at the 466-seat Founders' Theatre and the 99-seat Spring Lawn Theatre. Also under way is the re-creation of the Rose Playhouse, the original of which has stood on the South Bank of the London's Thames River since 1587.

Fodor'sChoice **Tanglewood** (⊠ West St. off Rte. 183 ☎ 413/637–5165, 617/266–1492, ★ 617/266–1200 tickets from Symphony Charge ⊕ www.bso.org), the 200-acre summer home of the Boston Symphony Orchestra, attracts thousands every year to concerts by world-famous performers from mid-June to Labor Day. The 5,000-seat main shed hosts larger concerts; the Seiji Ozawa Hall (named for the former BSO conductor—James Levine took the helm in 2003) seats around 1,200 and is used for recitals, chamber music, and more intimate performances by summer program students and soloists. One of the most rewarding ways to experience Tanglewood is to purchase lawn tickets, arrive early with blankets or lawn chairs, and have a picnic. Except for the odd celebrity concert, lawn tickets remain below $20, and concerts can be clearly heard from just about any spot on the lawn. Inside the shed, tickets vary in price, with most of the good seats costing between $38 and $100.

TANGLEWOOD

EACH JULY, THE BOSTON SYMPHONY PACKS up its instruments and heads for the Berkshire Hills and their summer retreat, Tanglewood. Perched on a steep rise overlooking the Stockbridge Bowl, Tanglewood is the heart of most every Berkshire summer vacation. Few music festivals in the country, and certainly none in New England, can compare to it terms of size, popularity, and scenic beauty. Each season more than 300,000 music lovers from around the world flock to Lenox with one goal in mind—a picnic concert at Tanglewood.

Founded in 1934, Tanglewood was originally called the Berkshire Musical Festival, and for the first two seasons the New York Philharmonic performed a series of concerts at the site. In 1936, the Boston Symphony Orchestra under the leadership of the great Russian conductor Serge Koussevitzky, arrived to replace them. The three concerts they performed over one steamy weekend in August drew more than 15,000 people. With the large canvas tent overflowing onto the surrounding lawns, Koussevitzky realized he had found a summer home for his orchestra. The following season, the BSO returned to Tanglewood and again met with great success. Indeed, so popular was the new festival, that when a thunderous storm arrived and drowned out Wagner's The Ride of the Valkyries, the patrons rushed into action, raising more than $30,000 for an indoor music pavilion. When Koussevitzky and his musicians arrived in 1938, they performed in a huge shed, capable of seating 5,000 people.

Since then, every July and August weekend, visitors arrive long before the concert begins, before the instruments are tuned, or the musicians don their tuxedos. They lay out their blankets, set up their tables and chairs, unpack their bags and buckets and baskets, put flowers in glass vases, uncork their wine bottles, light candles and settle in for the best people watching in the Berkshires.

Tanglewood has expanded its schedule to include mid-week concerts in the 12,000-seat Seiji Ozawa Hall, prelude concerts on Friday nights, and the bargain of all times, open rehearsals on Saturday mornings. The Tanglewood Jazz Festival over Labor Day weekend draws major jazz musicians and its attendance grows larger each year.

Sports & the Outdoors

Health & Fitness

Daily rates are available at the **Lenox Fitness Center & Spa** (✉ 90 Pittsfield-Lenox Rd., U.S. 7 and 20 ☎ 413/637–9893 ⊕ www.lenoxfitnesscenter.com), where everything from Pilates to kickboxing and tanning to waxing is available under one roof.

Hiking

Operated by the Massachusetts Audubon Society's system, the **Pleasant Valley Wildlife Sanctuary** (✉ 472 W. Mountain Rd. ☎ 413/637–0320 ⊕ www.massaudubon.org), abounds with beaver ponds, meadows, hardwood forests and woodlands. Its 1,400 acres and 7 mi of trails offer excellent bird- and beaver-watching. The nature center is open daily July to October. Canoe trips are also offered regularly on the Housatonic River and area lakes.

Horseback Riding

Travel along the beautiful shaded trails of Kennedy Park and Lenox Mountain and enjoy breathtaking views of Berkshire county when you book an hour, half-day, or overnight ride at **Berkshire Horseback Adventures** (✉ 293 Main St. ☎ 413/637–9090).

Shopping

Influenced no doubt by the artistic and historic influences of its venerable past and the dynamic cultural offerings of the present, Lenox is a creative, eclectic jumble of shops, galleries, and boutiques that is patronized by locals and tourists alike. Books, leather, jewelry, toys, health food, art, antiques, greeting cards, exotic liqueurs, and cheeses as well as clothing that sweeps the fashion spectrum make shopping in this small four-street downtown a vibrant and exciting treasure hunt.

Local sculptor **Andrew DeVries** (✉ 17 Franklin St. ☎ 413/637–3462) has his own shop and gallery, where he displays not only his sculptors but also sketches and watercolors.

Not your typical jacket and handbag leather store, **Berkshire Classic Leather & Silver** (✉ 74 Main St. ☎ 413/637–0727) is stocked with a wonderful blend of contemporary and eclectic items.

A local favorite, **The Bookstore** (✉ 11 Housatonic St. ☎ 413/637–3390) sells regional interest titles as well as books by regional authors.

At **Chocolate Springs** (✉ The Lenox Shops, 55 Pittsfield-Lenox Rd., U.S. 7 and 20 ☎ 413/637–9820) you can either order truffles, mousse cakes, and pastry picnic packs to go, or grab a table and indulge yourself in Chocolate Springs' "Asian Influenced Atmosphere."

At **Cose D'Argilla** (✉ 93 Church St. ☎ 413/637–8886) browse glass, pottery, jewelry, breathtaking Iris prints of photographs of Italy, and watercolors by contemporary New England artists, many at affordable prices.

For colorful clothing, toys, and accessories for newborns to preteens, visit the **Gifted Child** (✉ 72 Church St. ☎ 413/637–1191).

One of the foremost crafts centers in New England, **Hoadley Gallery** (✉ 21 Church St. ☎ 413/637–2814) shows American arts and crafts with a strong focus on pottery, jewelry, and textiles.

Every Friday afternoon from 3 to 7, rain or shine, locals gather at the **Lenox Farmer's Market,** in the parking lot of the **Lenox Shops** (✉ Pittsfield-Lenox Rd.), to buy locally grown edibles.

Nejaime's Wine Cellars (✉ 60 Main St., Lenox ☎ 413/637–2221) prepares excellent picnics-to-go and is also a top-flight wine-and-cheese store.

No one prepares picnics quite as elegant as **Perfect Picnics** (✉ 34A Main St. ☎ 413/637–3015). Since 1989, this small shop has been packing picnics for those coming to Tanglewood. Depending on your budget, you can choose from either the Perfect or the Ultimate Perfect Picnic.

R. W. Wise (✉ 81 Church St. ☎ 413/637–1589 ⊕ www.rwwise.com) produces high-quality creative jewelry and also sells estate and antique pieces.

RICHMOND

⑤ *6 mi west of Lenox.*

The jewel of this small, rural community between Pittsfield and West Stockbridge is Richmond Pond, a 226-acre pond with a town beach and state boat ramp. You won't find a sign announcing its location, however, as town residents, many of them part-time second-home owners, would just as soon keep it their own little secret. Other than Bartlett's Orchard, you'll have little reason to linger here, though driving through town on Route 41, otherwise known as the West Stockbridge–Richmond Road, is a more scenic, though time-consuming, alternative to U.S. 7.

Where to Stay

$$–$$$$ 🏠 **The Inn At Richmond.** On 27 acres of perennial gardens with a reflecting pool, meadows, and woodlands, the Inn at Richmond has some of the most spectacular views of the Berkshire Hills. Elegant accommodations are furnished with family heirlooms and such luxury touches as Caswell and Massey amenities, fine linens, port, sherry, and chocolate truffles. If you can pull yourself away from the plush country elegance of the parlor, library, and garden rooms, the inn is a mere 7 scenic miles from Tanglewood. An equestrian center is on the property, and the full, fresh Berkshire-grown breakfast is a sumptuous affair. ✉ *802 State Rd., 01254* ☎ *413/698–2566 or 888/968–4748* 🖷 *413/698–2100* ⊕ *www. innatrichmond.com* ⤴ *3 rooms, 3 suites, 2 cottages, 1 carriage house* ♿ *Some kitchens, cable TV, in-room VCRs; no smoking, no kids under 10* ▭ *MC, V* ⊺⊙⊦ *BP.*

Shopping

Its strategic location on a mountainside assures **Bartlett's Orchard** (✉ 575 Swamp Rd. ☎ 413/698–2559) the proper airflow necessary for prime apple growth. It, along with "rich, moisture-bearing soil," is responsible for the dependably juicy fruit sold at this Richmond farm stand. Whether you're just driving by with a yen for fresh-made cider and donuts or are in the market to pick a bushel of Macoun apples, Bartlett's is a satisfying roadside stop.

THE HILLTOWNS
BECKET, HINSDALE, PERU, WASHINGTON & WINDSOR

Strung out along remote stretches of Routes 8 and 9 north and east of Pittsfield, the Hilltowns of Central County are mountainous outposts, thickly wooded—rich with small brooks, streams, and ponds, and pleasantly isolated from the cultural engine that drives the rest of the Berkshire economy. Indeed, with the exception of second-home owners who have, in the past decade or so, decided they really do want to get away from it all not just for a weekend but for the rest of their lives, most hill towners have lived in these parts for generations. These sparsely populated rural communities are in many ways more like the Appalachians than the Berkshires. It is quite possible to head south out of Dalton on Route 8—through Hinsdale, Washington and Becket—and see barely a soul along the way. Though the entire county is as lush, scenic, and lovely as England's Lake District, it is in the Hilltowns of Becket, Hinsdale, Peru, Washington, and Windsor that you will discover the soft pleasure and deep silence of the Berkshire countryside.

A circular drive through Hinsdale, Washington and Becket is the easiest and best way to get a taste of the Hill Towns. Though none have anything resembling a village, the drive south on Route 8, which begins in Dalton, just east of Pittsfield, is a meandering, well paved road through cool forests and vast fields crowded with wildflowers. Pack a picnic and settle into this quiet land with its gentle views.

Ponds and streams appear with comforting regularity, and though you're never more than a half hour distant from the nearest gas station or supermarket, you can capture that off-the-beaten-trail magic. For the avid explorer, not afraid of getting a tad lost, there are tempting side roads that all seem to magically wend their way back to Route 8 just when you think you're never going to see a convenience store ever again.

Becket

6 *15 mi east of Lenox.*

With no shops, no general store, no bar or village café, and less than 2,000 residents, Becket gets its fair share of attention. Of all the Hill towns, Becket is far and away the most illustrious, most visited, and most varied. Jacob's Pillow, America's first dance festival, draws thousands of dance enthusiasts each summer and is the town's major tourist attraction. Down the road a piece, gracefully hidden in thick pine woods, is Becket's only famous resident, Arlo Guthrie, who has been playing host to hordes of musicians for the past four decades. And, last but not least, set in all its rustic finery at the top of a mountain, is the county's most unusual, enchanted, and adventurous restaurant, the Dream Away Lodge.

Becket's natural resources—its boisterous streams and abundant woodlands—were the silver spoons that launched its incarnation, a small but flourishing lumber industry that fueled the economy until 1927. When the Ballou Reservoir burst its earthen banks and a 25-foot wall of water tore through the narrow valley, which the settlers had chosen for its snug, comforting location, the town and its industrial life ended. Becket's luck seemed to have turned until Ted Shawn arrived with his wife, Ruth St. Denis, and a dream to popularize a revolutionary dance form rooted in theatrical and ethnic traditions rather than those of European ballet. The small hamlet was revitalized, and since the 1930s, Becket has hosted the Jacob's Pillow Dance Festival in what was the first of the many cultural venues that would create the vital tourism industry that is at the heart of the Berkshire economy.

Besides Shawn and Guthrie, a significant stream of celebrities has found its muse in the sweet, lush hills of this hidden jewel 19 mi southeast of Pittsfield. Paul Revere, the first visitor of note, arrived in 1780, a mere 15 years after Becket was established, to fashion a bell for the town's Congregational Church. Two decades later, Johnny Appleseed hiked to the top of the Jacob's Ladder Trail, which served as the trailhead for the Yellowstone Trail, on his way to Oregon.

If you haven't found a good place to picnic along Route 8 by the time you reach Becket, and you don't mind walking on a slightly rough trail, follow Route 8 through Becket to the junction with Route 20, cross over to Bonny Rigg Hill Road and follow the signs to **Becket Land Trust and Historic Quarry.** An integral part of Becket history, the Quarry was essential to the town's development, and it remains a hidden treasure for today's hikers.

Where to Eat

$-$$$ ✕ **Dream Away Lodge.** When the Dream Away reopened in 1998, folk-music fans hailed the revival of the "middle of nowhere" roadhouse once run by the late "Mama" Maria Fresca, a spirited hostess who befriended many performers (scenes from Bob Dylan's road-show movie *Renaldo and Clara* were filmed here). The bar menu consists of burgers, pastas, spicy fries, and the like; the dining room serves a four-course prix-fixe meal, which might include roast cilantro chicken or salmon fillet in puff pastry. Wednesday is music night, with acoustic folk, blues, and other traditional sounds. ⊠ *County Rd.* ☎ *413/623–8725* ▤ *No credit cards* ☽ *Closed Mon. and Tues.*

The Arts

For nine weeks each summer, Becket becomes a mecca of the dance world during **Jacob's Pillow Dance Festival** (⊠ 358 George Carter Rd., at U.S. 20 ☎ 413/327–1234 ⊕ www.jacobspillow.org), which showcases world-renowned performers of ballet, modern, and ethnic dance. Before the main events, showings of works-in-progress and even of some of the final productions are staged outdoors, often free of charge. You can picnic on the grounds or eat at the restaurant under the tent. To reach Jacob's

Pillow, follow Route 8 through Becket to U.S. 20. Turn right and follow U.S. 20 to George Carter Road; follow the signs from there.

Sports & the Outdoors

SKIING If you're looking for an adventure in wilderness skiing, **Canterbury Farm** (⊠ Fred Snow Rd. ☎ 413/623–0100 ⊕ www.canterbury-farms.com) should be at the top of your list. Surrounded by 2,000 acres of state and private land, the property offers 12 mi of broad trails groomed daily and appealing to every skill level. You can ski along brooks and stone walls, downhill ski on the Outer Limits Trail, glide your way to a hidden lake across fields of snow and through woods so silent you can hear a squirrel breathe. After you've got in some solid ski time, take a break in the cozy Berkshire room around the fireplace, where drinks, hot soup, and snacks are available. Ski rentals and lessons are available.

Washington

❼ *3 mi north of Becket.*

Incorporated in 1784, Washington was named after George Washington, and with its fertile soil, five sparkling lakes, and abundance of waterways, it attracted early settlers. Today the population hovers around 550, and most of its homes were built during the 1980s. Besides the shameful behavior of Mr. Watson, Washington's only claim to infamy is having been the birthplace of Edwin D. Morgan, the first chairman of the Republican National Committee.

Hinsdale

❽ *6 mi north of Washington.*

Settled in 1804, Hinsdale has little to offer other than the fact that it is ideally situated on Route 8 at the beginning of the hilltown drive described above.

At the **Partridgefield Trading Company** (⊠ 371 Old Dalton Rd., at Rte. 8 ☎ 413/655–0161) you can buy everything from teriyaki chicken wings and wine to amply stuffed sandwiches, pizza, and homemade soup. This deli–cum–liquor store, perched on the side of an inviting little brook, is also a good place to begin your exploration of the Hilltowns. Picnic tables are available brook-side, or pick up a lunch basket for the road.

Peru

❾ *5 mi east of Hinsdale.*

Apart from being highest town center in the state of Massachusetts, Peru—like its neighboring soulmates—serves as a bedroom community for Dalton, Pittsfield, and Springfield. More than half of this hilltop town consists of woodlands and its one historic site, the humble Garnet Mountain Monument, which commemorates the 15 soldiers killed in a plane crash on the mountain during World War II. Though originally named Partridgefield on July 4, 1771, after one of its original purchasers, the town was renamed Peru by Reverend John Leland three decades later because its mountainous landscape reminded him of the South American country.

Windsor

⑩ *10 mi north of Peru.*

Windsor, like its sister Hilltowns in Central County, was founded in the mid-18th century. Like the others, it was remote, and the long, harsh Berkshire winters made it inaccessible for the better part of six months out of the year. Far from the rail line, tucked snug and away from the clatter of commerce and transport that began to surface elsewhere in the country during the mid-19th and early-20th centuries, Windsor clung to the valley bottom, hidden from view. In the mid-1980s, however, Windsor began to draw an increasing number of families who worked in Pittsfield and were attracted by its rural lifestyle, low-priced real estate, and attractive countryside. Originally called Gageborough, the town was renamed Windsor in 1778 because so many of its early settlers had come from Windsor, Connecticut. Today, with pleasant woodlands, a few small farms, a smattering of mobile homes, and a family-owned, no-frills general store, the town fathers proudly describe the community as "a small town which behaves like a large family."

Sports & the Outdoors

HIKING The 3,000-acre **Notchview Reservation** (✉ Rte. 9 ☎ 413/684–0148 ⊕ www.thetrustees.org) provides 20 mi of trails that cut through field and forest and are popular with hikers, bird-watchers, and cross-country skiers.

A short walk from the parking lot on Route 9 brings you to **Wahconah Falls** (✉ Rte. 9 ☎ 413/442–8992). A good destination for an outing, especially during the Berkshire's vivid autumn season.

In a region full of rolling hills and mountain streams, **Windsor State Forest** (✉ River Rd. off Rte. 9 ☎ 413/663–8469) stands out for the spectacular beauty of cascading falls at Windsor Jamb. The popular day-use swimming area on the Westfield River provides a 100-foot sandy beach and picnic sites. The numerous trails and old roads that wind through the forest are favored by hikers, cross-country skiers, and snowmobilers.

PITTSFIELD

⑪–⑬ *10 mi north of Lenox.*

A mere agricultural backwater at the time of the American Revolution, the seat of Berkshire county grew steadily throughout the 19th century into an industrial powerhouse of textile, paper, and electrical machinery manufacturing. As recently as the 1930s, the WPA guidebook on Massachusetts described Pittsfield as possessing a "prosperous, tranquil look of general comfort and cultivation which makes it one of the most attractive industrial cities in the state." Alas, the city's economy took a nosedive following World War II, and much of that apparent prosperity diminished.

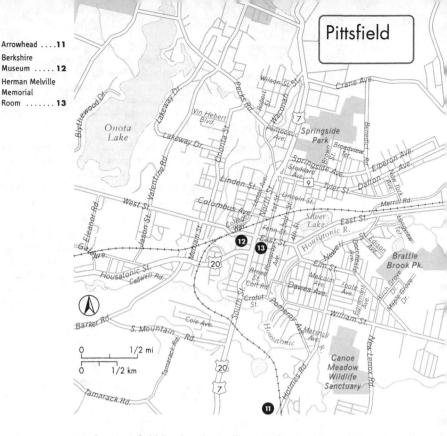

Pittsfield

Modern Pittsfield has brushed off some of its bruises and blemishes of the past several decades and reclaimed a number of intriguing industrial buildings. Still, this is a workaday city without the moneyed urbanity of Great Barrington or the quaint, rural demeanor of the comparatively small Colonial towns that surround it. Along North Street, several new shops and eateries have opened, perhaps signaling a return to downtown prosperity.

What to See

🕚 **Arrowhead,** the gold-painted house Herman Melville purchased in 1850, is 4 mi south of downtown Pittsfield; the underwhelming tour includes the study in which *Moby-Dick* was written; it is said that Melville found his whale in the graceful shape of Mt. Greylock, which is framed by its window. ✉ *780 Holmes Rd.* ☎ *413/442–1793* ⊕ *www.mobydick. org* 🎫 *$10* ⊙ *Late May–Oct., daily 10–5, with guided tours on the hr; Nov.–late May, weekdays by appointment.*

🕐 Opened in 1903, the **Berkshire Museum** houses three floors of exhibits, which display a varied and sometimes curious collection of objects relating to history, the natural world, and art. A highlight of the latter is a collection of Hudson River School paintings, including works by Frederic Church and Albert Bierstadt. An aquarium contains 26 tanks of sea creatures, including a touch tank; a 10-foot-high, 26-foot-long "Wally" the Stegosaurus highlights the Dinosaurs and Paleontology gallery. At the Dino Dig, kids and adults can dig together for touchable replicas of dinosaur bones. An ancient civilization gallery displays Roman and Greek jewelry and an ancient Egyptian mummy. ⊠ *39 South St.* ☎ *413/443–7171* ⊕ *www. berkshiremuseum.org* ▦ *$8* ◔ *Mon.–Sat. 10–5, Sun. noon–5.*

⓭ The **Herman Melville Memorial Room** at the **Berkshire Athenaeum** houses an extensive collection of books, letters, and memorabilia of the author of *Moby-Dick.* ⊠ *Berkshire Public Library, 1 Wendell Ave.* ☎ *413/499– 9486* ⊕ *www.berkshire.net/pittsfieldlibrary* ▦ *Free* ◔ *Call for hrs.*

Where to Eat

$$–$$$$ ✕ **Trattoria Rustica.** Owner–chef Davide Manzo's culinary skill is reflected in the bread and mozzarella he makes fresh each day, in the inspired use of spices, the freshness of his produce, the tender cuts of meat, and exotic fish he serves. Brick walls, tile floors, hand-painted dishes, lanterns, and an exposed kitchen where classic southern Italian dishes are prepared, combine to create a warm, intimate setting far from the sights and sounds of a city struggling to find its identity. ⊠ *McKay St.* ☎ *413/499–1192* ▭ *AE, D, MC, V.*

$$–$$$ ✕ **Dakota.** Moose and elk heads watch over diners, and the motto is "Steak, seafood, and smiles" at this large and popular chain restaurant, decorated like a rustic hunting lodge. Meals cooked on the mesquite grill include steaks and salmon, shrimp, and trout; the 32-item salad bar has many organic foods. A hearty Sunday brunch buffet includes Belgian pancakes, omelets, ham, lox and bagels, fruit, salads, and rich deserts. ⊠ *1035 South St.* ☎ *413/499–7900* ▭ *AE, D, DC, MC, V* ◔ *No lunch Mon.–Sat.*

$$ ✕ **Elizabeth's Borderland Café.** This small house with bright Mediterranean blue trim may sit at the far end of Pittsfield's East Street, past auto-body shops, car dealerships, and an abandoned GE plant, but its white walls and bright posters recall sunny days on distant Caribbean isles. Owner Tom Ellis has been serving up his delicious, "honest" Italian cuisine (six vegetarian pasta dishes and two daily nonpasta specialties) for nearly two decades. ⊠ *1264 East St.* ☎ *413/448–8244* ▭ *No credit cards* ◔ *Closed Mon. June–Oct. No lunch.*

¢–$$ ✕ **The Fighting Parson Tavern & Brewery.** The Fighting Parson immortalized by this Pittsfield tavern and brewery fired the first shot at the Battle of Bennington, in 1777. The Parson's heritage is found in the dark-wood confines of a restaurant that clings to the New England favorites of its namesake: Shepherd's Pie, country chicken, thick burgers, New York strip steaks, and fish-and-chips. Wash it all down with a pint of Bohemian pilsner, stout, or blond ale. ⊠ *34 Depot St.* ☎ *413/442– 2072* ▭ *AE, D, MC, V* ◔ *Closed Sun.*

¢ ✕ **Bellissimo Dolce.** At the far end of North Street, just when you think you've explored the dining options in downtown Pittsfield, you'll discover a tempting reason to pause for a cup of cappuccino and a sfogliattel. Its high ceilings, massive wood coffee bar, huge mirrors, hardwood floors, and opera music are as inviting as the cheesecake, focaccia, pastry, frittata, and quiche. ⊠ *444 North St.* ☏ *413/443–1792* ▭ *No credit cards.*

¢ ✗ **Digital.Blend.** Everyone in the country may have their own PC by now, but this Internet café still lures dot-comer's away from their techno-nests to enjoy flavorful coffee drinks. Along with macchiatos and steamers, Digital also serves panini, exotic wraps, and sandwiches. Internet access is $5 per hour and is provided in a quiet room separate from the café. ⊠ *76 North St.* ☏ *413/445–9991* ▭ *No credit cards* ⊘ *Closed Sun.*

Where to Stay

$$–$$$$ ⊞ **Thaddeus Clapp House.** Tucked away behind the Colonial Theatre, this elegant 19th-century grande dame is a gracious reminder of Pittsfield's Victorian years. Its suites are generously proportioned and decorated with Oriental rugs, antique furniture, and museum-quality art. Mrs. Clapp's bedroom includes a sweet little sunporch. All rooms have a wet bar, robes, and a decanter of port. ⊠ *74 Wendell Ave., 01201* ☏ *413/ 499–6840 or 888/499–6840* ⊟ *413/499–6842* ⊕ *www.clapphouse. com* ⇌ *8 suites* ♿ *In-room data ports, some in-room hot tubs, Internet, refrigerators, cable TV; no smoking* ▭ *AE, D, MC, V* �○| *BP.*

$–$$$$ ⊞ **Crowne Plaza Pittsfield.** The Crowne Plaza in downtown Pittsfield provides stunning views of the Berkshire Hills. Rooms are comfortable, and the property is well kept and convenient to restaurants, shops, and the Berkshire Museum. Two floors of rooms surround the large, glass-domed pool area, overlooked by a comfortable lounge that serves a credible buffet lunch. ⊠ *Berkshire Common, 1 West St., 01201* ☏ *413/499–2000 or 800/227– 6963* ⊟ *413/442–0449* ⊕ *www.crowneplaza.com* ⇌ *177 rooms, 2 suites* ♿ *2 restaurants, room service, in-room data ports, pool, gym, hot tub, sauna, bar, business services, meeting room, free parking* ▭ *AE, D, DC, MC, V.*

$$–$$$ ⊞ **White Horse Inn.** Standing on Pittsfield's busy South Street, this early-20th-century Colonial Revival home provides comfortable rooms, appointed with handsome colonial furnishings. The breakfast room has a wood-burning stove and overlooks a deck, where you can eat on warm summer mornings. ⊠ *378 South St., 01201* ☏ *413/442–2512* ⊟ *413/ 443–0490* ⊕ *www.whitehorsebb.com* ⇌ *8 rooms* ♿ *In-room data ports, cable TV; no smoking* ▭ *AE, D, MC, V* ○| *BP.*

The Arts

The **Berkshire Opera Company** (⊠ Koussevitsky Arts Center, 1350 West St. ☏ 800/588–9757) stage a variety of performances at Berkshire Community College's Koussevitzky Arts Center.

The **Shaker Mountain Opera** (⊠ Koussevitsky Arts Center, 1350 West St. ☏ 800/588–9757) presents fully staged operas, as well as Shaker for Kids productions, at Berkshire Community College's Koussevitsky Arts Center.

For the serious music lover, **South Mountain Concerts** (⊠ U.S. 7 and 20, 2 mi south of Pittsfield center ☏ 413/442–2106) is one of the most distinguished centers for chamber music events in the country. Set on the wooded slope of South Mountain, the 500-seat auditorium presents concerts every September Sunday at 3.

Sports & the Outdoors

Boating & Fishing

For guided canoe tours on the Housatonic River, contact **Berkshire Scenic Treks and Canoe Tours** (⊠ 151 Bullhill Rd. ☎ 413/442–2789).

Rent canoes, kayaks, sailboats, motorboats, and pontoons on Onota Lake at the **Onota Boat Livery** (⊠ 463 Pecks Rd. ☎ 413/442–1724).

Golf

A scenic 18-hole par-70 golf course, **Pontoosuc Lake Country Club** (⊠ Kirkwood Dr. ☎ 413/445–4217) sits on 100 acres. Greens fees are $30, and discounted twilight rates are available.

Hiking

Operated by the Massachusetts Audubon Society's system, **Canoe Meadows** (⊠ Holmes Rd. ☎ 413/637–0320) has 262 acres of fields, wetlands, woods, and croplands bordered by the Housatonic River. The sanctuary, which is open dawn to dusk Tuesday–Sunday, has 3 mi of nature trails and a small observation building overlooking a beaver wetland.

One of the highlights of the 65 acre **Pittsfield State Forest** (⊠ Cascade St. ☎ 413/442–8992) is its paved ¾-mi Tranquility Trail. There are also 13 rustic campsites and 18 with flush toilets. Campground office hours are 8 AM–10 PM, and the regular camping season is from May to October.

Skiing

BOUSQUET
SKI AREA

Other areas have entered an era of glamour and high prices, but Bousquet remains an economical, no-nonsense place to ski. The inexpensive lift tickets are the same price every day, and there's night skiing except Sunday. You can go tubing for just $10 for the day when conditions allow. ⊠ *101 Dan Fox Dr., 01201* ☎ *413/442–8316, 413/442–2436 snow conditions* ⊕ *www.bousquets.com.*

Child care. Bous-Care Nursery watches children age six months and up by the hour; reservations are suggested. Ski instruction classes are given twice daily on weekends and holidays for children ages five and up.

Downhill. Bousquet, with a 750-foot vertical drop, has 21 trails, but only if you count every change in steepness and every merging slope. Though this is a generous figure, you will find some good beginner and intermediate runs, with a few steeper pitches. There are three double chairlifts, two surface lifts, and a small snowboard park.

Summer and year-round activities. Play Bousquets uses three drop funnels to pour kids out into a large activity pool and enough twists and turns and chute-to-chutes to scare the pants off many parents. A miniature-golf course, 24-foot climbing wall, go-karts, Thrill Sleds, and a scenic chairlift make Bousquet a suitable reward for children who have stoically accompanied their parents to the assortment of galleries, concerts, and plays that are the area's major tourism resource. The facilities at the **Berkshire West Athletic Club** (⊠ Dan Fox Dr. ☎ 413/499–4600), across the street from Bousquet, include four handball courts, indoor and outdoor tennis courts, cardiovascular and weight machines, and indoor and outdoor pools.

Shopping

When the Lanesboro Mall opened up north of Pittsfield, locals abandoned Pittsfield's downtown for the promise of cheaper prices. The town's retailers sadly withdrew, leaving a dearth of vacant storefronts, empty theaters, and bleak luncheonettes. Today, two shopping options bookend North Street.

Greystone Gardens (⊠ 436 North St. ☎ 413/442–9291), Pittsfield's only vintage clothing store, sells an array of men's and women's apparel, jewelry, and accessories dating to the early 19th century, when seamstresses embroidered bodices, attached delicate handmade buttons, and turned hems.

USBluesware (⊠ 141 North St. ☎ 413/442–5533) has taken advantage of the recent craze in the retail apparel market for used designer clothing by opening a store in downtown Pittsfield. For bargain couture from Armani, Escada, and Channel, USBluesware is for you.

DALTON

⑭ *8 mi northeast of Pittsfield.*

The paper manufacturer Crane and Co., started by Zenas Crane in 1801, that supplies the cotton-fiber paper used in making U.S. currency, is the major employer in working-class Dalton. Just east of Pittsfield on Route 9, Dalton calls itself the ideal community in which to raise a family.

Exhibits at the **Crane Museum of Paper Making,** in the handsomely restored Old Stone Mill (1844), trace the history of American papermaking from the 18th century to the present. A museum since 1930, the building sits on the banks of the Housatonic River. It's an impressive space with rough-hewn oak beams and Colonial-style chandeliers. ⊠ *E. Housatonic St. off Rte. 9* ☎ *413/684–6481* ☜ *Free* ☉ *June–mid-Oct., weekdays 2–5.*

Where to Eat

¢ ✕ **Juice n' Java Coffee House.** This unassuming little café on Main Street serves fresh home-baked pastries, particularly muffins, which are downright memorable. Also available are specialty coffees, quiche, and designer sandwiches made on an Italian panini grill. The house drink specialties are numerous, from fruit smoothies to frozen cappuccinos, flavored lattes, and fresh-squeezed lemonade. ⊠ *661 Main St.* ☎ *413/684–5080* ▤ *AE, MC, V* ☉ *No dinner.*

Where to Stay

$$–$$$ ▣ **Dalton House.** Cheerful guest rooms decorated in an eclectic mix of Shaker and period furnishings, folk art, plants, and collectibles are spread among three interconnected buildings; the original structure was built in 1810 by a Hessian soldier. Common rooms include a living room with a stone fireplace and a sunny breakfast area. Two suites in the carriage house have sitting areas, exposed beams, and quilts. ⊠ *955 Main*

St., 01226 ☎ *413/684–3854* 🖷 *413/684–0203* ⊕ *www.thedaltonhouse. com* 🖙 *9 rooms, 2 suites* ⟡ *Cable TV, in-room data ports, pool; no kids under 8, no smoking* ⊟ *AE, MC, V* 🍽 *BP.*

LANESBOROUGH

⓯ *6 mi northwest of Dalton.*

North of Pittsfield, between Pontoosuc Lake and Mt. Greylock, Lanesborough is a rural suburban community with a small strip mall and minicommercial center along U.S. 7. The most accessible road to the summit of Mt. Greylock lies in Lanesborough, and with its myriad of hiking trails, along with go-karts, miniature golf, batting ranges, and family restaurants, Lanesborough is a extremely popular with families.

Where to Eat

¢–$ ✕ **Matt Reilly's.** Overlooking the Pontoosuc Lake, this eatery presents a large menu that includes not only fish but myriad sandwiches, from veggie to buffalo burgers. If the sunset seems promising, grab a table on the deck and order a fresh scallop roll or a plate of steamers. ✉ *750 S. Main St., U.S. 7* ☎ *413/447–9780* ⊟ *AE, D, MC, V.*

Sports & the Outdoors

Golf
Enhance your game while taking in the breathtaking views of the Berkshire Hills at the **Skyline Country Club** (✉ 405 S. Main St., U.S. 7 ☎ 413/445–5584). Greens fees for the 18-hole course are $22; 9 holes are $11.

Hiking
At 3,491 feet, **Mount Greylock State Reservation** (✉ Rockwell Rd. off U.S. 7 ☎ 413/499–4262) is the highest peak in Massachusetts, and on a clear day you can see a panorama of five states from its summit. There are 70 mi of trails, including a section of the Appalachian National Scenic Trail, and campsites. Snowmobiling is permitted once the road system is closed to auto traffic for the winter.

Water Sports
Operating out of Matt Reilly's Restaurant, **Wild 'N Wet Snow & Water & Bike Rentals** (✉ 750 S. Main St., U.S. 7 ☎ 413/445–5211), launches customers onto Pittsfield's scenic Pontoosuc Lake in paddleboats, pontoon boats, canoes, and Jet Skies. They also lead winter snowmobile tours throughout the Berkshires.

HANCOCK

⓰ *9 mi east of Lanesborough.*

Tiny, rural Hancock, the closest village to the Jiminy Peak ski resort, comes into its own during ski season. It's a great base for outdoor enthusiasts year-round, with biking and hiking options during summer. It is also home to one of the finest living-history museums in the Northeast, the Hancock Shaker Village.

Fodor'sChoice **Hancock Shaker Village** was founded in the 1790s, the third Shaker com-
★   munity in America. At its peak in the 1840s, the village had almost 300
inhabitants, who made their living farming, selling seeds and herbs, making medicines, and producing crafts. The religious community officially
closed in 1960, its 170-year life span a small miracle considering its population's vows of celibacy (they took in orphans to maintain their con-
stituency). Many examples of Shaker ingenuity are visible at Hancock
today: the **Round Stone Barn** and the **Laundry and Machine Shop** are
two of the most interesting buildings. Also on-site are a farm, some period gardens, a museum shop with reproduction Shaker furniture, a picnic area, and a café. ⊠ *U.S. 20, 6 mi west of Pittsfield* ☎ *413/443–0188
or 800/817–1137* ⊕ *www.hancockshakervillage.org* ✉ *$15, $10 in
winter* ☉ *Late May–late Oct., daily 9:30–5 for self-guided tours; late
Oct.–late May, daily 10–3 for guided tours.*

☼ Established in the 1930s, the 600-acre **Ioka Valley Farm** (⊠ Rte. 43
☎ 413/738–5915) is one of the best-known pick-your-own farms in the
Berkshires. You can pick berries all summer, then apples and pumpkins
in fall. In winter you can cut your own Christmas tree. Other activities
include hayrides, pedal tractors for kids, and a petting zoo with pigs,
sheep, goats, and calves.

Where to Stay

$$$ 🏨 **Country Inn at Jiminy Peak.** Massive stone fireplaces in its lobby and
lounge lend this hotel a ski-lodge atmosphere. The modern condo-style
suites accommodate up to four people and have kitchenettes separated
from living areas by bars with high stools; the suites at the rear of the
building overlook the slopes. Ski packages are available. ⊠ *Corey Rd.,
01237* ☎ *413/738–5500 or 800/882–8859* ⊟ *413/738–5513* ⊕ *www.
jiminypeak.com* ↩ *96 suites* ☖ *2 restaurants, kitchens, in-room VCRs,
miniature golf, 5 tennis courts, pool, gym, 2 hot tubs, 2 saunas, fish-
ing, hiking, cross-country skiing, downhill skiing, bar, video game room,
meeting room* ⊟ *AE, D, DC, MC, V.*

$ 🏨 **Hancock Inn.** This country Victorian inn, which dates from the early
1800s, provides cozy accommodations a mile from Jiminy Peak. Rooms
are appointed with period furnishings and floral wallpaper. Two small
dining rooms have fireplaces, stained-glass windows, and candles on the
tables. ⊠ *Rte. 43, 01237* ☎ *413/738–5873* ⊟ *413/738–5719* ⊕ *www.
thehancockinn.com* ↩ *6 rooms* ⊟ *AE, D, MC, V* ⦿ *BP.*

Sports & the Outdoors

Skiing

JIMINY PEAK   The Berkshires only full-service ski and snowboard resort, and the largest
in southern New England, Jiminy Peak is also a splendid spot to stay dur-
ing the fall folliage season. Additional adventures including a four-in-one
Euro-bungee trampoline, a two-story-high rock-climbing wall, summit
rides on the Berkshire Express chairlift, and mountain biking make it a
delightful alternative for families looking in summer. ⊠ *Corey Rd.,
01237* ☎*413/738–5500, 888/454–6469 outside Massachusetts, 413/738–
7325 snow conditions* ⊕ *www.jiminypeak.com.*

Child care. The nursery takes children from 6 months. Children ages 4–12 can take daily SKIwee lessons; those 6–15 can take a series of eight weekends of instruction with the same teacher. The kids' ski area has its own lift.

Downhill. With a vertical of 1,150 foot, 40 trails, and 9 lifts, Jiminy has near big-time status. It is mostly a cruising mountain—trails are groomed daily, and only on some are small moguls left to build up along the side of the slope. The steepest black-diamond runs are on the upper head walls; longer, outer runs make for good intermediate terrain. There's skiing nightly, and snowmaking covers 93% of the skiable terrain.

Other activities. Jiminy has a snowboard park and an old-fashioned ice rink.

Summer activities. The resort has a 3,000-foot alpine slide, a challenging 9-hole miniature golf course, rock climbing, mountain biking, tennis courts, swimming facilities, and trout fishing. You can ride up the mountain on a high-speed chairlift.

NORTH COUNTY

3

TAKE IN THE VIEWS
from the state's highest peak
in Mt. Greylock State Reservation ⇨*p.79*

DIG INTO A BURGER
at Miss Adams Diner ⇨*p.80*

WANDER AMONG THE RENOIRS
at Clark Art Institute ⇨*p.87*

BOOK A ROOM
in the art-filled Field Farm Guest House ⇨*p.93*

TAKE A SCENIC ROAD TRIP
along the Mohawk Trail ⇨*p.108*

By Gail M.
Burns

North County combines the natural beauty and leisurely pace of country life with the exciting cultural diversity of an urban area. Almost all of the towns in North County lie in the lush valleys along the Green and Hoosic Rivers, with the exception of Florida and Savoy, which are rightly known as hilltowns as they sit atop the spine of the Hoosac Mountain range to the east. The river valleys encircle Mt. Greylock in the center, and are bounded by the Taconic Range to the west, the Hoosac range to the east, and the Green Mountains of Vermont to the north.

The first settlers in the area came west across the Mohawk Trail into the Green and Hoosic valleys to claim the land between the Hoosac Range and the Hudson River for Massachusetts instead of New York. The state lines fluctuated greatly over the centuries as bickering went on over coveted farm land before settling along the spine of the Taconic Mountain Range. Fort Massachusetts was established in 1744 in what is now North Adams as a western outpost of civilization in the Bay State.

Until the arrival of the railroads in the mid-19th century the primary industry in North County was agriculture. With a way to transport goods out of the region, manufacturing opportunities began to take shape, especially in Adams, Cheshire, Clarksburg, and North Adams. Despite good river access, the economy in Williamstown, however, remained focused on agriculture and education, although as the 20th century progressed and automobiles made commuting to work feasible many wealthy executives from North Adams and Adams made their homes in town.

North County's manufacturing industry declined in the latter half of the 20th century, and its economy slowed. But toward the end of the 1980s, tourism generated by students and parents at Williams College and the Massachusetts College of Liberal Arts (then North Adams State College) coupled with the growing appeal of the Clark Art Institute (opened in 1955), the Williamstown Theatre Festival (established in 1954), and the natural beauty of the area created new interests and opportunities. At the start of the 21st century those opportunities paid off with the opening of the Massachusetts Museum of Contemporary Art (MASS MoCA), set in a 13-acre, 19th-century factory complex whose 26 buildings occupy nearly one-third of North Adams' downtown business district.

Because of their relative isolation from the rest of the state and county and from each other, the towns and cities in North County are fiercely independent. If you were to tell a native of Adams that he or she lived in the same region as a native of North Adams, they would tell you in no uncertain terms why you were wrong. But for the traveler the different personalities of each community make North County a fascinating place to visit.

North County can be explored both by car and on foot. Towns are close together, and Williamstown and North Adams, in particular, are good places to take a short stroll.

EXPLORING NORTH COUNTY

North County is the more mountainous and more rural section of the region. Mt. Greylock, at 3,491 feet, and its surrounding foothills dom-

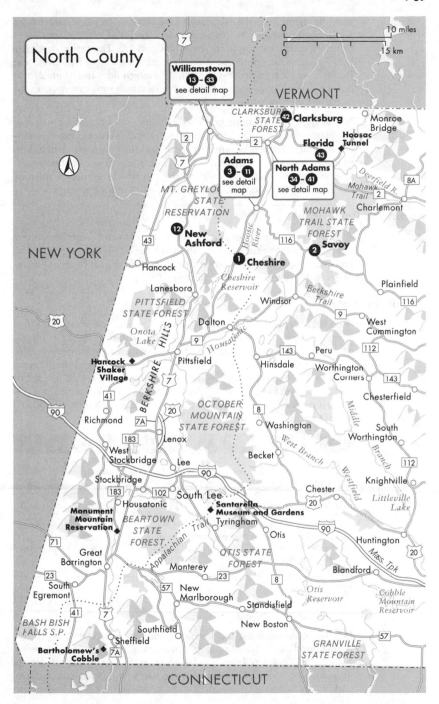

North County

VERMONT

NEW YORK

CONNECTICUT

0 ——————— 10 miles
0 ——————— 15 km

Williamstown
13 - **33**
see detail map

CLARKSBURG
STATE
FOREST
42 Clarksburg
Monroe
Bridge

Florida
43
Hoosac
Tunnel

Adams
3 - **11**
see detail
map

North Adams
34 - **41**
see detail map

Deerfield R.
Mohawk
Trail 2
8A

MT. GREYLOCK
STATE
RESERVATION

Charlemont

MOHAWK
TRAIL STATE
FOREST

12 New
Ashford

1 Cheshire

2 Savoy

Hancock

Lanesboro

Cheshire
Reservoir

Windsor

Berkshire
Trail

Plainfield

116

PITTSFIELD
STATE FOREST

Onota
Lake

Dalton

9

West
Cummington

Housatonic

143

Peru

112

Hancock ♦
Shaker
Village

BERKSHIRE HILLS

Pittsfield

Hinsdale

Worthington
Corners

143

Chesterfield

41

Richmond

7A

20

OCTOBER
MOUNTAIN
STATE FOREST

8

Washington

Middle Branch

South
Worthington

West Branch

112

183

Lenox

Becket

Westfield

Knightville

West
Stockbridge

Lee

90

Chester

Littleville
Lake

Stockbridge

183

102

South Lee

20

Housatonic

Santarella
Museum and Gardens
Tyringham

Monument
Mountain
Reservation ♦

BEARTOWN
STATE
FOREST

Otis

90

Huntington

20

71

Great
Barrington

Appalachian Trail

OTIS STATE
FOREST

Mass. Tpk.

23

Monterey

23

Blandford

South
Egremont

57

New
Marlborough

8

Otis
Reservoir

Cobble
Mountain
Reservoir

41

7

Standisfield

New Boston

57

BASH BISH
FALLS S.P.

Southfield

GRANVILLE
STATE FOREST

Bartholomew's ♦
Cobble

Sheffield

7A

inate the region. With the exception of the hilltowns of Florida and Savoy, all the communities in North County lie along the Hoosic River and its tributaries, which encircle the base of Greylock. The major roads are U.S. 7, which runs north–south on the western side of Mt. Greylock; Route 8, which runs north–south on the eastern side; and Route 2, also known as the Mohawk and Taconic trails, which runs east–west to the north of the mountain.

Williamstown, Clarksburg, and Florida border Vermont, and it's an easy trip from north Berkshire into Bennington and Windham counties in Vermont. Many people who work in north Berkshire choose to live in Vermont for its rural beauty and low cost of living. While visiting North County you may want to consider a trip "north of the border" to enjoy the great scenery, shopping, restaurants, and outdoor activities.

About the Restaurants

Although good American cuisine abounds in North County, the dining landscape has changed dramatically since the 1990s. You can now find restaurants specializing in Argentine, Indian, and Thai food, as well as offering unexpected twists on familiar dishes.

About the Hotels

With the exception of the more "out there" wilderness experiences, you can generally find any kind of lodging a short drive from the area's biggest attractions. High-end rooms tend to be spacious and beautifully decorated, and often have gas fireplaces or whirlpool tubs. And almost every window in every property has a view of mountains, rivers, forests, or meadows. Area lodgings fill up during peak fall foliage months, usually the last weeks of September and first few weeks of October. Book well in advance at these times.

WHAT IT COSTS					
	$$$$	$$$	$$	$	¢
RESTAURANTS	over $28	$20–$28	$12–$20	$8–$12	under $8
HOTELS	over $220	$170–$220	$120–$170	$80–$120	under $80

Restaurant prices are for a main course at dinner, excluding sales tax of 5%. Hotel prices are for two people in a standard double room in high season, excluding service charges and 5.7% state room occupancy tax. Williamstown levies an additional 4% lodging tax.

CHESHIRE

❶ *11 mi north of Pittsfield.*

In 1766 Nicholas Cook and Joseph Bennett, two Baptists from Rhode Island, purchased a territory then known as North Berkshire Township Number 6. This was later divided into tracts that would ultimately make up parts of not only Cheshire, but also Savoy, Lanesboro, Adams, and North Adams. Cook and Bennett hired Colonel Joab Stafford to survey their holdings and eventually ended up selling him 394 acres, which he and several other families settled and christened New Providence. Nearly a generation later, in 1793, the territory in and around this settlement was incorporated as Cheshire. The site of the original colony is now known as Stafford Hill in his honor.

The population of Cheshire gradually shifted from Stafford Hill toward the present village to be closer to the Hoosic River. The Berkshire Iron Furnace, the Dean Saw Mill, and the Cheshire Shoe Factory helped boost the town's economic development in the 19th century, as did the Crown Glass Company, which at one point was the area's largest employer. To power all this industry, local businessmen purchased 1,000 acres at the headwaters of the south branch of the Hoosic River and built a dam in 1869. The result was 418-acre Hoosac Lake, northern Berkshire's largest body of water. Also known as the Cheshire Reservoir, it is a lovely spot for boating, fishing, and picnicking.

The only town in North County to be crossed by the Appalachian Trail, Cheshire is known as a respite for hikers who often have their mail forwarded to them in care of the Cheshire Post Office. The recent addition of the Ashuwillticook Rail Trail should mean more changes for downtown Cheshire.

Fodor'sChoice
★ **Appalachian Trail.** Berkshire County is the only county in the state of Massachusetts traversed by the 2,100-mi Appalachian Trail, which winds from Georgia to Maine. The Berkshire County Chapter of the Appalachian Mountain Club helps maintain the 80 mi that run from the Connecticut border to the Vermont border. There is a parking lot where the Ashuwillticook and Appalachian trails cross, making Cheshire the perfect place for a day hike. If you head south on the trail, you'll quickly come to some lovely views back toward the Hoosic River Valley and the Greylock Range. ⊠ *Church St.* ☎ *413/443–0011* ⊕ *www. amcberkshire.org.*

★ ☺ **Ashuwillticook Rail Trail.** This section of the 11-mi paved path, which follows the route of an abandoned railroad line along the shores of Cheshire Lake, is one of the most beautiful. Free parking is available in Cheshire near Church Street, off Route 8 near the northern end of Hoosac Lake, and at Farnams Road between the lake's north and south basins. ⊠ *Church St.* ☎ *413/442–8928* ⊕ *www.mass.gov/dem/parks/asrt.htm.*

Cheshire Cheese Press Monument. This monument is a reproduction of the modified cider press used to create the enormous chunk of cheese the citizens of Cheshire presented to President Thomas Jefferson as a New Year's gift in 1802. ⊠ *Church and School Sts.*

need a break?
At the junction of the Appalachian and Ashuwillticook trails, in downtown Cheshire, is **Diane's Twist** (⊠ 13 Main St. ☎ 413/743–9776 ☾ Closed Labor Day–Memorial Day), where owner Diane Ramer scoops out a dozen delicious flavors made at the local Crescent Creamery. Stop for a sundae or stock up on bottled water and snacks for the rest of your hike.

CloseUp
THE CHEESE THAT CHANGED AMERICA

O N A DUSTY STREET CORNER IN CHESHIRE, on a patch of land known as Leland Park, sits a concrete replica of a converted cider press. It's an odd monument, and all the more so when you know the full story behind this odd slice of New England history.

In the late 18th century, in order for a town to be incorporated, it needed a church with its own pastor. And it couldn't be the church of the town's choosing—it had to be the official state religion, an offshoot of the faith of the Puritans who had settled the region, called the Congregational Church. The beliefs of the majority of a town's residents made no difference to the Commonwealth. In fact, members of other denominations were even not recognized as Christians.

Cheshire had been founded by Baptists. Residents of towns like Cheshire and nearby Adams, founded by Quakers, knew they could either submit to the will of the state and establish a Congregational Church, or they would have to challenge the law.

In the hard-fought 1800 presidential campaign, Cheshire was the only Berkshire town that favored Thomas Jefferson, who had led the fight to end state religion in Virginia. In 1801 the Reverend John Leland, a fiery and eccentric Baptist preacher who had also joined the struggle for religious freedom in Virginia, hatched a scheme that would simultaneously honor the president with a fitting tribute from Cheshire and call attention to the plight of Congregationalists in New England.

Cheshire was a town with many fine dairy herds. Leland convinced local dairy farmers to band together to produce an enormous wheel of cheese using milk from every cow in region. Accounts vary as to exactly how large the wheel was, but it was enormous: at least 1,235 pounds, 4 feet in diameter, and 12 inches thick. There was not a cheese press large enough to create it, and so a cider press was called into service.

The cheese was hauled over the frozen ground on a sled drawn by a team of oxen or by six horses, depending on the teller of the tale, to the banks of the Hudson River. From there it was shipped by boat to the nation's capital. Leland preached in various ports along the route, gaining national notoriety. Leland presented the cheese to Jefferson on New Year's Day in 1802 in the East Room of the White House in the presence of foreign diplomats, Supreme Court justices, and members of Congress. Eyewitnesses reported that the cheese bore the slogan: REBELLION TO TYRANTS IS OBEDIENCE TO GOD.

At the time, Jefferson was fascinated by the recent discoveries of woolly mammoth fossils. In fact, he had christened the East Room, the largest room in the White House, the "Mammoth Room," thinking that it was large enough to house even a member of that extinct species. The Cheshire Cheese became known as the Mammoth Cheese, and from that time on the word mammoth came into the vernacular in reference to anything of great size.

After receiving the cheese, Jefferson wrote a letter to Baptist leaders in Danbury, Connecticut, in which he coined the phrase "the wall of separation between church and state."

Stafford Hill Monument. This monument is a fieldstone replica of a tower in Newport, Rhode Island, which was long rumored to have been built by Norse explorers back in the 1100s. The view from the top is one of the most striking in the Berkshires. Erected in 1927 by the Massachusetts Sons of the American Revolution to mark the grave of Cheshire founder Col. Joab Stafford, the monument commemorates his heroism in the 1777 Battle of Bennington. Stafford was the commander of the Silver Greys, the local companies of Berkshire County men who volunteered for the revolutionary cause. ⊠ *Stafford Hill Rd.*

Where to Eat

$–$$ ✕ **Lakeside.** On the shores of Hoosac Lake, this friendly-family eatery has some great views from the dining room. The restaurant is near the Ashuwillticook Rail Trail, so it's an excellent place to take a break. The American fare—beef, chicken, veal, and pasta dishes—is good and reasonably priced. ⊠ *287 S. State Rd.* ☎ *413/743–7399* ▤ *MC, V.*

¢–$$ ✕ **Christina's.** A pizza place south of downtown Cheshire, Christina's has a few tables inside and a few picnic tables outside. The menu is Italian, and the short dessert menu lists such delights as chocolate raspberry cake and Bavarian cheesecake. ⊠ *41 Main St.* ☎ *413/743-7272* ▤ *No credit cards* ☉ *Closed Mon.*

Where to Stay

★ **$–$$** 🖼 **Harbour House Inn.** The only place to stay in Cheshire, Harbour House Inn is one of the most picturesque B&Bs in North County. Innkeepers Eva and Sam Amuso have turned this 18th-century farmhouse into an elegant and inviting inn. It's so quiet that you completely forget that you are right on Route 8. ⊠ *725 N. State Rd., 01225* ☎ *413/ 743-8959* ⊕ *www.harbourhouseinn.com* ⇄ *6 rooms, 1 suite* ▤ *AE, D, MC, V* �🍽 *BP.*

Sports & the Outdoors

Hoosac Lake, more correctly called Cheshire Reservoir, covers 418 acres in Cheshire and Lanesboro. Horn's Beach, a recreation area at Shadowland Cove in the northwestern corner of the lake, is open daily in summer. It's a great spot for canoeing and kayaking, and there are many picnic areas along its shores.

Shopping

At the **E. L. Martin Farm Stand** (⊠ 594 Windsor Rd. ☎ 413/743–9154) the Martin family sells sweet corn, winter squash, cucumbers, and other produce in season, and hay and eggs all through the year. At **Lightwings Farm** (⊠ Farnams Causeway ☎ 413/743–4425), Lucia Saradoff sells grapes, asparagus, and tomatoes, all grown free of herbicides or pesticides. There's also honey and beeswax candles. Call ahead before you stop by, as the shop closes when the season is over.

★ ☺ At **Whitney's Farm Stand** (⊠ 1775 S. State Rd. ☎ 413/442–4749), Eric and Michelle Whitney have turned his grandfather's farm stand into a theme park. You'll find something for the kids no matter when you stop by, from an Easter egg hunt in spring to a high-summer corn festival to a corn maze in fall. There are pick-your-own blueberries and pumpkins in season. All year there hayrides, pony rides, and a petting zoo.

Locals rave about the treasures to be found at the **Cheshire Auction Gallery** (✉ 110 South St. ☎ 413/743–2485 ⊕ www.atticgold.com). Owner Alan Hamilton and his wife Sandra Young have more than 30 years experience buying and selling antiques and collectibles. Auctions are held at 11 AM every third Saturday.

A modest antique store, **Winter Brook Farm Antiques** (✉ 450 N. State Rd. ☎ 413/743–2177 ⊕ www.winterbrookfarm.com) conceals a surprising specialty. They deal in reproductions of hard-to-find hardware. Looking to match a drawer pull on that Victorian sideboard? Or a handle on that Hepplewhite cupboard? The friendly folks at Winter Brook will try to help.

SAVOY

❷ *9 mi east of Cheshire.*

A real estate skirmish began the history of Savoy. When the state needed money in 1762, it auctioned off 10 townships. The successful bidder for Savoy asked for his money back, saying that the land had been misrepresented. The territory, measuring 6 square mi, was then awarded to Col. William Bullock in 1771. By the end of the Revolutionary War, 35 families lived in Savoy.

By the 19th century, Savoy had a remarkable range of industry, including newfangled steam sawmills, box manufacturers, tanneries, and printing shops. Equally diverse was the town's religious community, with Baptists, Congregationalists, Methodists, and Adventists all worshiping in Savoy. A Shaker community lived in Savoy from 1817 to 1821. The only Shaker home still standing is at 31 Barnard Road. It was built by Nathan Haskins, son of the town's first minister. He, his wife, and their two sons all became Shakers. Their older son, Orrin, was a renowned furniture maker, and his work is on exhibit at several Shaker museums. Along the the Lewis Hill Trail into Savoy State Forest is a Shaker cemetery.

Half of the land in the township is protected by the Savoy Mountain State Forest. In addition, parts of Mohawk Trail State Forest and Windsor State Forest are in Savoy. The Westfield and Chickley rivers have their headwaters in Savoy, and anglers have discovered excellent fly-fishing there. With all this wilderness, Savoy is an ideal place to enjoy the beautiful Berkshires.

Properly known as a "glacial erratic," **Balance Rock,** an enormous boulder, was left balancing on a small protrusion as glaciers retreated after the ice age more than 10,000 years ago. There are actually two "balance rocks" in Savoy Mountain State Forest—this one near Tannery Road and another off the Loop Trail at South Pond. Both are as spectacular but less well-known than their cousin at Balance Rock State Park in Lanesboro.

Formerly known as Savoy Mountain, **Borden Mountain** is the township's highest peak. Topped by a fire tower, it has lovely views from the summit in all directions. ⊠ *Adams Rd.*

Built around 1863 by members of the Advent Society, **Brier Chapel** was active for a number of years. Legend has it that the congregation erected the chapel in a single day while the owner of the land was out of town. He was enraged to find the building on his property and demanded payment of $10. He later donated the money back to the church. The bell, which still hangs from its original rope, was donated by former Gov. W. Murray Crane. The chapel is currently used for concerts, lectures, and town events. ⊠ *Chapel Rd.*

A very small portion of the **Mohawk Trail** is in Savoy. The stretch is along the Cold River between Florida and Charlemont. This portion of the road lies in the Mohawk Trail State Forest. ⊠ *Black Brook Rd.* ⊕ *www. mohawktrail.com.*

At the **Savoy Elementary School** stands School Number 7, the last remaining one-room schoolhouse in use in Berkshire County. Built early in the 19th century, the school was moved from the corner of Chapel and Loop roads to its present location in 1885. Today it is used as a preschool classroom. ⊠ *26 Chapel Rd.* ☎ *413/743–1992.*

The state acquired the first bit of land for **Savoy Mountain State Forest** in 1917. Today the preserve covers more than 11,000 acres. Miles of wooded trails are used by hikers in all seasons. Spectacular natural features include Bog Pond, with its floating bog islands, Tannery Falls, and two "balance rocks." Campsites are in an old apple orchard, a reminder that this wild forest was cultivated farmland not too long ago. Log cabins overlooking South Pond are available for rental year-round, although the regular camping season is from Memorial Day through Columbus Day. ⊠ *Central Shaft Rd.* ☎ *413/663–8469* ⊕ *www.mass. gov/dem/parks/svym.htm* ✉ *$5 parking fee* ☉ *Daily.*

Formerly called High Falls, **Tannery Falls** acquired is current name because the 110-foot cascades powered a tannery until 1870. The falls are on Ross Brook, which passes 200 feet west of Tannery Brook. Here you'll find an unusual series of waterfalls in the slanting bedrock. ⊠ *Tannery Rd.*

Sports & the Outdoors

Fishing
The 8½-mi **Chickley River** runs from the slopes of Borden Mountain to its confluence with the Deerfield River in Hawley. It's stocked with trout and salmon. The **Westfield River** flows for more than 50 mi through 16 towns. It is one of the most beautiful and pristine of the rivers of southern New England. In the 1990s, 43 mi of the upper Westfield, including the portion through Savoy, were designated "Wild and Scenic" by the National Park Service. It offers excellent trout fishing.

Horseback Riding
One of the best riding stables in the area, **GreenBriar Farm** (⊠ 100 Jackson Rd. ☎ 413/743–5127) conducts private and group lessons. The sta-

ble has outdoor and indoor rings and a beautiful hunt course. Trail rides are available.

Snowmobiling

Savoy usually gets the greatest snow accumulation in Berkshire County. With an ever-growing fleet of groomers, the **Kanary Kats Snowmobile Club** (⌧ 20 Old Dalton Rd. ⊕ www.savoykanarykats.org) traverses miles of some of the best trails in North County.

Shopping

Known for its Romney sheep, **Good Shepherd Farm** (⌧ 142 Griffin Hill Rd. ☎ 413/743–7916) sells sheepskins, fleece for hand-spinners, yarn, and hand-knitted wool hats.

ADAMS

❸–**⓫** *8 mi northwest of Savoy.*

At the base of Mt. Greylock, Adams has spectacular views of the Greylock Range from just about everywhere in town. Although the 3,491-foot summit of the state's highest peak is in Adams, you can't reach it by car without driving through nearby North Adams or Lanesboro.

Settled largely by Quakers, Adams was first known as the East Hoosuck Plantation. An important remnant of the town's heritage is the 1782 Friends Meeting House, surrounded by the Maple Street Cemetery, which is without headstones because the Quakers did not believe in individual grave markers. The congregation's most famous member was Susan B. Anthony (1820–1906), abolitionist, educator, and women's rights activist. She lived here only until her family moved in 1826.

In 1778 the town was incorporated as Adams, after Massachusetts revolutionary war leader Sam Adams. A century later the arrival of the railroads had swelled the population of the northern part of town to the point that the township was split into two parts, creating Adams and North Adams. Adams, however, is known as the "mother town." You know you have arrived in downtown Adams when you are greeted by the 1902 statue of President William McKinley in front of the handsome Adams Free Library, for which McKinley laid the cornerstone.

With the railroads came several waves of immigrants. By the early 20th century five different languages—French, Polish, German, Italian, and English—were preached from town pulpits on Sunday mornings. There is a Jewish community, and several Syrian and Lebanese names can still be found on the town census. The most recent immigrant group to the town were the Polish, and their influence is still strong. St. Stanislaus Kostka Church, at the corner of Hoosac and Summer streets, maintains the only remaining parochial elementary school in north Berkshire, and the nearby Polish National Alliance is still a town social center. To this day Adams is one of the most ethnically diverse communities in the area.

Every August the town celebrates its most famous daughter with five days of festivities known as Susan B. Anthony Days. Regular events include sidewalks sales, historic walks, and a Victorian lawn party. Also in summer is the annual Agricultural Fair. A prince and princess are crowned, prize pigs are judged, and bumper cars collide during three festive days full of cotton candy and fried dough. In early December the town gathers for Adams Holly Days, during which Santa Claus arrives on a fire truck. And the Adams Alert Hose Company No. 1 warms up the winter months with the Annual Alerts Ball, a local tradition since 1877. Dressed in their elegant white and buff uniforms, the company has won numerous prizes for its parade appearances through the years.

a good walk

Begin your walk at the **Discover the Berkshires Visitors Center** ▶ ❸. Parking is off Depot Street. From here it's a short walk west along Hoosac Street to McKinley Square, where you find two handsome Catholic churches, St. Thomas Aquinas (1897) and Notre Dame des Septs Douleurs (1887). Also facing the square are the **Adams Free Library**❹ and the **President William McKinley Statue** ❺. McKinley was a frequent visitor to the town during his presidency. A left turn takes you down Park Street. Stay on the east side of the street to find the **Armory Block** ❻ and the historic **Park Street Firehouse** ❼. Once you reach the end of Park Street, turn left. The **Town Common** ❽ is recognizable by the little gazebo on your right. Proceed up the hill on Center Street, across the **Ashuwillticook Rail Trail** ❾ and the Hoosic River, until you make a left turn onto **Summer Street** ❿. For a few blocks the tree-lined street is bordered by handsome Victorian era homes on either side. Once you have passed the intersection with Spring Street, you will find yourself in a shopping district. The imposing edifice of **St. Stanislaus Kostka Church** ⓫—with its school, convent, and other structures—marks the intersection of Summer and Hoosac streets.

What to See

❹ **Adams Free Library.** The second floor of this library was originally used as a meeting place for veterans of the Civil War, and today part of it houses the collection of the Adams Historical Society. The handsome yellow-brick building is trimmed with marble quarried at the former Adams Marble Company. President William McKinley laid the building's cornerstone in 1897 and placed a time capsule underneath containing items of the day. The 40,000-book collection includes the New England Historical and Genealogical Register. ✉ *92 Park St.* ☎ *413/ 743–8345* ✆ *Free* ☾ *Mon.–Thurs. 10–8, Fri. 10–6.*

❻ **Armory Block.** Built in 1914, the Armory of Company M was modeled after a Norman medieval castle. When National Guard Company M moved out early in 2004, the state took control of this property ✉ *39–45 Park St.*

★ ☾ ❾ **Ashuwillticook Rail Trail.** This 11-mi section of an abandoned railway between Adams and Lanesboro attracts snowshoers and cross-country skiers in winter and bikers, hikers, and in-line skaters the rest of the year. The paved path winds through the Hoosic River Valley between Mt. Greylock and the Hoosac Range, passing the shores of Hoosac Lake. The section between Adams and Cheshire is covered with thick forests. The northern terminus of the trail is beside the Discover the Berkshires Vis-

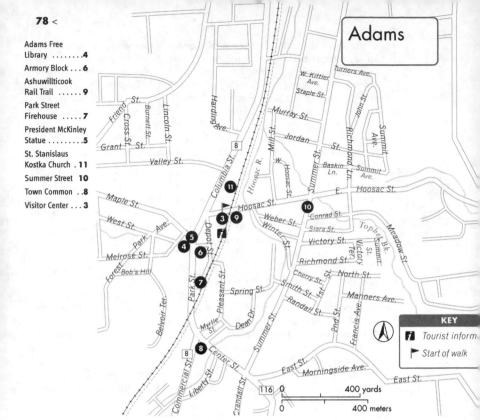

itors Center. ✉ *3 Hoosac St.* ☎ *413/442–8928* ⊕ *www.mass.gov/dem/ parks/asrt.htm* ✉ *Free* ☉ *Daily.*

★ ❸ **Discover the Berkshires Visitors Center.** This state-of-the-art facility houses an interactive exhibit on Berkshire County. This is an excellent place to start your visit to north Berkshire, since there are racks and racks of free brochures and maps and a courteous and knowledgeable staff that can answer questions. Ideally situated at the northern terminus of the Ashuwillticook Rail Trail, the center makes a perfect starting point for outdoor activities or for exploring the downtown sights. There are restrooms, vending machines, a small gift shop, and picnic tables. ✉ *3 Hoosac St.* ☎ *413/743–4500 or 800/237–5747* ⊕ *www.berkshires.org* ✉ *Free* ☉ *Weekdays 8:30–5.*

❼ **Park Street Firehouse.** Former home of the Adams Alerts Hose Company No. 1 and the current home of the Adams Ambulance Service, this 1891 brick building is listed on the National Register of Historic Places. ✉ *47 Park St.* ☎ *413/743–1929* ⊕ *www.adamsalerts.com.*

❺ **President William McKinley Statue.** McKinley was a friend of the Plunkett family, which owned the Berkshire Cotton Manufacturing Company, better known as the Berkshire Mills. During his presidency from 1897 to 1901 he supported legislation and tariffs that helped make the mill complex in Adams one of the largest in the country. McKinley visited Adams on three occasions during his presidency amid much fanfare. Shortly after his assassination in 1901, Adams town leaders commissioned well-known sculptor, Augustus Lukeman, to create the statue of the 25th president; it was unveiled on October 10, 1903. On Columbus Day weekend in 2003, the 100th anniversary of this event was observed with a McKinley impersonator delivering portions of speeches McKinley delivered in Adams. ⊠ *McKinley Sq.*

⓫ **St. Stanislaus Kostka Church.** This Roman Catholic church is the newest house of worship in Adams, having been erected in 1902 by Polish immigrants. An unusual stained-glass window depicts the Bolshevik trio of Trotsky, Lenin, and Stalin. St. Stan's also operates the sole remaining parochial school in North County, staffed by nuns who reside in the on-site convent. ⊠ *25 Hoosac St.* ☏ *413/743–0041.*

⓾ **Summer Street.** The portion of Summer Street between Route 116 and Hoosac Street is part of a National Register Historic District. The southern stretch is lined with beautiful Victorian-era homes, and the northern end is a quaint shopping district. St. Stanislaus Kostka Roman Catholic Church occupies the southeast corner of Summer and Hoosac streets.

❽ **Town Common.** A small patch of greenery at a busy intersection, the Town Common has free outdoor concerts and movies in the summer. ⊠ *Rtes. 8 and 116.*

off the
beaten
path

★

THE EAST HOOSUCK QUAKER MEETING HOUSE – The original settlers in Adams lived in the area for 15 years before they started building this Quaker Meeting House, saying they were less interested in creating a monumental house of worship than in living their lives according to their religious beliefs. Construction began in 1782 and finished four years later. The Quaker community in Adams reached its peak in 1819, when a total of 40 local families were members. After a steady decline, the last official meeting in the old meeting house took place in 1842. The Adams Historical Society now owns the property, and opens it to the public in summer. On the last Sunday in August, the Society of Friends Descendants holds an annual meeting in the building, which includes a half hour of silence. The surrounding Maple Street Cemetery is without headstones because the Quakers did not believe in monuments to their dead. ⊠ *Friend and Maple Sts.* ⊕ *www.adamshistorical.org/ quakermh.htm* ☒ *Free* ☉ *Memorial Day–Labor Day, Sun. 1–4.*

FodorśChoice
★

MT. GREYLOCK STATE RESERVATION – At 3,491 feet, Mt. Greylock is the highest peak in Massachusetts. Acquired in 1898, the towering peak is the centerpiece of what became the first state park. Construction of the 100-foot Veterans War Memorial tower at the summit began in 1931 and was completed in 1933. Always plagued by problems with water and ice damage, the structure received a major $1 million makeover in 1997 and is once more open to the public. Its bright beacon is visible on all but the stormiest nights. Intended to honor those lost in World War I, the inscription at the base of the memorial tower reads: ERECTED BY MASSACHUSETTS IN GRATEFUL RECOGNITION OF THE LOYALTY AND SACRIFICE OF HER SONS AND DAUGHTERS. IN WAR THEY WERE FAITHFUL EVEN UNTO DEATH. While the summit and a large portion of the Mt. Greylock State Reservation are in Adams, you cannot access the summit by car from the town. To drive to the summit, head north on Route 8 into North Adams, and then turn west on Route 2. Take Notch Road on your left about a mile out of the city. To hike to the summit, take the precipitously steep Thunderbolt Trail from the top of Thiel Road or the more circuitous Gould Trail from the end of Gould Road. ⊠ *Summit of Mt. Greylock* ☎ *413/499–4262* ⊕ *www.mass. gov/dem/parks/mgry.htm* ⊠ *$2 parking fee* ⊗ *Memorial Day–Columbus Day, daily 9–5.*

SUSAN B. ANTHONY BIRTHPLACE – The Federal-style house where Susan Brownell Anthony was born on February 15, 1820, was built after her father Daniel Anthony married Lucy Reed in 1817. Daniel Anthony was a Quaker Abolitionist and a successful cotton manufacturer. Although Susan, the second of their eight children, lived here only until she was six, she returned to visit throughout her life. The house is a currently private residence and can be viewed only from the road. ⊠ *67 East Rd.*

Where to Eat

★ $ ✕ **Miss Adams Diner.** A genuine slice of Americana, the Miss Adams Diner, originally Worcester Lunch Car No. 821, was delivered to town on December 7, 1949. The original porcelain panels on the front have been covered over by an unfortunate stone facade, but the interior retains its small-town diner charm. There have been many owners over the past few years. At one point it offered an eclectic menu which, while delicious, seemed jarringly out of place in a diner. The current owners serve tasty, traditional diner fare, but regardless of what's on the menu, if you want the experience of eating in a real, hot-off-the-rails dining car, you can't pass up the Miss Adams. ⊠ *53 Park St.* ☎ *413/743–5300* ⊟ *MC, V.*

$ ✕ **Pizza Jim's.** A tiny hole in the wall with no seating, Pizza Jim's makes great Italian-style food for takeout. The delicious pizzas are neither too crispy nor too greasy. ⊠ *85 Commercial St.* ☎ *413/743–9161* ⊟ *No credit cards.*

Where to Stay

$–$$ 🏠 **Mount Greylock Inn.** The Inn, a lovely Queen Anne Victorian, was built in 1887 for Daniel and Amanda Burt and their four children. Rooms are bright and appointed with period furnishings, some with four-poster beds. On most days, a Continental breakfast is served, but on Saturday there's a choice of omelets, pancakes, or French toast with maple syrup. ⊠ *6 East St., 01220* ☎ *413/743–2665* 🖨 *425/795–5373* ⊕ *www. mountgreylockinn.com* 🛏 *4 rooms* ♿ *No a/c, no room TVs, no kids under 5* ⊟ *MC, V* ⑩ *CP.*

¢ ▦ **Bascom Lodge.** This rustic lodge was built atop the state's highest peak by the Civilian Conservation Corps in the 1930s. It is named in honor of Rev. John Bascom, one of the first commissioners of Mt. Greylock State Reservation, who called the mountain "our daily pleasure, our constant symbol, our ever renewed inspiration." Stone fireplaces, soaring ceilings with hand-cut oak beams, and a porch with large windows provide an ideal atmosphere for enjoying the finest views in the Berkshires. The lodge has everything from coed dorms that accommodate nine guests to private rooms. Bathrooms are shared and individual shower units with adjacent changing areas offer privacy. Blankets, sheets, pillows, and towel are provided. Dinner is served family-style, and is sure to satisfy the heartiest appetite. ⊠ *Mt. Greylock Summit, 01220* ☎ *413/443–0011 or 413/743–1591* ⊕ *www.naturesclassroom.org* ↝ *8 rooms with shared baths* ⚐ *No a/c, no room phones, no room TVs* ⊟ *No credit cards* ⊙ *Closed late Oct.–mid-May.*

Sports & the Outdoors

No matter what outdoor activity you enjoy—hiking, biking, canoeing, rock climbing, kayaking, snowshoeing, or cross-country skiing—you'll find the equipment you need at **Berkshire Outfitters** (⊠ 8 Grove St. ☎ 413/743–5900 ⊕ www.berkshireoutfitters.com), one of Berkshire County's best-known sporting goods retailers. Owner Steve Blazejewski and his knowledgeable staff can help you with maps and suggestions of where to go.

Golf

Forest Park Country Club (⊠ 41 Forest Park Ave. ☎ 413/743–3311), is a 9-hole public course designed by Alex Findlay in 1901. The fairways are narrow with small greens, so you must place your shots well. There are no water hazards and only about seven bunkers. Greens fees are under $20. The course is open March 15 to December 1.

Hiking

The **Thunderbolt Ski Trail,** site of the U.S. Eastern Amateur Ski Association Championships in 1935 and 1936, is now a hiking trail. This is the steepest and most challenging of the trails to the summit of Mt. Greylock, as the climb from the Old Thiel Farm at the end of Thiel Road in Greylock Glen ascends 2,175 feet in just under 2 mi. The trail was named after a famous roller coaster, which should give you an idea what to expect. As you near the summit, the Thunderbolt Trail crosses the Appalachian Trail.

From Gould Road in Greylock Glen you can access the **Bellows Pipe Trail,** also known as Thoreau's Ascent because writer Henry David Thoreau used this route to climb Mt. Greylock in 1844. This is a moderate to strenuous climb of about 2½ mi. The wind funneling through the notch between Mt. Greylock and Ragged Mountain creates a sound like a blacksmith's bellows, which gives the trail its name. The Bellow's Pipe Trail intersects both the Thunderbolt and the Appalachian trails. **The Gould Trail** (formerly known as the Peck's Brook Trail) and the **Cheshire Harbor Trail,** which connect near the summit, are alternate hiking routes that start from West Mountain Road.

If hiking up the eastern face of Mt. Greylock is your goal, then start from downtown Adams. From McKinley Square you can easily reach many beautiful trails. An excellent map is available at the **Discover the Berkshires Visitors Center** (⊠ 3 Hoosac St. ☎ 413/743–4500 or 800/237–5747 ⊕ www.berkshires.org).

Shopping

Shopping in Adams is eclectic and surprising. Howland Avenue, Park Street, and Commercial Street—all local names for Route 8—have the highest concentration of retail establishments. Don't miss the historic shopping area on Summer Street and the flourishing stretch of Hoosac Street that connects Summer Street to Route 8 at McKinley Square. From July to early October, the downtown **Adams Farmer's Market** (⊠ Depot St.) sells locally grown produce every Wednesday from 1 to 4.

★ The **Interior Alternative** is for folks who want to decorate their homes without emptying their wallets. The store carries discounted wallpaper, bedding, and throw pillows. There are bolts and bolts of beautiful fabrics suitable for upholstery and draperies for those handy with a needle, as well as some ready-made draperies and accessories. Upstairs you'll find a wide selection of attractive area rugs. It's open 10–5 Monday to Saturday. ⊠ *5 Hoosac St.* ☎ *413/743–1986* ⊕ *www.fschumacher.com/corp/crp_alt.htm.*

Housed in an early-20th-century school building, the **Crafters Cottage & Olde Schoolhouse Gifts** (⊠ 23 Park St. ☎ 413/743–2640) stocks a wide variety of items made by local artists and artisans. You'll find everything from jewelry to furniture.

☺ The young (and young at heart) enjoy **Jeepers Creepers** (⊠ 19 Hoosac St. ☎ 413/743–4799), a family-run establishment filled with gag gifts,
☺ collectibles, and helium balloons. **What Kids Want** (⊠ 31 Park St. ☎ 413/743–7842) carries educational toys. There's an old-fashioned soda fountain where ice cream and homemade goodies are served.

NEW ASHFORD

⑫ *12 mi west of Cheshire.*

One of the smallest communities in the Commonwealth, New Ashford has fewer than 200 citizens. The town was called New Ashford Plantation in 1762, after the fort made of ash logs that was home to the earliest settlers. New Ashford was not incorporated until 1836. Even then the community grew very slowly. In 1885 the *Berkshire County Gazetteer* noted that "no doctor or lawyer has ever been located in town."

Nearly 40% of the land in New Ashford is part of the Mt. Greylock State Reservation. The view from the summit of Saddle Ball Mountain, a part of the Mt. Greylock Range, is considered one of the grandest in the area. In the 1930s a portion of 2,700-foot-high Brodie Mountain was opened as a ski resort, but today it is used only on weekends and for snow-tubing.

THE GAMBLER'S CHURCH

LEGEND HAS IT THAT THE MONEY FOR THE *New Ashford Church came from a group of gamblers who frequented the tavern that once sat next door.* They are said to have been turned from their wicked ways by the firebrand preacher, Baptist Elder John Leland. Whether this is fact or fiction remains unclear, but the dice pattern on the underside of the eaves of the steeple lends some credibility to the tale.

Built in 1828, the pretty little church never had a permanent minister or an official congregation. It was used on and off by a Methodist group in the late 19th and early 20th century. Completely abandoned in 1951, the church was literally crumbling until a prominent citizen took an interest in the property. By the early 1990s, restoration work had begun. A concert marked its rebirth in 1994.

Although plain and boxy on the outside, inside the church is all curves. Upon entering the vestibule, you are met with the semicircular wall of the back of the chancel. A curved door in the wall, now closed off, used to provide access to the chancel from the vestibule. The ceiling is also gracefully rounded. Simple dark-wood pews in three sections face the chancel, and a balcony surrounds the nave on three sides.

The interior colors, which have been faithfully reproduced from the original plans, start with the dark brown of the earth used for the floor, doors, and pews, rise to the beige of the fields and forests on the walls, and end with the sparkling sky blue of the dome.

Attractively preserved and landscaped, **Mallery Homestead** marks the site of the original Mallery family homestead, circa 1770, which gave this road its name. The Mallerys were a founding family in New Ashford, and the homestead is said to be haunted. The house burned down when a young man's clothes hung out to dry before the fireplace caught fire in early 20th century. ✉ *Mallery Rd.*

Many markers in the older section of **New Ashford Cemetery** are missing, and records of burials were destroyed in a house fire. ✉ *Cemetery Rd.* ☎ *413/339–5504.*

Built in 1828, the **New Ashford Church** was originally a nondenominational house of worship paid for by townspeople "subscribing" to its construction. There never was a permanent minister or congregation, although it was often used for Methodist services. Closed and crumbling for 40 years, the church reopened in 1994 with a concert, the first event held there since 1951. ✉ *155 Mallory Rd.* ☎ *413/458–1083* ⊕ *www. berkshire.net/chc.*

Dating from 1792, the **Old Schoolhouse** is believed to be the oldest one-room schoolhouse in the country. The site is also notable because after women won suffrage in 1920, the first American woman to cast a vote in a national election did so here. The polls in New Ashford opened at 7:30 AM, earlier than any other town on the East Coast. ⊠ *Mallery Rd.*

Where to Eat

★ **$$$–$$$$**   ✕ **The Mill on the Floss.** Since 1973 the Champagne family has served French country cuisine in this 18th-century farmhouse perched above a babbling brook. The authentic antiques and open kitchen create a mood that is at once intimate and elegant. One of the best (and most expensive) restaurants in North County, it is considered a special treat by locals—a spot to celebrate an anniversary, engagement, or graduation. ⊠ *342 U.S. 7* ☎ *413/458–9123* ⊟ *AE, MC, V* ⊘ *Closed Mon. No lunch.*

Where to Stay

$–$$ ⌸ **The Springs Motor Inn.** Built to house the crowds when the ski resort down the road was booming, this motel is without much architectural interest. But if you are headed for a weekend of skiing at Jiminy Peak or snow-tubing at Brodie, the rooms are clean and comfortable. ⊠ *U.S. 7, 01237* ☎ *413/458–5945* ⇗ *42 rooms* ♿ *Microwaves, refrigerators, outdoor pool* ⊟ *AE, MC, D, DC, V.*

Sports & the Outdoors

Hiking

Nearly 40% of New Ashford is part of the **Mt. Greylock State Reservation** (⊠ Rockwell Rd. ☎ 413/499–4262 or 413/499–4263). All of the mountain trails can be accessed from Greylock Road, off the east side of U.S. 7. The summits of Sugarloaf (1,890 feet), Saddle Ball Mountain (3,247 feet), and many other scenic lookouts are in this town.

Skiing

Brodie Mountain (⊠ U.S. 7 ☎ 413/443–4752 ⊕ www.skibrodie.com) no longer opens its slopes to downhill skiers. Now it's the domain of snow-tubing aficionados and open only on weekends.

Shopping

At **Jennings Brook Farm** (⊠ 83 Beech Hill Rd. ☎ 413/458–5274) Steve and Maureen Jennings make Massachusetts Maple Syrup on wood-fired boilers. Visit during sugaring season, between late February and early March.

WILLIAMSTOWN

⑬–㉝ *9 mi north of New Ashford.*

The fortunes of Williamstown and Williams College are forever intertwined. The center of the town and the center of the campus are one, which means that the handsome college buildings mingle with the attractive private homes and small businesses along the main streets.

Settled in 1753, Williamstown was given the unfortunate name of West Hoosuck Plantation. Colonel Ephraim Williams, a member of a wealthy and powerful family, wrote a will bequeathing money to maintain a school in the community, provided that it change its name to Williamstown. After Williams was killed in the Battle of Lake George in 1755, the town acceded to his wishes. In 1791 the Williamstown Free School opened in a building on Main Street. Soon afterward, the trustees petitioned the Massachusetts Legislature to convert the free school into a college. The petition was granted, and Williams College opened its doors on October 9, 1793.

Colonel Williams would probably be surprised to see what became of his bequest to the little township of West Hoosuck. Williams College is one of the top private liberal arts schools in the nation, enrolling 2,000 students from around the world. He would be pleased, no doubt, that the varsity teams at Williams are referred to as the Ephs (short for Ephraim), and on occasion men's teams are called Ephmen and women's teams are called Ephwomen.

Early in the 20th century, an innkeeper called Williamstown "The Village Beautiful," and a sign with that slogan remains at the top of Spring Street. Today, locals take great pride in the community's natural beauty. At the confluence of the Green and Hoosic rivers in what is sometimes referred to as the Purple Valley, the town and its surroundings are breathtaking in all seasons. Williamstown has hundreds of acres of preserved land, including a portion of Mt. Greylock State Reservation.

a good tour

Williamstown has a very definite center, squeezed up into the northeast corner of the township. The rest of the land in town is rural or residential. The southeastern portion of the town is in the **Mt. Greylock State Reservation** ⑬ and the northwestern portion is occupied by **Hopkins Memorial Forest** ⑭.

Starting from the downtown Williamstown, head east on Main Street. Take a right onto Adams Road. The road forks almost immediately, and you should bear right onto Stratton Road. This will take you uphill past the historic **Stratton Inn** ⌐ ⑮. There are many fine views of the Taconic Range, particularly from the sharp turn where Stratton Road becomes Blair Road and begins its descent into the Green River Valley. At the bottom of the hill, take a left on Green River Road. You will pass the intersection with Hopper Road at **Mount Hope Park** ⑯ on your left and the **Old Stone Church** ⑰ on your right. When you come to the **Store at Five Corners** ⑱, you are in the center of the area known as South Williamstown, once a separate community. Nearby is the **Little Red Schoolhouse** ⑲ and the South Lawn Cemetery. If you brought a picnic lunch, head across the street to **Bloedel Park** ⑳.

Continue on Green River Road to U.S. 7. Take Hancock Road (or Route 43) south a short distance, then turn right onto Sloan Road. As you pass through the lovely pastures, you might want to stop at **Field Farm** ㉑. When Sloan Road meets Oblong Road, take a right. There are some magnificent views of Mt. Greylock from here. Stay on Oblong Road past the former **Sinclair Lewis Estate** ㉒. At the end of Oblong Road, take a right on ends at Torrey Woods Road. This will take you onto the stretch of Route 2 known as the **Taconic Trail** ㉓. Take a hard left and continue

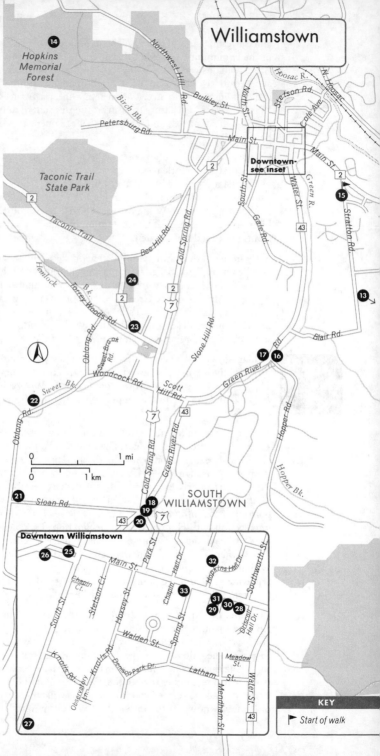

Williamstown

until you reach Bee Hill Road, then take a right. This narrow, unpaved road brings you back to the center of town. The Williamstown Rural Lands Foundation has a pair of parking areas along this road where you can stop to admire the view, set out on hikes, or tour **Sheep Hill ㉔**.

Bee Hill Road brings you to Cold Spring Road, or U.S. 7. Continue on this route as it turns into Main Street, which will take you to **Field Park ㉕** and the **Williamstown House of Local History ㉖**. Next, take a right on South Street, which will take you past some beautiful homes, to the **Clark Art Institute ㉗**. Continue past the museum to where South Street becomes Gale Road. Turn left on Water Street, where you will pass the oldest house in town, dating from 1767, at the intersection with Latham Street, and continue back to Main Street. Take a left on Main Street and drive over Consumption Hill past the **Hopkins Observatory ㉘** and **Williams College Museum of Art ㉙** on your left, and **Griffin Hall ㉚** and **Thompson Chapel ㉛** on your right. Behind Thompson Chapel is the **Chapin Library of Rare Books & Manuscripts ㉜**. At the corner of Spring Street is the **First Congregational Church ㉝**.

What to See

㉚ Bloedel Park. Despite its unassuming appearance, Bloedel Park has played a major part in the history of South Williamstown. A number of historic buildings, now gone, were once located on this spot. In 1724 it was the site of a mill and hatter's shop. A blacksmith lived here in 1796, followed by a merchant. A post office and general store occupied the site from the 1820s until the 1920s. ✉ *U.S. 7 and Rte. 43.*

★ **㉜ Chapin Library of Rare Books & Manuscripts.** At Williams College, this library contains original copies of the four founding documents of the United States—the Declaration of Independence, the Articles of Confederation, the Constitution, and the Bill of Rights. You'll also find 50,000 books, 40,000 manuscripts, and illustrations dating from as far back as the 9th century. Every Independence Day the Library sponsors an open house for viewing of the rare documents and readings by actors from the Williamstown Theatre Festival. Chapin Library is on the second floor of Stetson Hall, behind Thompson Chapel. ✉ *26 Hopkins Hall Dr.* ☎ *413/ 597–2462* ⊕ *www.williams.edu* ✉ *Free* ☉ *Weekdays 10–noon and 1–5.*

㉗ Clark Art Institute. In the early 1950s, Robert Sterling and Francine Clary

Fodor's Choice Clark were looking for a home for their art collection—away from major
★ cities and therefore not subject to the threat of nuclear attack that seemed so imminent in the Cold War era. The Clark Art Institute opened to the public in 1955 and has already undergone two major expansions, with a third in the planning stages. One of the nation's notable small art museums, the Clark has more than 30 paintings by Renoir (among them *Mademoiselle Fleury in Algerian Costume*) as well as canvases by Monet and Pissarro. *The Little Dancer,* an important sculpture by Degas, is another exceptional work. Other items include priceless English silver, European and American photography from the 1840s through the 1910s, and Flemish and Dutch masterworks from the 17th and 18th centuries. The Clark also has an excellent research library, which is open the public. Admission is free on Tuesday. ✉ *225 South St.*

☎ *413/458–2303* ⊕ *www.clarkart.edu* ✉ *July–Oct. $10; Nov.–May free* ⊙ *Sept.–June, Tues.–Sun. 10–5; July and Aug., daily 10–5.*

㉑ **Field Farm.** A 316-acre nature preserve has a mixed hardwood and pine forest, freshwater marshes, open meadows, two streams, and a small spring-fed pond. More than 4 mi of trails are excellent for hiking, snow-shoeing, and cross-country skiing. At the northern end of the property is the 42-acre Caves Lot, where small streams disappear into a series of underground channels carved into the limestone bedrock. Two houses grace the grounds at Field Farm. The main house, designed in 1948 by Edwin Goodell, is now an elegant B&B. The Folly, built as a guest house, was designed in 1966 by Ulrich Franzen. Modern sculptures, including works by Richard M. Miller and Herbert Ferber, are found in the garden. ⊠ *554 Sloan Rd.* ⊕ *www.thetrustees.org* ✉ *Free* ⊙ *Daily, sunrise to sunset.*

㉕ **Field Park.** This remnant of the village green that ran the length of Main Street once served as a common grazing area. The park, which opened to the public in 1878, was the site of the first and second meeting houses of the First Congregational Church. The first meetinghouse was a crude building with one door, few windows, and no chimney. It was moved in 1798 to make way for a larger meetinghouse. The second meetinghouse, larger and more dignified, burned on January 21, 1866. Field Park is now home to the **1753 House,** a replica of the town's first freestanding structure. ⊠ *U.S. 7 and Rte. 2* ⊕ *www.mass.gov/dem/parks/svym.htm.*

㉝ **First Congregational Church.** In 1886 this Romanesque Revival style brick church was built at the corner of Main Street and Chapin Hall Drive. In 1914, changing tastes prompted church officials to rebuild the church in the neoclassical style, modeled in part on an 18th-century church in Old Lyme, Connecticut. The church is active to this day, with regular Sunday services. ⊠ *906 Main St.* ☎ *413/458–4273* ⊕ *www.fccwilli.org.*

㉚ **Griffin Hall.** Constructed in 1828, this former chapel was designed by the college's third president, Edward Dorr Griffin. Originally called the Brick Chapel, it was christened Griffin Hall in 1859. For a time it was the home of Williamstown National Bank, which opened in 1884 in the office of the college treasurer. In 1904 Griffin Hall was moved northeast to bring it into line with the new Thompson Chapel. A small monument to the college's Civil War dead stands in front of Griffin Hall. ⊠ *844 Main St.*

⑭ **Hopkins Memorial Forest.** A 2,500-acre nature preserve, Hopkins Memorial Forest occupies the northwest corner of the state at the border of New York and Vermont. The forest has miles of trails suitable for hiking and horseback riding. A 4½-mi figure-eight loop is maintained in winter for cross-country skiing. Throughout the year, the forest is home to many festivals, including the Fall Festival, Maple Sugar Days, and Spring Field Day. The Rosenburg Center is at the eastern entrance. It has public restrooms and a first-aid station. The museum in the lobby is used for interpretive displays relating both to the forest and to the region. ⊠ *271 Northwest Hill Rd.* ☎ *413/597–4353* ⊕ *www.williams. edu* ✉ *Free* ⊙ *Daily.*

★ ☾ ㉘ **Hopkins Observatory.** The oldest existing observatory in the United States, the Hopkins Observatory was built between 1836 and 1838 by Professor Albert Hopkins and his students from stone they quarried themselves on East Mountain. That building now houses the Milham Planetarium and Mehlin Museum of Astronomy. Originally located in the center of the quad, it was moved to the far end in 1908, then to its present location in 1961. The domed ceiling of the planetarium was covered with painted stars until the projector was installed in 1963. ✉ *829 Main St.* ☎ *413/597–2188* ⊕ *www.williams.edu* 🎫 *Free* ☉ *Daily.*

⑲ **Little Red Schoolhouse.** This one-room schoolhouse was built in 1865, replacing the original building dating from 1810. It functioned as the public school for South Williamstown until 1962. The Williamstown Cooperative Nursery School has rented space in the building ever since. The South Williamstown Community Association continues to hold meetings in the building. ✉ *New Ashford Rd.* ☎ *413/458–8668.*

⑬ **Mt. Greylock State Reservation.** A portion of the 11,000-acre Mt. Greylock State Reservation occupies the southeast corner of Williamstown. The primary trails onto the property are the Hopper Trail (reached from Hopper Road) and the Roaring Brook Trail (from Roaring Brook Road). The summits of Stoney Ledge (2,560 feet) and Mt. Prospect (2,690 feet) are located near Williamstown. ✉ *Rockwell Rd.* ☎ *413/499–4262 or 413/499–4263* ⊕ *www.mass.gov/dem/parks/mgry.htm* 🎫 *Free* ☉ *Daily dawn to dusk.*

⑯ **Mount Hope Park.** An agricultural experiment on a grand scale, Mount Hope Farm was a major economic force in Williamstown during the first half of the 20th century. At its height the farm occupied more than 1,300 acres and was noted for its success in using genetic principles to improve the yield of potatoes and to boost the production of poultry and dairy cattle. Mount Hope Park is a small recreational area near what used to be the main gates to the property. Many of the farm buildings, including the million-dollar cow barn, can still be seen today. ✉ *Hopper and Green River Rds.*

⑰ **Old Stone Church.** Built in 1835, the Old Stone Church served as the Baptist Church for most of its first 100 years. After a new church was built on Main Street, the congregation voted to close the old one in 1937. The building stayed shuttered for more than 30 years. A local college professor bought the church and converted it into a private residence in the 1970s. ✉ *Green River Rd.*

☾ ㉔ **Sheep Hill.** Sheep were raised here in the late 19th century, hence the name. You can visit the farmhouse where Art and Ella Rosenburg and their son lived when they kept a milking herd here for more than 50 years. From the top of the hill on Bee Hill Road hikers can reach the Fitch Trail and the Running Pine Trail. ✉ *Access from Bee Hill Rd. or Cold Spring Rd.* ☎ *413/458–2494* ⊕ *www.wrlf.org* 🎫 *Free* ☉ *Grounds, daily dawn–dusk; farmhouse, weekdays 9–5.*

㉒ **Sinclair Lewis Estate.** In 1946, Nobel Prize-winning author Sinclair H. Lewis purchased the 600-acre Thorvale Farm on the Torrey Plateau west of Oblong Road. During the two years Lewis lived there he wrote *Lucy*

Jade and most of *Kingsblood Royal* and *The God-Seeker*. Lewis left Williamstown, and the United States, in 1948, but when he died in Rome in 1951, he was still legally a Williamstown resident and so his will was filed in Berkshire County Probate Court. The building was used as a monastery between 1952 and 2002. ✉ *Olbong Rd.*

Southlawn Cemetery. At the end of an unmarked dirt road, this cemetery was established in 1769 on land donated by the town's first settler, Isaac Stratton. Many early residents are buried beneath the wonderful gravestones, which include one shaped like a tree trunk with vines twining about it. ✉ *U.S. 7* ☎ *413/458–8657* 🎟 *Free* ☉ *Daily 7–dusk.*

⓲ Store at Five Corners. The nation's oldest continuously operated country store, the Store at Five Corners was built as a tavern in 1770. The first South Williamstown post office was located here in 1827. In 1830 the second story and the Greek-Revival portico were added. It was operated as Steele's Store from 1905 to 1978, when it became known as the Store at Five Corners. Inside are gourmet specialties from around the world. The full-service delicatessen serves soups, sandwiches, and New York–style bagels. ✉ *U.S. 7 and Rte. 43* ☎ *413/458–3176 or 888/ 745–1770* ⊕ *www.thestoreatfivecorners.com.*

⓯ Stratton Inn. In 1790 Elijah Smedley built the post-and-beam portion of this home. When he married Lucy Smedley in 1828, they expanded the home by adding the brick facade. The main building later served as a stagecoach stop, a speakeasy, a motel, and—more recently—as research offices for the Getty Foundation. It was moved to its current location from the land now occupied by the Orchards Hotel in 1984, at which time many of the beautiful old apple trees were destroyed. ✉ *63 Stratton Rd.* ☎ *413/458–1303.*

㉓ Taconic Trail. Built between 1925 and 1930, the Taconic Trail runs from Williamstown to Troy, New York. Also known as Route 2, the portion that runs through Massachusetts is steep and scenic. The RRR Brooks Trail and the Shepherd's Well Trail entering Hopkins Memorial Forest can be accessed from the road, and the beautiful 35-mi Taconic Crest Trail crosses the road at the summit just over the New York border. ✉ *Rte. 2.*

㉛ Thompson Chapel. This imposing stone chapel, which sits on the grounds of Williams College, was built between 1903 and 1904. The west transept window, dedicated to President James A. Garfield (an 1856 graduate), was created by noted 19th-century stained-glass artist John LaFarge. ✉ *860 Main St.* ☎ *413/597–2483* ⊕ *www.williams.edu.*

> **need a break?** Formerly known as Cold Spring Coffee Roasters, **Tunnel City Coffee** (✉ 100 Spring St. ☎ 413/458–5010) has moved into spacious new quarters. Grab a cup of Green Mountain Coffee and a freshly baked cookie. Whether you're in the mood for an ice-cream cone on the summer evening or a bowl of soup on a winter's day, the place to stop is **Lickety-Split** (✉ 69 Spring St. ☎ 413/458–3436), a branch of which is at Mass MoCa. There are plenty of tasty smoothies, shakes, and sundaes.

🐾 ㉙ **Williams College Museum of Art.** When you enter the Williams College
Fodor'sChoice Museum of Art, you are greeted by Louise Bourgeois' *Eyes.* Compris-
★ ing one of the finest college art museums in the country, the collection
contains approximately 12,000 pieces. Small enough to be enjoyed in
an afternoon, the museum is always filled with thought-provoking exhibits. The original octagonal structure facing Main Street was built as
a library in 1846. ⊠ *15 Lawrence Hall Dr.* ☏ *413/597–2429* ⊕ *www.
williams.edu* ⊠ *Free* ☉ *Tues.–Sat. 10–5, Sun. 1–5.*

🐾 ㉖ **Williamstown House of Local History.** When Herbert Sanford Botsford bequeathed his house to the town for use as the public library in 1940, he
stipulated that the second floor be occupied by an exhibit about the town's
history. When the library moved to Main Street, so did this charming
display. There is a children's discovery room and a series of changing
exhibits on different aspects of life in Williamstown. The extensive
archives are used by those conducting genealogical or historical research. ⊠ *1095 Main St.* ☏ *413/458–2160* ⊕ *www.milnelibrary.org*
⊠ *Free* ☉ *Weekdays 10–noon.*

Where to Eat

$$$ ✕ **Mezze Bistro & Bar.** This is, without a doubt, Williamstown's hot spot.
Fodor'sChoice On summer evenings it's not uncommon to find yourself rubbing el-
★ bows with stars from the Williamstown Theatre Festival. The interior
mixes urban chic and rustic charm, with hardwood floors and exposed-
brick walls. The spectacular menu is always in flux, but don't be sur-
prised to encounter sashimi with watercress alongside filet mignon with
roasted root vegetables. ⊠ *16 Water St.* ☏ *413/458–0123* ⊕ *www.
mezzerestaurant.com* ⩘ *Reservations essential* ☰ *AE, D, MC, V*
☉ *No lunch.*

$$–$$$ ✕ **Hobson's Choice.** Everyone in Williamstown knows Hobson's. This
Fodor'sChoice chef-owned restaurant is known for its expertly prepared seafood and
★ steaks. The menu also features freshly made desserts. The decor, with
wood paneling and exposed beams, invites you to linger. You feel as if
you've traveled back in time to an early-19th-century tavern. ⊠ *159 Water
St.* ☏ *413/458–9101* ☰ *AE, MC, V.*

$$–$$$ ✕ **Taconic.** One of the larger restaurants in Williamstown, Taconic is a
popular site for parties and receptions. The menu features poultry, beef,
veal, seafood, and pasta in familiar dishes and new combinations. The
portions are generous, and the atmosphere is warm and welcoming.
⊠ *1161 Cold Spring Rd.* ☏ *413/458–9499* ⊕ *www.taconicrestaurant.
com* ☰ *AE, D, DC, MC, V.*

$–$$$ ✕ **Chopsticks.** This is not your run-of-the-mill Chinese place—it also fea-
tures an array of Japanese and Korean dishes, such as *job chae* with
chicken, beef, or vegetables; and salmon teriyaki. Sushi lunch is also available. Many meals are cooked with a flourish right at your table. ⊠ *412
Main St.* ☏ *413/458–5750* ☰ *AE, D, MC, V.*

★ $$ ✕ **Spice Root.** Inside this mango-colored dining room, a bountiful menu
of exotic entrées, including kabobs, curries, and plenty of vegetarian
choices is served. If you're new to Indian cuisine, the staff is always ready
to explain how each dish is prepared. ⊠ *23 Spring St.* ☏ *413/458–5200*
☰ *No credit cards.*

$–$$ ✕ **Hot Tomatoes.** If you like your pizza thin and crispy, then Hot Toma-toes is for you. Locals rate this as the best pizza place in the area. The list of toppings is impressive. Stop by in the morning for delicious New York–style bagels and the *New York Times.* ⊠ *100 Water St.* ☏ *413/458-2722* ▭ *MC, V.*

$–$$ ✕ **Michael's.** This eatery, run by the Nikitas family, serves a mix of en-trées from Italy and their native Greece. You can't go wrong with spe-cialties such as lasagna, veal Parmesan, and fettuccine Alfredo. For dessert try Cindy's baklava or Pappa Charlie's rice pudding. You may have to wait for a table on Friday and Saturday nights. Why the odd architecture? Michael's was originally an A&W Root Beer stand. ⊠ *460 Main St.* ☏ *413/458-2114* ⌕ *Reservations not accepted* ▭ *MC, V* ☉ *Closed Sun. and Mon.*

★ **$–$$** ✕ **Moonlight Diner & Grille.** Locals love this place for its funky atmosphere, its cheerful service, and its reasonable prices. There's also great break-fast fare served all day long. The 1950s diner decor isn't just for show—you can get real soda fountain drinks, malts, and thick milk shakes. The Moonlight also stays open late for the night owls. ⊠ *408 Main St.* ☏ *413/458-3305* ▭ *D, MC, V.*

★ **$–$$** ✕ **Thai Garden.** A delightful addition to Spring Street, this restaurant serves authentic dishes made with Thai herbs and spices. The menu warns you that dishes such as stir-fried squid and spicy fish fillet are for the ad-venturous, while the steamed ginger salmon and tamarind duck are for more timid palates. Beverages such as Thai iced coffee are nicely pre-sented. Desserts include homemade custard, coconut-and-ginger ice cream, and chilled lychees. ⊠ *27 Spring St.* ☏ *413/458-0004* ▭ *AE, D, MC, V.*

¢–$$ ✕ **Chef's Hat.** You'll be hard pressed to find a table at this diner on Sun-day morning, when just about everyone in town seems to stop by for a hot breakfast. The decor is a little dreary, but the food is all-American and is served fast and hot. Check out the century-old countertop. ⊠ *905 Simonds Rd.* ☏ *413/458-5120* ▭ *D, MC, V* ☉ *Closed Mon. No din-ner Tues. and Wed.*

$ ✕ **Desperados.** Authentic Mexican food is what you get at Desperados, where they make all their own salsas and sauces. Many of the dishes arrive at your table sizzling. Check out desserts such as flan and fried bananas. ⊠ *246 Main St.* ☏ *413/458-2100* ▭ *AE, D, MC, V.*

★ **$** ✕ **Pappa Charlie's Deli.** No trip to Williamstown is complete without a visit to Pappa Charlie's. This legendary deli serves a huge variety of sand-wiches, many named after famous actors who have appeared at the Williamstown Theatre Festival, such as the Blythe Danner (tuna, sprouts, tomato, Swiss cheese, avocado, and mayonnaise on whole wheat) and the Mary Tyler Moore (bacon, lettuce, tomato, and avocado). ⊠ *28 Spring St.* ☏ *413/458-5969* ▭ *No credit cards.*

★ **¢–$** ✕ **Helen's Place.** More than a deli, Helen's prepares creative wraps, sandwiches, and salads for the dining rooms and a variety of nicely pre-pared items are available for takeout. Regular specialties include organic salmon that is smoked right on the premises. For a quick pick-me-up, there's a fresh fruit and vegetable juice bar. ⊠ *60 Spring St.* ☏ *413/458-1360* ▭ *MC, V* ☉ *Closed Sun. and Mon.*

¢ ✕ **Arugula Cocina Latina.** This dapper storefront with a few tables scattered about is mostly a lunch spot, but you can order dinner until 8 PM. With contemporary art lining the walls and piped-in Latin jazz filling the air, you'd expect to find this nifty hole-in-the-wall on a side street in Miami's Little Havana. Cuban sandwiches are the best reason to make the trip here, but the great chorizo sandwiches, empanadas, salads, and rich, creamy hot chocolate also satisfy. ⊠ *25 Spring St.* ☎ *413/458–2152* ⊟ *AE, D, MC, V* ⊙ *Closed Sun.*

Where to Stay

★ **$$$–$$$$** ✕▦ **The Orchards Hotel.** Although it's near Route 2 and surrounded by parking lots, this thoroughly proper, if rather stuffy, hostelry compensates with a beautiful courtyard filled with fruit trees and a pond stocked with koi. English antiques furnish most of the spacious accommodations. The inner rooms, which have windows looking onto the courtyard, are best for summer stays. The outer rooms have less-distinguished views, but their fireplaces add appeal for winter visits. The restaurant ($$$–$$$$) serves such creative fare as sautéed scallops with a banana–shiitake salad. ⊠ *222 Adams Rd., 01267* ☎ *413/458–9611 or 800/225–1517* 📠 *413/458–3273* ⊕ *www.orchardshotel.com* 🛏 *49 rooms* ♭ *Restaurant, some refrigerators, pool, gym, hot tub, sauna, bar, meeting room* ⊟ *AE, DC, MC, V.*

★ **$$–$$$$** ▦ **Field Farm Guest House.** Built in 1948, this guesthouse contains a fine collection of art on loan from Williams College. The former owners, who gave part of their own art collection to the college, donated the 296-acre property to the Trustees of Reservations, which runs it as a B&B. The large windows in the guest rooms have expansive views of the grounds. Three rooms have private decks; two rooms have working tile fireplaces. You can prepare your own simple meals in the pantry. The grounds, open to the public, have miles of hiking trails. ⊠ *554 Sloan Rd., 01267* ☎☎ *413/458–3135* ⊕ *www.berkshireweb.com/trustees/field.html* 🛏 *5 rooms* ♭ *Tennis court, pool; no kids under 12* ⊟ *D, MC, V* ⍟ *BP.*

$$–$$$ ▦ **Williams Inn.** What this lodging lacks in architectural charm it more than makes up for with the warmth of its innkeepers, Carl and Marilyn Faulkner. The other thing the Williams Inn has going for it is an excellent location within many shops and restaurants. The large and attractive dining room serves breakfast, lunch and dinner, and the Sunday brunches are legendary. The smaller pub features live entertainment on the weekends. ⊠ *Field Park, at the northern intersection of Routes 7 and 2, 01267* ☎ *413/458–9371* 📠 *413/458–2767* ⊕ *www.williamsinn.com* ♭ *Restaurant, pool, hot tub, sauna, pub, meeting rooms; no smoking* ⊟ *AE, D, DC, MC, V.*

$–$$$ ▦ **Williamstown Bed & Breakfast.** This attractive Victorian is within walking distance of all the great shopping, dining, and cultural attractions of Williamstown. Owners Kim Rozell and Lucinda Edmonds make a marvelous morning muffin. ⊠ *30 Cold Spring Rd., 01267* ☎ *413/458–9202* ⊕ *www.williamstownbandb.com* 🛏 *3 rooms* ♭ *No kids under 12, no smoking* ⊟ *No credit cards* ⍟ *BP.*

$$ 🏨 **Berkshire Hills Motel.** All the rooms at this two-story brick-and-clapboard motel are furnished in Colonial style. The lounge has a fireplace, and guests are free to use the barbecue grill on the deck. Although the motel is close to the road, the spacious grounds encompass a brook and beautiful woodlands. The motel is about 3 mi south of Williamstown. ✉ *1146 Cold Spring Rd., 01267* ☎ *413/458–3950 or 800/388–9677* 🖷 *413/458–5878* ⊕ *www.berkshirehillsmotel.com* ⟳ *21 rooms* ⚘ *Pool, meeting room; no smoking* ⊟ *AE, D, MC, V* ⦿ *CP.*

$–$$ 🏨 **Maple Terrace Motel.** Just east of town, the Maple Terrace Motel is wrapped around a pretty and private courtyard. The rear of the property faces a horse farm, and in summer you can relax in the pool while watching the beautiful animals grazing on the sloping pastures. The property is within easy walking distance from town. Its best asset may be the warm Swedish hospitality of owners Kjell and Ann Truedsson. ✉ *555 Main St., 01267* ☎ *413/458–9677* ⊕ *www.mapleterrace.com* ⟳ *15 rooms, 2 apartments* ⚘ *Refrigerators, in-room VCRs, outdoor pool, playground* ⊟ *AE, DC, MC, V* ⦿ *CP.*

★ $–$$ 🏨 **Steep Acres Farm.** Steep Acres Farm and its sister property, the Birches at Steep Acres, are operated by two generations of the Gangemi family. The lodgings are perched upon a knoll in the neighborhood known as White Oaks. The rooms are cozy and attractive, and breakfast is served in a handsome country kitchen or on a terrace overlooking the grounds. Located on a 54-acre working farm, the property features rolling meadows and beautiful birch woods. There is a private pond for swimming or rowing. ✉ *520 White Oaks Rd., 01267* ☎ *413/458–3774* ⟳ *7 rooms* ⊟ *No credit cards* ⦿ *BP.*

¢–$$ 🏨 **1896 House Country Inn & Motels.** This attractive property south of town offers a variety of lodging options. Two motels—Brookside and Pondside—each have their own style. The rooms at Brookside are Colonial-inspired, with maple furniture and warm and inviting Waverly fabrics. Pondside rooms are bright and flowery with Laura Ashley fabrics. The elegant and romantic Barnside suites are quite grand. Each is individually appointed in period style. Enjoy a creatively prepared three-course breakfast in an intimate breakfast room. ✉ *910 Cold Spring Rd., 01267* ☎ *413/458–8125 or 888/666–1896* ⊕ *www.1896house.com* ⟳ *30 rooms, 6 suites* ⚘ *Cable TV, restaurant, outdoor pool; no smoking* ⊟ *AE, D, DC, MC, V* ⦿ *CP.*

★ $ 🏨 **River Bend Farm.** This 18th-century tavern has period details to make you feel cozy and with just enough modern conveniences to make you comfortable. On the National Register of Historic Places, the Colonel Benjamin Simonds house at River Bend Farm is an authentic 1770 Georgian Colonial home. All the guest rooms are sprinkled with antique pieces—chamber pots, washstands, wing chairs, and spinning wheels. Some bedrooms have wide-plank walls, curtains of unbleached muslin, and four-poster beds with canopies or rope beds. A gracious library awaits you downstairs. The kitchen contains an open-range stove and an oven hung with dried herbs. ✉ *643 Simonds Rd., 01267* ☎ *413/458–3121* ⊕ *www.cycle-logical.com/riverbend* ⟳ *4 rooms with shared bath* ⚘ *No a/c, no room phones, no room TVs* ⊟ *No credit cards* ⊘ *Closed Nov.–Mar.* ⦿ *CP.*

The Arts

The locals will tell you that Williamstown rolls up the sidewalks at 10 PM, but that isn't quite true. During the academic year, the online **Williams Weekly Calendar** (⊕ www.williams.edu/dean/calendar) provides information on goings on at the college. The **Williams College Department of Music** (✉ 54 Chapin Hall Dr. ☎ 413/597–3146 ⊕ www.williams.edu/music) publishes its own calendar for its fall and spring concert series.

Fodor'sChoice
★
At the Adams Memorial Theatre, the **Williamstown Theatre Festival** (✉ 1000 Main St. ☎ 413/597–3400 or 413/597–3399 ⊕ www.wtfestival.org) is the summer's hottest ticket. From June to August, the long-running production presents well-known theatrical works with famous performers on the Main Stage and contemporary works on the Nikos Stage.

On Tuesday evenings in August, the **Williamstown Chamber Concerts** (☎ 413/458–8273) present a variety of chamber music ensembles in the auditorium at the Clark Art Institute. April is enlivened by the **Williamstown Jazz Festival** (☎ 800/214–3799 ⊕ www.williamstownjazz.com). You can hear big name musicians in concert or catch rising stars at the Intercollegiate Jazz Festival.

Beautiful foliage isn't the only reason to travel to Williamstown in October. The **Williamstown Film Festival** (☎ 413/458–9700 ⊕ www.williamstownfilmfest.com) fills local movie theaters in Williamstown and North Adams with cutting-edge cinema. You also have a chance to hear from famous and almost-famous filmmakers at seminars and social events. One of the few remaining independent theaters in the area, **Images Cinema** (✉ 50 Spring St. ☎ 413/458–5612 ⊕ www.imagescinema.org) presents an exceptional variety of independent, foreign, and classic films throughout the year.

The works at the elegant **Harrison Gallery** (✉ 39 Spring St. ☎ 413/458–1700 ⊕ www.theharrisongallery.com) focus on landscapes and images from the Northeast. Emerging as well as established artists share the space, with new exhibits every month. You'll find authentic Asian antiquities ranging from priceless Ming pieces to utilitarian country furniture and folk art at the **LiAsia Gallery** (✉ 31 Spring St. ☎ 413/458–1600 ⊕ www.liasiagallery.com). Housed in a historic neighborhood market, the **Plum Gallery** (✉ 112 Water St. ☎ 413/458–3389 ⊕ www.plumgallery.com) has the best in contemporary art surrounded by century-old woodwork.

Sports & the Outdoors

The **Green River** flows 11 mi from its headwaters on Sugarloaf Mountain in New Ashford to its confluence with the Hoosic River in Williamstown. There are several nice spots to picnic or fish along its banks, and locals enjoy taking a dip in some of its quieter pools or rafting along its gentle course in summer months. The 489-acre Green River Wildlife Management Area is near the Five Corners intersection.

Golf

Waubeeka Golf Links (⊠ 137 New Ashford Rd. ☎ 413/458–8355 ⊕ www.
waubeeka.com), open April–November, is an excellent public 18-hole,
par 72 course with beautiful views of Mt. Greylock, Brodie Mountain,
and the Taconic Range. Greens fees are $30 weekdays and $35 on
weekends.

Fodor'sChoice The 18-hole **Taconic Golf Club** (⊠ 19 Meacham St. ☎ 413/458–3997)—
★ an 18-hole, par-71 course—permits nonmembers to play Tuesday–Friday. On the 14th hole, a stone marker indicates the site of legendary
golfer Jack Nicklaus' first hole-in-one, made while he was competing
in the national junior championships.

Hiking

There are hundreds of miles of beautiful trails for hikers of all levels in
Williamstown. The **Williams Outing Club** (⊠ Siskind House ☎ 413/597–
2711) is the authority on the area's outdoor activities. They publish a
great book, *The North Berkshire Outdoor Guide*, with a topographi-
cal map. **The Mountain Goat** (⊠ 130 Water St. ☎ 413/458–8445 ⊕ www.
themountaingoat.com) sells gear for all outdoor sports. The company
also organizes local hikes through the wilderness.

Horseback Riding

Rustic **Oakhollow Farm** (⊠ 651 Henderson Rd. ☎ 413/458–9278),
home of the Williams College Riding Club, has access to miles of trails.
DeMayo's Bonnie Lea Farm (⊠ 511 North St. ☎ 413/458–3149 ⊕ bon-
nieleafarm.tripod.com) is the place to go for trail rides. The farm is near
miles of trails along the scenic Hoosic River.

Ice-skating

There's ice-skating from November to March at **Lansing Chapman Rink**
(⊠ Latham St. ☎ 413/597–2283).

Swimming

⟲ Named after a beloved elementary school teacher, **Margaret Lindley Park**
(⊠ Cold Spring Rd. ☎ 413/458–5985) has been Williamstown's official swimming hole since 1962. The pond is filled seasonally by divert-
ing and (nominally) warming the waters of Hemlock Brook. From
mid-June to Labor Day there are lifeguards on duty from 11 to 7. **Sand
Springs Pool** (⊠ 158 Sand Springs Rd. ☎ 413/458–5205) has been famous for its 74° spring water for more than two centuries. The water
flows along an underground fault from a natural thermal spring 4,500
feet below, at a constant rate of 450 gallons per minute. There is a swimming pool, indoor and outdoor hot tubs, and a snack bar. From May
to September it's open weekdays 11 to 7:30 and weekends 10 to 8.

Tennis

One of the town's best kept secrets is the **Williamstown Town Tennis Court**
(⊠ Main St. ☎ 413/458–9341), just east of the bridge over the Green
River. It's available on a first-come, first-served basis. The **Williams College Tennis Courts** (⊠ Stetson Rd. and Lynde La. ☎ 413/597–3151) has
24 clay and hard-surface outdoor courts available for a small membership fee in summer. Reservations are required.

Shopping

For 30 years, Samuel and Elizabeth Smith have tilled and tended **Caretaker Farm** (✉ 210 Hancock Rd. ☎ 413/458–4309), one of the oldest continuously operating organic farms in New England. And since 1991, Caretaker has been growing organic produce—raspberries to rutabagas—for 215 subscribing households. The farm is a social hub for its members, who socialize over the rows of green beans and the bins of scallions, lettuce, and spinach. On a historic farm in South Williamstown, **Green River Farms** (✉ 2480 Green River Rd. ☎ 413/458–2470 ⊕ www.greenriverproduce.com) bills itself as the "agri-tainment" capital of northern Berkshire County. You can pick your own fruits and vegetables in season or visit the farm store for everything from locally grown produce to homemade pies. There's a petting zoo and ice-cream shop for the kids. Local farmers and artisans gather in the parking lot at the southern end of Spring Street for the **Williamstown Farmer's Market** (✉ Spring St. ☎ 413/458–3365). It's open on Saturday from 8 to noon between late May and early October.

The Cottage (✉ 24 Water St. ☎ 413/458–4305) has a wide array of clothing, jewelry, glassware, pottery, and table linens. At **Library Antiques** (✉ 70 Spring St. ☎ 413/458–3436 ⊕ www.libraryantiques.com), you can browse an array of prints, paintings, and antiquarian books. **Funky Room** (✉ 95 Water St. ☎ 413/458–9394) is all the rage with teens and twentysomethings. Older folks will also enjoy poking through the inexpensive home accessories, clothing, and gadgets. Some people consider tiny **Toonerville Trolley** (✉ 131 Water St. ☎ 413/458–5229) the best music store in the world. One thing they appreciate is the vast musical knowledge of proprietor Hal March. Toonerville carries hard-to-find jazz, rock, and classical recordings.

Water Street Books (✉ 26 Water St. ☎ 413/458–8071) is large enough to have a great selection but small enough to feel inviting. The children's department is impressive and most Saturday mornings you'll find kids listening to a story or making a craft project. Jam-packed with every imaginable toy and game, **Where'd You Get That?** (✉ 100 Spring St. ☎ 413/458–2206 ⊕ www.wygt.com) also benefits from the warmth and enthusiasm generated by owners Ken and Michele Gietz. **Wild Oats** (✉ 248 Main St. ☎ 413/458–8060 ⊕ www.wildoats.coop) started out as a food co-op, but now it is open to everyone. Its locally grown produce can't be beat.

NORTH ADAMS

34–**41** *6 mi east of Williamstown.*

The second-largest community in Berkshire County, North Adams was simply a part of neighboring Adams until 1878. Farmers had not been interested in the swampy, flood-prone land, but loggers were lured by the stands of virgin pines and the abundant rivers. Water continued to be the area's most valuable resource as the industrial revolution took hold. Textiles became the major industry of North Adams beginning in 1799.

By the late 19th century, the Freeman Print Works, the Sampson Shoe Company, and O. Arnold & Company were the largest employers.

The explosion of manufacturing increased the ethnic diversity of North Adams. Known today as the City of Steeples, North Adams has Italian, Irish, and French Roman Catholic churches, a Full Gospel Tabernacle, as well as Methodist, Baptist, Congregational, and Episcopal churches. Until recently a Unitarian-Universalist church, a Christian Science reading room, and a Reformed Jewish synagogue were all within walking distance of Monument Square. The former two have closed their doors, but Congregation Beth Israel recently moved to a beautiful new home in the west end of the city.

In the 1980s North Adams fell on hard times. After nearly two centuries, it was clear that manufacturing was no longer the backbone of the local economy. The heart of the city was filled with decaying mills. In 1986 Thomas Krens, then director of the Williams College Museum of Art, spearheaded the idea of transforming the mills into museums to exhibit works of contemporary art too large to fit into standard galleries. Like the Hoosac Tunnel, it took longer than anyone thought to make this a reality. But on Memorial Day weekend in 1999, the doors of the Massachusetts Museum of Contemporary Art were finally opened.

a good walk

Begin your walk near the northwest end of Main Street, across the street from City Hall. Here the **Monitor Monument** ㉞ ☞ marks the location of the blast furnace for the North Adams Iron Works. It was one of many industrial buildings that once stood in the heart of North Adams. Looking north, you can see the city's largest mill, now the home of the **Massachusetts Museum of Contemporary Art** ㉟. Cross the street to City Hall, where a small footbridge behind the building leads to **Western Gateway Heritage State Park** ㊱.

Proceed east on Main Street. The two-story yellow-brick house at 49–61 Main Street is the **Empire Building** ㊲, constructed in 1912. It is now home to a pair of arts organizations. At the corner of Main and Holden streets you'll see the two **Blackinton Blocks** ㊳, built by one of the city's wealthiest mill owners. Continuing on, the New Kimbell Building at 85 Main Street was the first building in North Adams to be built on steel pilings. Look for the lions' heads between the fifth-floor windows and along the roof. Farther down Main Street, the Hoosac Savings Bank Building was designed by architect H. Neill Wilson of Pittsfield. If you have very sharp eyes, or a good imagination, you may be able to see the ghoulish faces atop the columns between the fourth-floor windows. Next in line, the Dowlin Block was the work of Edwin Thayer Barlow, a North Adams architect who helped design the facade of the New York Public Library. Just west of the intersection with Eagle Street, the art deco Mohawk Theater was one of the few commercial buildings constructed in North Adams during the Great Depression.

This brings you to the intersection of Main, Eagle, and Ashland streets, just below Monument Square. Take a detour down narrow Eagle Street, a vestige of the city's earliest years. Look up to see the remains of some old painted signs, including one advertising Enna Jettick's shoes for $5

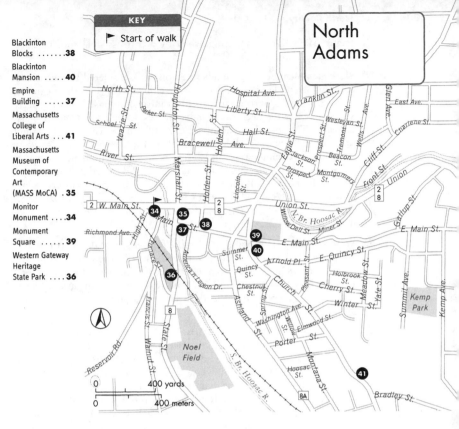

North Adams

to $6. Return to Main Street and continue until you reach **Monument Square** ㉟. At the head of the public park is the magnificent 1869 **Blackinton Mansion** ㊵, home of the public library since 1898.

Make sure to wander down nearby Church Street, the best collection of Victorian homes in Berkshire County. The street, which is virtually intact, includes at least one outstanding example of every architectural style of the period. Walking down Church Street you can imagine horse-drawn carriages and ladies with parasols under the spreading elm trees. About half a mile down Church Street is the campus of the **Massachusetts College of Liberal Arts** ㊶.

What to See

㊳ **Blackinton Blocks.** Sanford Blackinton (1797–1885) was one of the wealthiest and most influential of the 19th-century mill owners in North Adams. These buildings at the corner of Holden and Main streets are two of his most important contributions to the way the city looks today. The first Blackinton Block on Holden Street is an ornate Italianate brick structure designed by Marcus Fayette Cummings of Troy, New York, the architect who had the single greatest impact on the architecture of North Adams during its Victorian heyday. The second Blackinton Block, facing Main Street, is distinguished by a fortress-style roof parapet. ⊠ *Holden and Main Sts.*

★ ⓰ **Blackinton Mansion.** This handsome home is considered the most outstanding example of Second Empire architecture in Berkshire County. In 1863 textiles baron Sanford Blackinton purchased this property when he made the decision to move his residence away from his massive mill. The cost of the home was $75,000, an astronomical amount at the time. Blackinton resided here until his death in 1885, and his widow Eliza remained until she died in 1896. Albert C. Houghton, the first mayor of North Adams, purchased the mansion and donated it to the city as the public library. In 2003 construction began on an eastern wing, which will enable the library to expand its collection. ⊠ *74 Church St.* 📠 *413/662–3133* ⊕ *www.naplibrary.com* ☉ *Mon., Tues., Thurs. 9–8, Wed., Fri. 9–5, Sat. 9–1.*

⓷ **Empire Building.** This building is on the former site of the North Adams House, a lodging where writer Nathaniel Hawthorne stayed during the summer of 1838. Several decades later it was the site of a grand hotel called the Wilson House and the Empire Theater. Both burned to the ground a few months after Theodore Roosevelt spoke on this site in 1912. ⊠ *49–61 Main St.*

⓸ **Massachusetts College of Liberal Arts.** In 1894 state officials inaugurated the North Adams Normal School, a two-year teachers' college. The original campus consisted of two buildings that can still be seen on Church Street, Murdock Hall and Smith House. The oldest building on the MCLA campus, Murdock Hall was named in 1922 after the school's first principal Frank Fuller Murdock. It was built of yellow brick and white marble between 1894 and 1897 to house the original North Adams Normal School and for years was the only building on campus. The college currently is planning to renovate and restore its most historic structure. Smith House is a handsome yellow-brick mansion with stately white columns and a graceful portico. Traditionally the home of college presidents, it is currently used for special functions and to house visiting dignitaries. In 1997, after being known as the State Teachers College at North Adams and North Adams State College, the institution changed its name to the Massachusetts College of Liberal Arts. ⊠ *375 Church St.* 📠 *413/662–5000* ⊕ *www.mcla.mass.edu.*

☾ ⓵ **Massachusetts Museum of Contemporary Art (MASS MoCA).** This industrial
Fodor'sChoice complex was part of Harvey Arnold & Co., which manufactured fab-
★ rics from 1862 to 1940. In 1999, after it had sat empty for more than a decade, the building opened to much fanfare as the nation's largest center for contemporary performing and visual arts. Six of the factory buildings have been transformed into more than 250,000 square feet of galleries, studios, performance venues, cafés, and shops. Exhibits and performances include everything from art exhibitions to dance and music concerts to film presentations. ⊠ *87 Marshall St.* 📠 *413/664–4111* ⊕*www.massmoca.org* 🎟*$10* ☉*June–Sept., daily 10–6; Sept.–June, Wed.–Mon. 10–5.*

③④ **Monitor Monument.** This monument to the city's industrial past marks the location of the blast furnace of the North Adams Iron Works. It is believed that the iron for the *USS Monitor,* the ironclad warship used in the Civil War, was smelted here. Further back in history, this site is thought to have been the intersection of the two Indian trails, the Pontoosuc Trail and the Mohawk Trail. ☒ *Main St.*

③⑨ **Monument Square.** Surrounded by the Congregational, Methodist, and Baptist churches is this memorial to the local soldiers who died during the Civil War. The simple marble statue, depicting a soldier at parade rest, was dedicated on Independence Day in 1878. During the Civil War, North Adams furnished an unusually large number of soldiers in proportion to the population of the town. The pedestal reads: PRESENTED TO THE TOWN OF NORTH ADAMS BY THE LADIES SOLDIERS AID SOCIETY. A few months before the statue's centennial, it was shattered during a traffic accident, but was pieced back together in time for a July 4, 1981, rededication. ☒ *Main and Church Sts.*

★ ☾ **North Adams Museum of History & Science.** North Adams' best kept secret, this museum has more than 25 permanent exhibits on three floors of a building that was once part of an railroad yard. A store sells a number of North Adams Historical Society publications. ☒ *Western Gateway Heritage State Park, Bldg. 5A State St.* ☏ *413/ 664–4700* 🖅 *Free* ☉ *Jan.–Apr., Sat. 10–4, Sun. 1–4; May–Dec., Thurs.–Sat. 10–4, Sun. 1–4.*

★ ☾ ③⑥ **Western Gateway Heritage State Park.** Located on the old Boston & Maine railroad yard, this state park includes a visitor center with exhibits that trace the impact that train travel had on the region. A 30-minute documentary provides a look at the intense labor that went into the construction of the nearby Hoosac Tunnel. ☒ *115 State St.* ☏ *413/ 663–6312* ⊕ *www.state.ma.us/dem/parks/wghp.htm* 🖅 *Free* ☉ *Visitor center, daily 10–5.*

Where to Eat

★ **$$–$$$** ✕ **Gramercy Bistro.** Occupying what was once a downtown diner, this casual, upbeat eatery has developed a loyal following. The intimate space, with a wood-beam ceiling and walls lined with black-and-white photos of the town, serves an eclectic mix of sandwiches and salads. Come by on weekends for the memorable brunch. ☒ *24 Marshall St.* ☏ *413/ 663–5300* ▭ *AE, MC, V* ☉ *Closed Tues. No lunch.*

★ **$–$$** ✕ **Eleven.** This eatery is incredibly chic, and its setting in the courtyard of the Massachusetts Museum of Contemporary Art adds to the ultra-modern ambience. The decor is space-age in a retro George Jetson kind of way. You can get away cheap with an individual pizza topped with caramelized onion, mushroom, and fontina, or splurge on a grilled tuna salad with mixed greens, cherry tomatoes, caper berries, and caper vinaigrette. ☒ *1111 MASS MoCA Way* ☏ *413/662–2004* ▭ *AE, D, MC, V.*

$–$$ ✕ **Freightyard Restaurant & Pub.** In a festive space near Heritage State Park, this busy eatery serves half-pound burgers, prime rib dinners, and other down-home favorites. Dinner is served until 11, and the bar keeps going long after that. ⊠ *Heritage State Park, Furnace St.* ☎ *413/663–6547* ☰ *AE, MC, V.*

★ **$-$$** ✕ **Jae's Inn.** Eclectic Pan-Asian fare, served with grace and style in a renovated country house, is what you'll find here at this branch of the Boston chain. A jazz trio plays every Thursday evening, and it's possible to combine an afternoon at the in-house spa with a lunch or dinner. Entrées range from a spicy Korean hot-stone bibim bab to a standard filet mignon. Nigiri sushi and hosomaki are also available. ⊠ *1111 S. State St.* ☎ *413/664–0100* ☰ *AE, D, DC, MC, V.*

$-$$ ✕ **Joga Café.** At this small café, the modern and intimate decor complements the menu's light fare. The panini are among many of the delicious offerings. This place caters to the late-night crowd and sometimes hosts live jazz and blues. During the warmer months you can eat outside. ⊠ *23 Eagle St.* ☎ *413/664–0126* ☰ *MC, V.*

$ ✕ **Desperados.** An instant hit when it opened in 2004, this Mexican eatery is near the Massachusetts College of Liberal Arts. The great food, low prices, and casual atmosphere are a natural draw for the college crowd, as well as for families looking for a fun place to take the kids. ⊠ *138 Ashland St.* ☎ *413/662–2177* ☰ *AE, D, DC, MC, V.*

¢ ✕ **Jack's Hot Dog Stand.** A North Adams institution since 1917, this hole in the wall is where locals go for a frank. It also serves burgers and fries any way you like them. There is minimal seating, so be prepared to eat your wiener on the run. ⊠ *12 Eagle St.* ☎ *413/664–9006* ☰ *No credit cards.*

¢ ✕ **Lickety-Split.** Inside the Massachusetts Museum of Contemporary Art, this café serves soups and sandwiches that are delicious and bountiful. Lickety-Split also serves Berkshire Ice Cream, nice when you're looking to cool down on a hot day. ⊠ *87 Marshall St.* ☎ *413/663–3372* ☰ *AE, MC, V* ☉ *No dinner.*

☾ ¢ ✕ **Pedrin's Dairy Bar.** This seasonal burger joint is listed in the *Guinness Book of World Records* for having the world's longest menu. This is a bit misleading, as the accolade refers to the physical size of the menu, which is painted on boards that wrap around the top of this diner-style building. The food is standard short-order American—burgers, hot dogs, fries. This is a take-out joint, but a few picnic tables are scattered around the grounds. That this is a summer-only treat makes it even more beloved by locals. ⊠ *1360 Curran Hwy.* ☎ *413/664–9540* ☰ *No credit cards.*

Where to Stay

$$-$$$$ ▥ **Porches Inn.** These once-dilapidated mill workers' houses dating from
Fodor'sChoice 1890s were refurbished to become one of New England's quirkiest ho-
★ tels. The decor strikes a perfect balance between high-tech and historic—rooms have a mix of retro '40s and '50s lamps and bungalow–style furnishings along with such contemporary touches as stunning bathrooms with slate floors, hot tubs, and mirrors fashioned out of old window frames. Some two-room suites have loft sleeping areas reached by spiral staircases. Suites have pull-out sofas and can sleep up to six. ⊠ *231 River St., 01247* ☎ *413/664–0400* ⊕ *www.porches.com* ➷ *40 rooms, 12 suites* ♿ *Cable TV, some in-room hot tubs, some kitchens, pool, hot*

tub, sauna, in-room data ports, exercise equipment, bar, concierge, business services, meeting room, dry cleaning, laundry service. ⊟ *AE, MC, V* ⦿ *CP.*

★ $-$$$ ▦ **Blackinton Manor B&B.** Dan and Betsy Epstein's meticulously restored 1849 Italianate mansion is furnished with antiques. The Epsteins are both professional musicians, and they often host concerts and chamber music workshops. Several of the elegantly appointed guest rooms have pianos. The mansion, one of many in the city built by textiles baron Sanford Blackinton, is notable for its intricate wrought-iron balconies, floor-to-ceiling windows, a spacious bay window, and decorative corbels. ⊠ *1391 Massachusetts Ave., 01247* ☎ *413/663–5795 or 800/ 795–8613* ↩ *5 rooms* ♿ *Some in-room hot tubs, pool; no kids under 7, no smoking* ⊟ *MC, V* ⦿ *BP.*

★ $$ ▦ **Jae's Inn.** Owner Jae Chung has completely renovated this turn-of-the-20th-century building into a delightful, comfortable lodging. Each of the country-style guest rooms is equipped with a whirlpool tub, and several have French doors leading outside. The in-house spa provides a full range of relaxing treatments and beauty services. The hotel is about 2 mi south of downtown North Adams. ⊠ *1111 S. State St., 01247* ☎ *413/664–0100* ⊟ *413/664–0105* ⊕ *www.jaesinn.com* ↩ *11 rooms* ♿ *In-room DVD players, in-room hot tubs, outdoor pool, tennis court, spa, shop* ⊟ *AE, D, DC, MC, V* ⦿ *CP.*

¢-$$ ▦ **Holiday Inn Berkshires.** Solid and safe, this hotel has spacious rooms with wonderful views of the mountains. Steeples, the restaurant on the ground floor, has a popular weekly pasta bar and outdoor dining in warm weather. The hotel also has an indoor pool and a fitness center in the basement, making it a good choice when the temperatures drop. The location on Main Street means you're within walking distance of downtown shops and restaurants. ⊠ *40 Main St., 01247* ☎ *413/663–6500 or 800/465–4329* ⊟ *413/663–6380* ⊕ *www.holidayinnberkshires.com* ↩ *86 rooms* ♿ *Restaurant, indoor pool, exercise equipment, sauna, hot tub, meeting rooms* ⊟ *AE, D, DC, MC, V.*

The Arts

The historic Beaver Mill, which occupies 27 acres of woodland adjacent to Natural Bridge State Park, houses the **Contemporary Artists Center** (⊠ 189 Beaver St. ☎ 413/663–9555 ⊕ www.thecac.org), a 130,000-square-foot artists' residence and studio. The center has a small café that hosts exhibits. **Inkberry** (⊠ 63 Main St. ☎ 413/664–0775 ⊕ www.inkberry.org) is a nonprofit center for the literary arts. It offers in-person and online workshops geared toward every skill level of writer; book groups, and a reading series that brings established writers into the community.

Northern Berkshire Creative Arts (⊠ 2610 MASS MoCA Way ☎ 413/663–8338 ⊕ www.nbcreativearts.org), runs a broad range of classes in the creative arts, both traditional and contemporary, which are open to everyone. **Main Street Stage** (⊠ 57 Main St. ☎ 413/663–3240 ⊕ www. mainstreetstage.org) is a tiny storefront theater dedicated to producing new works and classics. Performances usually take place on weekends.

A new community theater group, **Mill City Productions** (✉ 59 Summer St. ⊕ millcityproductions.tripod.com), presents small shows every other month at St. John's Episcopal Church. Monthly between September and May, the **Railway Café** (✉ 59 Summer St. ☎ 413/664–6393) presents folk and contemporary musicians and groups in concert at St. John's Episcopal Church on Summer Street.

Sports & the Outdoors

Bowling

The **Mount Greylock Bowl** (✉ 41 Roberts Dr. ☎ 413/663–3761), is a family-friendly 10-pin bowling alley. The lanes are open Wednesday and Saturday nights in summer, and every night in winter. If candlepin bowling ☺ is your thing, head on over to **Valley Park Lanes** (✉ 1274 Curran Hwy. ☎ 413/664–9715). You'll find 18 lanes, as well as an arcade.

Hiking

★ A hidden gem in the city is **Natural Bridge State Park** (✉ Rte. 8 ☎ 413/663–6392 ⊕ www.mass.gov/dem/parks/nbdg.htm), a 30-foot span that crosses Hudson Brook. The marble arch at the center of this 49-acre park sits in what was a marble quarry from the early 1880s to the mid-1900s. There are picnic sites, hiking trails, and well-maintained restrooms. In winter the park is popular for cross-country skiing. To reach the **Notch Brook Cascades** (✉ Marion Ave.), take the scenic trail beginning on Marion Avenue. It travels along Notch Brook for about a ½ mi before reaching the waterfalls that drop through remarkable folds of rock.

The northeast corner of **Mt. Greylock State Reservation** (✉ Notch Rd. ☎ 413/499–4262 ⊕ www.mass.gov/dem/parks/mgry.htm) is in North Adams, accessible by car via Notch Road between May and October. Parking is available at the base of the Bernard Farm Trail.

Ice-Skating

Managed by the Massachusetts College of Liberal Arts, the **Vietnam Veterans Memorial Skating Rink** (✉ 375 S. Church St. ☎ 413/662–5112 ⊕ www.vvmsrink.org) offers free recreational skating and hosts ice-hockey teams and figure skating groups from throughout the Berkshires.

Swimming

Congenially known as Fish Pond, **Windsor Lake** (✉ Bradley St. and Kemp Ave. ☎ 413/663–7333) is a fairly small body of water, but it provides a host of recreational opportunities. The southeastern corner of the lake has picnic tables and grills, a swimming area patrolled by lifeguards, and restrooms. There is a bandstand with free outdoor concerts in summer. You can also enjoy canoeing or kayaking.

Shopping

New shops are popping up all over the city. Most of the interesting shops are on and near Main Street. Merchants draw shoppers with Winter-Fest and SummerFest, as well as special events on the first Friday of every month.

The flagship store of **eZiba Store** (⊠ 1112 MASS MoCA Way ☎ 413/664–6888 ⊕ www.eziba.com) stocks beautiful and useful handmade items, including jewelry, pottery, clothing, and small furnishings. You'll be surprised at the many types of natural-fiber clothing and accessories available at **Galadriel's** (⊠ 105 Main St. ☎ 413/664–0026). Take a peak inside the jewelry case where pendants, pins, bracelets, and rings set with semi-precious stones sparkle.

Owner Margot Sanger has filled **Legacy** (⊠ 38 Holden St. ☎ 413/664–8118 ⊕ www.legacycraftsarts.com) with a fascinating collection of antiques and hand-made items. She sells beautiful yarns and supplies for knitting and needlework. The shop runsweekly crafts workshops for children and adults. The heart of downtown North Adams is **Papyri Books** (⊠ 49 Main St. ☎ 413/662–2099 ⊕ www.papyribooks.com). This small and inviting independent bookstore sells new and used volumes. It also hosts readings, book signings, art exhibits, and concerts.

From the fabulous to the funky, you'll find vintage clothes and accessories from the mid-20th century at **Skiddoo Vintage & Modern** (⊠ 38 Eagle St. ☎ 413/664–8007). This is authentic retro—no knockoffs here.

Housed in the former J. J. Newberry storefront, **Moulton's General Store** (⊠ 75 Main St. ☎ 413/664–7770) sells Berkshire Ice Cream, Green Mountain Coffee, and all the penny candy you can eat.

Delftree Mushroom Farm (⊠ 234 Union St. ☎ 413/664–4907 or 800/243–3742) raises Japanese shiitake mushrooms inside a 19th-century mill. You can no longer tour the growing facilities (mushrooms don't grow in gardens, and in this case they are grown inside a dark, damp old mill building), but there is a retail shop here.

CLARKSBURG

42 *3 mi northeast of North Adams.*

Rural Clarksburg occupies a narrow strip of land beside the Vermont border. The reason to stop here is the spectacular setting, with views south toward Mt. Greylock and north along the valley formed by the north branch of the Hoosic River between the Hoosac Range and the Green Mountains.

The township contains both Clarksburg State Park and Clarksburg State Forest, which explains why 42% of the land is protected from development. Through what is literally an odd twist, only the elbow of the famous Hairpin Turn on the Mohawk Trail is in Clarksburg, while the rest of the road travels through Williamstown, North Adams, Florida, and Savoy. Clarksburg's lone restaurant, the Golden Eagle, is here, but you can only get there by going out of Clarksburg, down into North Adams, and halfway up the trail.

Clarksburg State Park is small and pretty, centered on Mausert's Pond, which is suitable for swimming, canoeing, kayaking, and fishing. Picnic tables make this a popular spot for family outings. A system of easy hiking trails winds around the pond. There are also 50 campsites with wheelchair-accessible restrooms. ✉ *1199 Middle Rd.* ☎ *413/664–8345* ⊕ *www.mass.gov/dem/parks/clsp.htm* 🅿 *$5 parking* 🕑 *Daily.*

The **Clarksburg Town Library,** housed in Clarksburg Elementary School, is unremarkable except for one window that was made by the Clarksburg Farmer's Glassworks. Between 1812 and 1814, local farmers operated a glassworks that produced utilitarian goods. Generally operations of this kind were owned and operated by business owners, so this collaboration among farmers was unique. The company's raw materials were quarried in the town of Washington, in central Berkshire County. ✉ *711 W. Cross Rd.* ☎ *413/664–6050* 🕑 *Nov.–Apr., Mon. and Tues. 10–4:30, Wed. 10–7:30, Fri. and Sat. 10–3; May–Oct., Mon. and Wed. 10–7:30, Tues. 10–3.*

The 13-room **R. D. Musterfield House,** built on a field used during the Revolutionary War, is of plank construction with hand-hewn beams marked with Roman numerals and held together with wooden pegs. It has six stone fireplaces. There is a secret room under the attic accessible only by removing a tread on the stairway; some claim it was used to hide runaway slaves on the Underground Railroad. The private home, listed on the Historic American Buildings Survey, was built in 1785 with an addition constructed in 1805. ✉ *Middle Rd.*

The 2,800-acre **Clarksburg State Forest** occupies the northwest corner of the township, sitting against the Vermont state line. This is an unspoiled wilderness area, accessible only via the Appalachian Trail, from the traffic light on Route 2 at Phelps Avenue in North Adams or the Pine Cobble Trail off Pine Cobble Road in Williamstown. ✉ *Clarksburg* 🅿 *Free* 🕑 *Daily.*

Where to Eat

$–$$$ ✕ **The Golden Eagle.** Reservations are a must at the Golden Eagle because it boasts one of the best views in Berkshire County. Perched at the elbow of the famous Hairpin Turn on the Mohawk Trail, it looks out in Mt. Greylock, the Taconic Range, and the Green Mountains of Vermont. North Adams and Williamstown are nestled in the valley below. Sunsets are spectacular from the balcony. The food is standard American, well-prepared and reasonably priced. To get here, drive east from North Adams or west from Florida on Route 2. ✉ *1935 Mohawk Trail* ☎ *413/663–9834* ⊕ *www.baygo.com/berkshires/ restaurants/goldeneagle* ⚱ *Reservations essential* 🖃 *AE, D, MC, V* 🕑 *Closed Tues.*

Sports & the Outdoors

The **North Adams Country Club** (✉ 641 River Rd. ☎ 413/663–7887 or 413/664–9011) has a pretty 9-hole golf course that was designed and built in 1903 by Orrin E. Smith, who remodeled it in 1939. The small greens are fast, and the narrow fairways are rolling. Water hazards come into play on three holes. Reserved tee times are required on weekends.

FLORIDA

43 *9 mi southeast of North Adams.*

Many visitors have had their picture taken standing hip-deep in snow next to the sign reading WELCOME TO FLORIDA. There are many theories about how this village—known as the "Switzerland of Berkshire County"—got its incongruous name. Historians speculate that the name may have been chosen because not long before it was incorporated the United States purchased Florida from the Spanish. Florida, the last township to join Berkshire County, was incorporated in 1805.

There are two distinct sections of Florida, the community on Florida Mountain and the community down by the Deerfield River. Over the years there has been great rivalry between these two communities, especially during the late 19th and early 20th century when the lower section was booming during construction of the Hoosac Tunnel. This project inspired many innovations in rock excavation, including the use of nitroglycerin, pneumatic drills, and electric blasting caps. During the 22 years it took to bore the 4¾-mi tunnel, 195 workers died. Work began in North Adams on January 8, 1851, and it wasn't until Thanksgiving Day, November 27, 1873, that a final blast opened the remaining rock between the West End and the Central Shaft, and the Hoosac Tunnel was complete. The first train passed through the tunnel on February 9, 1875. Regular passenger service between Boston and Troy was instituted in 1876. The last passenger train traversed the tunnel in 1958. Before you travel to Florida, you might want to pay a visit to Western Gateway Heritage State Park in North Adams, which explains the long and arduous process that created the Hoosac Tunnel.

The town takes special pride in its mascot, Rudy the Rutabaga. He marches in the Fall Foliage Parade in North Adams and many other area events. The purple-topped rutabaga, known locally as the Florida Mountain turnip, is said to be tastier than any other in the world. Very few farmers grow them now, and quite a scandal erupted in 2000 when folks were discovered trying to pass off ordinary rutabagas as Florida Mountain turnips. The townspeople have recently revived the Florida Turnip Festival, held each year in October. The highlight of this gala celebration is the crowning of the turnip king and queen, turnip contests, and a round of turnip songs from the Hoarse Chorus. Don't worry—there's also an appearance by Rudy.

The Deerfield River, which runs beside the town, contains brown, rainbow, and brook trout. Florida residents have long claimed that fish caught in their stretch of the river are larger than those from anywhere else in the Berkshires. Some of the best white-water rafting experiences in the Northeast can be had on the rivers around Florida. Nearby are plenty of opportunities for hiking, mountain biking, and horseback riding, as well as snowshoeing, snowmobiling, and cross-country skiing.

The **Bear Swamp Visitors Center**, underneath the Bear Swamp complex, which straddles the Deerfield River, comprises two hydroelectric stations with a combined maximum capacity of 625 megawatts. The center has a slide show as well as other displays about the history of the power station. ⊠ *River Rd.* ⊞ *Free* ☉ *Daily.*

Work on the 1,028-foot-deep **Central Shaft,** near the center of Hoosac Mountain, was begun in 1863, 12 years after construction on the Hoosac Tunnel commenced. On October 17, 1867 an explosion ignited the wooden building that stood over the Central Shaft, and 13 miners trapped inside the shaft were killed by falling debris and poisonous fumes. With its pumps destroyed, the shaft filled with the water. The contractors quit, and work on the shaft immediately halted. The Central Shaft was finally finished in 1870, after seven years' work. Once it was completed, teams were lowered down into shaft so they could dig toward both portals. On Thanksgiving Day in 1873, a final blast opened the remaining rock between the West End and the Central Shaft, and the Hoosac Tunnel was complete. Today the Central Shaft is fenced in and capped with a large ventilating fan that makes a fearful roar and emanates a dreadful stench of diesel fumes whenever a locomotive passes underneath. A memorial to the deceased tunnel workers is planned. ⊠ *Central Shaft Rd.*

Owned by the power company that operates Bear Swamp, the **Dunbar Brook Picnic Area** is a popular spot for hiking on the Dunbar Brook Trail, launching a kayak on the Deerfield River, or just enjoying the beauty of the valley. Many white-water rafting events use the Dunbar Brook Picnic Area as the starting point. ⊠ *River Rd.* ⊞ *Free* ☉ *Daily.*

★ In 1976 the American Society of Civil Engineers awarded the Hoosac Tunnel national landmark status, and placed a bronze plaque on the **Eastern Portal.** If you look to the left of the portal you can still see the scar in the rock face made during an aborted attempt to begin tunneling from this end. On March 16, 1853, an immense cast-iron boring machine known as Wilson's Patented Stone-Cutting Machine, after its inventor Charles Wilson, bored about 10 feet into the rock and then ground to a halt, wedged into its own hole. It remained there for several decades until it was finally removed and sold for scrap. Passengers used to disembark at the Eastern Portal to board Vermont-bound trains operated by the now defunct Hoosac Tunnel & Wilmington Railroad, affectionately known by locals as the Hoot, Toot & Whistle. ⊠ *River Rd.*

The huge bronze **Elk on the Trail** was erected in 1923 by the Massachusetts Elks Clubs to honor fellow lodge members who had fallen in World War I. A plaque reads: IN EVERLASTING MEMORY OF OUR DEPARTED BROTHERS. On the day of its dedication, June 17, 1923, despite the fact that the Mohawk Trail had been recently paved, the band could not get up the mountain for the ceremony, and so the participants were forced to sing the national anthem a cappella. ⊠ *Mohawk Trail.*

Fodor's Choice There is no more beautiful stretch of highway in Berkshire County than
★ Route 2 as it traverses the town of Florida. Although the road is known as the **Mohawk Trail** all the way from Orange to Williamstown, this section around the famous Hairpin Turn is what most people think of when they use the term. The road roughly traces the route of a trail used by

the Native Americans. As automobile travel took over in the 20th century, the old route was widened. The first 13 mi—from Charlemont, through Florida, and into North Adams—opened on October 22, 1914, and were designated a "scenic tourist route" by the legislature. ⊕ *www. mohawktrail.com.*

Hiking, snowshoeing, snowmobiling, and wilderness camping are permitted in wild and rugged **Monroe State Forest.** Along the Dunbar Brook you'll discover lovely waterfalls, along with the occasional pool in which you can take a dip. From Raycroft Road, take the Spruce Hill Trail to the top of Spruce Mountain for some of the most beautiful views in the region. ⊠ *Tilda Hill Rd.* ☎ *413/339–5504* ⊕ *www.mass.gov/dem/ parks/mnro.htm* ⊠ *$5 parking fee* ☉ *Daily.*

The first roadside tourist cabins in America were erected in 1914, the same year the road was officially opened to vehicular traffic, at **Whitcomb Summit,** the highest point on the Mohawk Trail. The cabins now on the summit currently have been in operation since 1920. Rumor has it that back in the 1930s there was a small ski area with a rope tow and an open slope known as the Elk Practice Slope located at Whitcomb Summit. ⊠ *229 Mohawk Trail* ☎ *413/662–2625 or 800/547–0944* ⊕ *www. whitcombsummit.com* ☉ *Daily.*

Where to Stay

¢–$ 🏨 **Whitcomb Summit.** People stay at this motel for its eye-popping views. The motel rooms, appointed with modern furnishings, have a three-state view across the mountains of Massachusetts, Vermont, and New Hampshire. The rustic cabins at this out-of-the-way lodging have been in continuous operation since 1920. All have mountain views, but do not have refrigerators or cooking facilities. ⊠ *2229 Mohawk Trail, 01247* ☎ *413/ 662–2625 or 800/547–0944* ⊕ *www.whitcombsummit.com* ⌨ *18 rooms, 8 cabins* ⌂ *Pool* ⊟ *AE, D, MC, V* ☉ *Closed Nov.–Apr.*

Sports & the Outdoors

Hiking

The easternmost section of Florida, known as Drury, is within the borders of the **Mohawk Trail State Forest** (⊠ Rte. 2 ☎ 413/339–5504 ⊕ www.mass.gov/dem/parks/mhwk.htm ⊠ $5 parking ☉ Daily). You can hike the Mahican-Mohawk Trail, a path once used by Native Americans that connected the Connecticut and Hudson rivers, from Florida to North Adams. You can access the forest on foot from Drury Road, South County Road, or anywhere along Route 2 east of the large sign reading STEEP HILL.

Two chunks of **Savoy Mountain State Forest** (⊠ Central Shaft Rd. ☎ 413/ 663–8469 ⊕ www.mass.gov/dem/parks/svym.htm ⊠ $5 parking ☉ Daily) are in Florida. From the forest headquarters on Central Shaft Road, take Busby Trail up Spruce Hill for some beautiful views of the Hoosic River Valley and the Greylock Range. From South County Road, a trail leads up to the 2,195-foot eastern summit, which affords lovely vistas to the north and east.

Snowmobiling

Snowmobiling is permitted in the state parks in and around Florida. If you want to find the best trails, contact the **Florida Mountaineers Snowmobile Club** (⊕ www.floridamountaineers.com).

Swimming

Beautiful **North Pond** (⊠ Central Shaft Rd. ☎ 413/663–8469), in Savoy Mountain State Forest, is the town's official swimming hole. The spring-fed pond has a sandy beach and is refreshingly cold even on the hottest days. Picnic tables are available.

White-Water Rafting

The Deerfield River is one of the most remote, pristine rivers in the region. It is very popular with white-water rafting enthusiasts, and several companies lead trips along this section of the river.

Crab Apple Whitewater (⊠ Mohawk Trail ☎ 800/553–7238 ⊕ www.crabapplewhitewater.com) conducts a variety of full- or half-day rafting trips. A trip down the Monroe Bridge section of the Deerfield River includes heart-stopping rapids with such names as "Devil's Odds," "Landslide," "Dragon's Tooth," and "The Terminator." At **Moxie Outdoor Adventures/Wilderness Plus** (⊠ 1 Thunder Rd. ☎ 800/866–6943 ⊕ www.wild-rivers.com/aaa/raftingmass.html) you can take exciting white-water trips on the Dryway and the Zoar Gap on the Deerfield River. The outfitter also leads float trips on the river's quieter stretches and rents inflatable two-person "funyaks" for individual adventures.

With its own outfitting store, **Zoar Outdoor** (⊠ Rte. 2 ☎ 800/532–7483 ⊕ www.zoaroutdoor.com) is the oldest of the firms leading white-water adventures on the Deerfield River. Zoar also offers canoe and kayak clinics and instruction. Rock climbing and biking trips are also available.

Shopping

Einar and Judith Oleson produce real Florida Mountain maple syrup at **Circle J Maple Syrup** (⊠ 48 Oleson Rd. ☎ 413/663–7604). Their sugar house, where they boil sap the old-fashioned way, is a ½ mi south of Route 2. The Hoosac Tunnel crosses under the Mohawk Trail at the Eastern Summit, which is marked by the **Eastern Summit Gift Shop** (⊠ Mohawk Trail ☎ 413/663–6996). From the parking area there's a spectacular three-state view. On a clear day you can see to Mount Monadnock in southern New Hampshire.

THE PIONEER VALLEY

4

IMMERSE YOURSELF IN ART
at the Springfield Quadrangle ⇨*p.116*

STEP BACK TO COLONIAL TIMES
on a walk through Old Sturbridge Village ⇨*p.119*

LINGER OVER AN ITALIAN BRUNCH
at Spoleto in Northampton ⇨*p.132*

REDISCOVER YOUR CHILDHOOD
inside the Eric Carle Museum
of Picture Book Art ⇨*p.138*

REST YOUR HEAD UNDER A CANOPY
at Deerfield Inn ⇨*p.143*

By Dave
Simons

THE MAJESTIC CONNECTICUT RIVER, the wide and winding waterway that runs through the heart of Western Massachusetts, is home to a string of historic settlements. These communities are part of the Pioneer Valley, which formed the western frontier of New England from the early 1600s until the late 1900s. The river and its fertile banks first attracted farmers and traders, and later became a source of power and transport for the earliest industrial cities in America.

Educational pioneers came to this region as well and created a wealth of major colleges including Mt. Holyoke, America's first college for women; Amherst; Smith; Hampshire; and the University of Massachusetts. Northampton and Amherst, two hubs of higher learning, serve as the valley's cultural hubs; with the rise of the telecommunications era, both have become increasingly desirable places to live, drawing former city dwellers who relish in the ample natural scenery, sophisticated cultural venues, and lively dining and shopping.

Pioneer Valley, which gave birth to radical political thought via the Abolitionist movement and other movements, continues to wholeheartedly embrace Utopian values and left-wing politics, particularly in the towns of the upper valley, where anti-war protesters and Wal-Mart boycotters regularly make national headlines and a white-domed peace pagoda gleams in the afternoon sun. Though not nearly as strident as it was, the *Valley Advocate,* the region's weekly newspaper, still serves as a mouthpiece for the area's left-leaning inhabitants.

And yet the Pioneer Valley is anything but one-dimensional. In sharp contrast to politically energized locales like Amherst and Northampton, nearby Hadley, Hatfield, Whately, and Sunderland are soft-spoken farming communities, where aging tobacco sheds (still yielding a fine crop) stand alongside fields of corn and potatoes and where the predominantly Polish-American residents blast polka music on the way to the dump each Saturday. Springfield, the largest city in the region, lends a businesslike attitude with its knot of insurance companies and manufacturing concerns.

For a small region in a small state, the Pioneer Valley offers an amazingly diverse range of attractions throughout the year. In spring, visitors come to sample the maple syrup harvest at any of the dozens of sugaring shacks that grace the region; in fall, many of the same people return to see the hillsides transformed into a stunning blaze of red and gold. In Springfield, hoops enthusiasts from around the world relive the days of Larry Bird and Magic Johnson at the newly refurbished Basketball Hall of Fame. The colleges around Amherst, Northampton, and South Hadley host an endless parade of nationally known performing artists, political speakers, and literary heroes, as well as a full slate of collegiate sports.

EXPLORING THE PIONEER VALLEY

The middle and northernmost sections of the Pioneer Valley—known as the Upper Valley—remain mostly rural and tranquil; farms and small towns reveal typically New England architecture. To the south, Lower Valley locales such as Holyoke and Springfield are chiefly industrial but

4

Maple Sugaring

If you happen to be driving through the Pioneer Valley in early spring, you'll notice that most of the maple trees in the area are oozing a sweet colorless substance into big metal buckets. The valley's sugaring shacks are a hot ticket as folks come from miles away to get a dose of freshly prepared maple syrup, perhaps dripping over a stack of hot raspberry pancakes. There are dozens of sugar houses around the region; for a complete list, check the Massachusetts Maple Association's Web site at www.massmaple.org.

Country Fairs

The Pioneer Valley hosts its share of country fairs and festivals throughout the year, but two of the biggest and best arrive within weeks of each other every September. A five-day event beginning on Labor Day weekend, the Three County Fair in Northampton—the oldest continuously operating agricultural fair in the country—includes horse pulls, demolition derbies, and thoroughbred horse racing. In mid-September comes the really big show: the Eastern States Exposition, called the Big E, held on Memorial Avenue. One of the largest fairs in the country, it features nearly three weeks of fun including carnival rides, crafts shows, and top-drawer musical talent.

---

have come a long way toward reinventing themselves over the past decade. Residents see these as two distinct regions. The folks who live on the farms around Shelburne Falls, for example, might not find much in common with the people who work in the factories of Chicopee, even though the towns are only 40 mi apart. Arrange your trip according to your own expectations: if you fancy offbeat boutiques and wide-open spaces, you'll want to spend your time in the Upper Valley; if you prefer homemade kielbasa and interesting museums, start your trip in Springfield and work your way through the Lower Valley.

The Pioneers Valley's main thoroughfare is I–91, the major north–south highway that runs adjacent to the Connecticut River from Springfield north to the Vermont border; U.S. 5 and Route 10 run parallel to I–91. Route 116 runs north from the Holyoke region through South Deerfield before turning west toward Conway and the Berkshire foothills. Travelers heading east–west are served by Route 9, which connects the towns of Amherst, Hadley, and Northampton; the Massachusetts Turnpike, which connects Boston with Springfield; and Route 2, which connects Boston to the top of Pioneer Valley. A fine public transportation system called the Pioneer Valley Transit Authority connects most of the region with a system of bus routes.

About the Restaurants

When visiting the Pioneer Valley, be sure to bring your appetite; the region claims some of the state's most memorable restaurants. Tops is downtown Northampton, so reminiscent of Manhattan's trendy SoHo

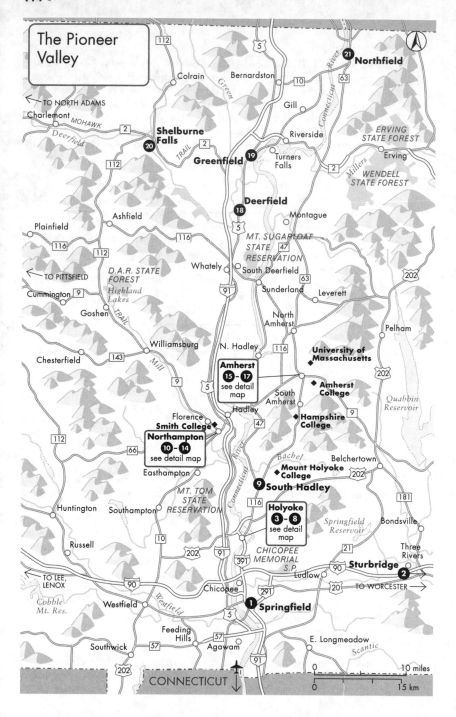

The Pioneer Valley

TO NORTH ADAMS ←

Charlemont

MOHAWK

Deerfield

Colrain

Bernardston

Gill

Riverside

Turners Falls

Northfield 21

Shelburne Falls 20

TRAIL

2

Greenfield 19

ERVING STATE FOREST

Erving

WENDELL STATE FOREST

Millers

Ashfield

Deerfield 18

Montague

Plainfield

116

112

D.A.R. STATE FOREST

Highland Lakes

TO PITTSFIELD ←

Whately

South Deerfield

MT. SUGARLOAF STATE RESERVATION 47

Sunderland

63

Leverett

202

Cummington 9

Goshen

TRAIL

Mill

Chesterfield

143

Williamsburg

9

N. Hadley

North Amherst

Pelham

University of Massachusetts

Amherst 15 - 17 see detail map

Hadley

South Amherst

Amherst College

202

Quabbin Reservoir

Florence

Smith College

Northampton 10 - 14 see detail map

66

Easthampton

47

Hampshire College

9

Bachel

Belchertown

Mount Holyoke College

202

Huntington

Southampton

MT. TOM STATE RESERVATION

9 **South Hadley**

116

Holyoke 3 - 8 see detail map

Springfield Reservoir

181

Bondsville

Russell

10

202

91

391

CHICOPEE MEMORIAL S.P.

21

Three Rivers

TO LEE, LENOX ←

90

Westfield

Chicopee

Ludlow

291

90 **Sturbridge** 2

20 TO WORCESTER →

Cobble Mt. Res.

Westfield

5

1 **Springfield**

Feeding Hills

57

E. Longmeadow

Scantic

Southwick

57

Agawam

202

91

CONNECTICUT

0   10 miles

0   15 km

neighborhood that locals call it Noho. Here you'll find everything from Chinese to Cajun. The homemade kielbasa and thin-crust pizza made in the Springfield area are well worth the trip. While exploring the back-roads of the Upper Valley, you'll find scores of bistros, bakeries, and sand-wich shops; during harvest season, be sure to pull up to a local farm stand for a bag of locally grown apples or a freshly baked pumpkin pie.

About the Hotels

You'll find a wide range of lodgings throughout the Pioneer Valley, many at prices that won't empty your wallet. Chain hotels can be found along the main thoroughfares from Springfield to Greenfield, offering ameni-ties such as indoor pools, fitness facilities, and the like, while the north-ern part of the region offers smaller inns and B&Bs, many of which have great views of the surrounding countryside.

WHAT IT COSTS					
	$$$$	$$$	$$	$	¢
RESTAURANTS	over $28	$20–$28	$12–$20	$8–$12	under $8
HOTELS	over $220	$170–$220	$120–$170	$80–$120	under $80

Restaurant prices are for a main course at dinner, excluding sales tax of 5%. Hotel prices are for two people in a standard double room in high season, excluding service charges and sales tax.

Timing

The peak season in the Pioneer Valley is autumn, when college home-comings, apple and pumpkin harvesting, and brilliantly colored foliage make this one of the most populated regions in the entire Northeast. The concentration of colleges and universities means the region is bustling between September and May. With students taking a break, summer is a nice quiet time to explore the college towns of Amherst and Northamp-ton while enjoying the many summer theater and music festivals.

SPRINGFIELD

❶ *90 mi west of Boston; 30 mi north of Hartford, Connecticut.*

Springfield is perhaps best known around the country as the birthplace of basketball, the game devised by local gym instructor James Naismith in 1891 as a last-minute attempt to keep a group of unruly teenagers occu-pied during the winter months. Today, Springfield's newly designed Bas-ketball Hall of Fame stands as a permanent shrine to Naismith and the legions of basketball heroes who made the game a worldwide phenomenon.

The only bona fide metropolis in Western Massachusetts, Springfield is the largest city in the Pioneer Valley. Yet this city of 150,000 retains much of the traditional charm of its earlier years, with old-style produce mar-kets and clothing stores sandwiched in between the glossy facades of the high rise office buildings. Inspired by Northampton's thriving music scene, Springfield has many fine old buildings around Worthington

Street that host live music throughout the week. Springfield has something Northampton doesn't: its own symphony orchestra, which performs at stately Symphony Hall from autumn to spring.

The city served as a major munitions arsenal during the American Revolution. A cornerstone of American politics was laid in Springfield in 1787 when a group of Pioneer Valley farmers, led by Shutesbury's Daniel Shays, attempted to take over the local munitions armory on State Street to protest the seizure of their land for nonpayment of taxes. Though what became known as Shays' Rebellion ultimately failed, Shays' act of defiance would serve as a blueprint for generations of civil libertarians.

You can glimpse Springfield's prosperous industrial past by exploring either of the city's most noted neighborhoods: the Maple Hill Historic District, which preserves several lavish mansions from the 1840s through the 1920s, and the McKnight Historic District, where you'll see a bounty of ornate Queen Anne, Tudor Revival, and Italianate Victorian houses. Self-guided tour brochures of both neighborhoods are available at the Greater Springfield Convention & Visitors Bureau.

FodorśChoice
★

One of the most ambitious cultural venues in New England, the **Springfield Museums at the Quadrangle** includes four impressive facilities. The most modest of them, the **Connecticut Valley Historical Museum** contains mostly quirky temporary exhibits such as a collection of toy soldiers or a room full of locally made violins. The main draw here is the in-depth genealogical library, where folks from all over the world come to research their family trees. The must-see **George Walter Vincent Smith Art Museum** houses a fascinating private art collection that includes 19th-century American paintings by Frederic Church and Albert Bierstadt. A Japanese antiquities room is filled with armor, textiles, and porcelain, as well as carved jade and rock-crystal snuff bottles. The **Museum of Fine Arts** has paintings by Gauguin, Monet, Renoir, Degas, Winslow Homer, and J. Alden Weir, as well as 18th-century American paintings and contemporary works by Georgia O'Keeffe, Frank Stella, and George Bellows. Rotating exhibits are open throughout the year. The **Springfield Science Museum** has an Exploration Center of touchable displays, the oldest American-built planetarium, an extensive collection of stuffed and mounted animals, dinosaur exhibits, and the African Hall, through which you can take an interactive tour of that continent's flora and fauna. The latest addition to the Quadrangle is the **Dr. Seuss National Memorial,** an installation of five bronze statues set around the grounds and depicting scenes from Theodore Geisel's famously whimsical children's books. Born in Springfield on 1904, Geisel was inspired by the animals at Forest Park Zoo, where his father served as director. The statues include a 4-foot Lorax and a 10-foot Yertle the Turtle. ⊠ *220 State St., at Chestnut St.* ☎ *413/263–6800* ⊕ *www. quadrangle.org* ▦ *$7* ⊘ *Wed.–Fri. noon–5, weekends 11–4.*

FodorśChoice
★

In 2003, nearly 20 years after it first opened its doors along the banks of the Connecticut River, the **Naismith Memorial Basketball Hall of Fame—** dedicated to Springfield's own Dr. James Naismith, who invented the game in 1891—opened a greatly improved complex right next door. This

80,000-square-foot facility includes a soaring domed arena, dozens of high-tech interactive exhibits, and video footage and interviews with former players. The Honors Rings pay tribute to the hall's nearly 250 enshrinees. ⊠ *1150 W. Columbus Ave.* ☎ *413/781–6500 or 877/446–6752* ⊕ *www.hoophall.com* ≊ *$16* ☺ *Daily 9:30–5:30.*

Before Harley-Davidsons ruled the road, the greatest thing on two wheels was the Indian Motorcycle. The **Indian Motorcycle Museum,** in one of the original production buildings, pays homage to the 50-year reign of the Indian Motorcycle Manufacturing Company. ⊠ *Hendee St.* ☎ *413/737–2624* ≊ *$5* ☺ *Open daily 10–4.*

☺ **Forest Park,** Sprinfield's leafy 735-acre retreat, is an ideal retreat for families. Hiking paths wind through the trees, paddleboats navigate Porter Lake, and a hungry ducks float on a small pond. The zoo where Theodore Geisel—better known as Dr. Suess—found inspiration for his children's books is home to nearly 200 animals, from black bears and bobcats to emus, lemurs, and wallabies. ⊠ *Off Sumner Ave.* ☎ *413/787–6461 or 413/733–2251* ≊ *$4.50* ☺ *Zoo: mid-Apr.–Labor Day, daily 10–5; Labor Day–mid-Nov., daily 10–4; mid-Nov.–mid-Apr., weekends 10–3.*

need a break?
Springfield's South End is the home of a lively Little Italy that supports some excellent restaurants, as well as **La Fiorentina Pastry Shop** (⊠ 883 Main St. ☎ 413/732–3151), which has been doling out heavenly pastries, butter cookies, and coffees since the 1940s.

☺ Four mi southwest of Springfield is **Six Flags New England,** the region's largest theme park and water park. It contains more than 160 rides and shows, including Batman–The Dark Knight floorless roller coaster and Superman–Ride of Steel, the tallest and fastest steel coaster on the East Coast. ⊠ *1623 Main St., Agawam* ☎ *413/786–9300* ⊕ *www.sixflags. com* ≊ *$40* ☺ *Late Apr.–late May and early Sept.–late Oct., Fri. and Sat. 10–10; late May–early Sept., daily 10–10.*

Where to Eat

$$–$$$ ✕ **School Street Bistro.** It's worth the trip 15 mi west to Westfield to sample first-rate contemporary cooking at this stately downtown eatery housed in a vintage 19th-century factory building. Top picks include Black Angus tenderloin with a mushroom-Gorgonzola demiglace and grilled salmon with a port wine reduction. Thin-crust pizzas and tasty salads are also available. ⊠ *29 School St.* ☎ *413/562–8700* ☐ *AE, D, MC, V* ☺ *No lunch weekends.*

$–$$$ ✕ **Nadina's Café Lebanon.** This casual eatery, a short walk down the hill from the Springfield Museums at the Quadrangle, serves such authentic Lebanese dishes as lamb shank simmered in tomato sauce, charbroiled swordfish kabobs, and falafel with sesame sauce. There's live belly-dancing on some Saturday evenings. ⊠ *141 State St.* ☎ *413/737–7373* ☐ *AE, D, DC, MC, V* ☺ *No lunch weekends.*

$–$$$ ✕ **Student Prince and Fort Restaurant.** Named after a 1930s operetta, this downtown restaurant has been a local favorite since 1935. People keep coming back for the classic German cuisine—bratwurst, schnitzel, and sauerbraten—as well as for the smoked pork chops with apple sauce and the broiled shrimp with garlic butter. As you wait, gaze at the collection of more than 2,000 beer steins. ⊠ *8 Fort St.* ☎ *413/734-7475* ▭ *D, DC, MC, V.*

★ $ ✕ **Red Rose.** Outfitted with massive chandeliers and revolving dessert displays, the Red Rose is a big, brassy eatery where everyone from couples to huge parties can feel right at home. Go for the light and sumptuous eggplant Parmesan, one of the best items on the menu of Italian favorites. If you order a pizza, you might as well ask for a box—you'll never finish it in one sitting. ⊠ *1060 Main St.* ☎ *413/739-8510* ▭ *AE, MC, V.*

$ ✕ **Theodore's.** "Booze, blues, and barbecue" are the specialties of this popular downtown restaurant, which stays open until 2 AM on weekends. You can dine saloon-style in the booths near the bar or in a small adjacent dining room. The decor is yard-sale chic, with framed old-time advertisements lending a whimsical air. The kitchen turns out standard pub fare—nothing special, but more people come here for the blues than the burgers. ⊠ *201 Worthington St.* ☎ *413/736-6000* ▭ *AE, MC, V* ⊘ *No lunch weekends.*

Where to Stay

$$ ✕🏨 **Springfield Marriott.** One of the few business hotels in the Pioneer Valley, the Springfield Marriott makes a good base for vacationers, especially on weekends when the rates drop precipitously. Contemporary furnishings adorn the rooms, some of which face the Connecticut River. The restaurant, Currents ($$–$$$$), is far better than you might expect of a chain hotel. Dine on such creative contemporary dishes as Block Island swordfish with sweet-potato fries, citrus pesto, and ginger, garlic, and lime marinade. ⊠ *Boland and Columbus Sts., 01115* ☎ *413/ 781-7111 or 800/229-9290* 🖷 *413/731-8932* ⊕ *www.marriott.com* ⇗ *264 rooms* ⚭ *Restaurant, room service, indoor pool, health club, hot tub, sauna, 2 bars, business services, parking (fee)* ▭ *AE, D, DC, MC, V* ⦿ *CP.*

$–$$ 🏨 **Sheraton Springfield Monarch Place.** The Sheraton's atrium-style lobby is an impressive sight; the views from the west-facing club-level suites are gorgeous. This landmark hotel is convenient to the Basketball Hall of Fame, Six Flags New England, and all of Springfield's downtown points of interest. Tip: Try the impeccable cheeseburgers from the lobby-level Peter's Grille. ⊠ *1 Monarch Pl., 01115* ☎ *413/263-2078* 🖷 *413/734- 3249* ⊕ *www.sheraton-springfield.com* ⇗ *325 rooms, 16 suites* ⚭ *Restaurant, pub, in-room data ports, some in-room hot tubs, some refrigerators, gym, sauna* ▭ *AE, DC, MC, V.*

Nightlife & the Arts
Nightlife

Worthington Street, the city's nightlife center, is lined with bars, clubs, and cafés. **Caffeine's,** (⊠ 254 Worthington St. ☎ 413/731-5282), a contemporary bar and restaurant, hosts live music duos and combos on weekends.

The Pour House (✉ 280 Worthington St. ☎ 413/732–7934), a beautifully refurbished vintage pub, frequently stages such regional faves as NRBQ and the Ray Mason Band. If you're in the mood for a fresh Guinness draft, stop off at **Tilly's Irish Pub** (✉ 1390 Main St. ☎ 413/732–3613), another weekend live-music haunt.

The Arts

The city's nonprofit theater company, **CityStage** (✉ 1 Columbus Center ☎ 413/733–2500 or 413/788–7033), showcases musicals, dramas, and comedies. Performing at Symphony Hall, the **Springfield Symphony Orchestra** (✉ 75 Market Pl. ☎ 413/733–2291) gives concerts year-round.

Shopping

In the heart of downtown Springfield, **Tower Square** (✉ 1500 Main St. ☎ 413/733–2171 ⊕ www.visittowersquare.com) is home to a wealth of thriving retailers, among them Hannoush Jewelers, Edwards Books, and Longmeadow Flowers & Gifts, and also includes the CityWalk Cafe, a full-service food court.

STURBRIDGE

❷ *34 mi east of Springfield; 55 mi southwest of Boston; 20 mi southwest of Worcester.*

On the western edge of the Pioneer Valley, Sturbridge is a faithful mockup of an early-19th-century New England town. The town's prime location makes it a popular stop for travelers. Its main thoroughfare, U.S. 20, has a bounty of art galleries, antiques shops, and country inns.

Incorporated in 1738, Sturbridge was initially a region rich in lead, and paved the way for the first lead mine to be worked in the United States. In the years that followed, Sturbridge, like many Massachusetts towns, saw an influx of manufacturing concerns, including an abundance of sawmills, cotton mills, and grist mills.

Fodor'sChoice Sturbridge is best known for **Old Sturbridge Village,** one of the country's
★ finest re-creations of a Colonial-era village. Modeled on an early-19th-century New England town, the 200-acre site has more than 40 historic buildings that were moved here from other towns. Some of the village houses are filled with canopy beds and elaborate furnishings; in the simpler, single-story cottages, interpreters wearing period costumes demonstrate home-based crafts like spinning, weaving, and shoe-making. The village store contains an amazing variety of goods necessary for everyday life in the 19th century. There are several industrial buildings, including a working sawmill. On the informative boat ride along the Quinebaug River, you can learn about river life in 19th-century New England and catch a glimpse of ducks, geese, turtles, and other local wildlife. ✉ *1 Old Sturbridge Village Rd.* ☎ *508/347-3362 or 800/ 733-1830 ⊕ www.osv.org ☜ $20 ۞ Apr.–Oct., daily 9–5.*

At **Hyland Orchard & Brewery,** you can pick your own peaches, apples, and other fruit, depending on the season. Take a tour of the state-of-the-art brewery, check out the farm animals, or join a scenic hayride in the fall. ✉ *199 Arnold Rd.* ☎ *508/347–7500* ⊕ *www.hylandbrew.com* ▣ *Free* ⊙ *Daily.*

> **off the beaten path**
>
> **WORCESTER ART MUSEUM** – This museum provides a comprehensive survey of art from around the world, with especially strong concentrations of Islamic, pre-Columbian, Chinese, and Korean works. Highlights in the European galleries include works by William Hogarth and Paul Gauguin. American highlights include paintings by Copley, Cole, and Edward Hicks and silver service by Paul Revere. The museum is about 20 mi northeast of Sturbridge. ✉ *55 Salisbury St., Worcester* ☎ *508/799–4406* ⊕ *www. worcesterart.org* ▣ *$8* ⊙ *Wed., Fri., and Sun. 11–5, Thurs. 11–8, Sat. 10–5.*

Where to Eat

$$–$$$ ✕ **Cedar Street.** This eatery, housed in a modest but charming Victorian
Fodor'sChoice house, sits just off Main Street. Inside, candlelit tables decked with
★   fresh flowers fill the intimate dining room. The menu tends toward the simple but creative, with an emphasis on healthful cooking. Choices include handmade parsnip ravioli with walnut pesto as well as molasses-brined pork chop with a mango-rum glaze, fried plantains, and a ginger-coconut custard. ✉ *12 Cedar St.* ☎ *508/347–5800* ▭ *AE, MC, V* ⊙ *Closed Sun. No lunch.*

$$–$$$ ✕ **Salem Cross Inn.** On a verdant 600-acre estate, the Salem Cross occupies a Colonial building built by the grandson of Peregrine White, the first child born on the *Mayflower.* It's a fitting legacy for a restaurant that prides itself on re-creating the Early American dining experience, both in terms of decor and dishes. A favorite event is the occasional Drover's Roasts, when prime rib is spiced and slow-roasted for hours in a fieldstone pit. A lavish and lengthy feast follows. Other times you'll find traditional American and Continental fare, such as broiled lamb chops and baked stuffed fillet of sole with lobster sauce. The eatery is 12 mi northwest of Sturbridge. ✉ *Rte. 9, West Brookfield* ☎ *508/867–8337* ▭ *AE, D, MC, V* ⊙ *Closed Mon. No lunch Sat.*

$$–$$$ ✕ **Tavern at Old Sturbridge Village.** Opposite the visitor center at Old Sturbridge Village, this eatery is a window to the past. The decor recalls a vintage taproom, with wide-plank floors, authentic period-style lighting fixtures, and re-created 19th-century cutlery. The menu, however, tends toward the nouvelle, with such entrées as roast duck with cranberry-barley hash, baby beets, and an apple-brandy sauce. Fireplace-cooking demonstrations are occasionally hosted. ✉ *1 Old Sturbridge Village Rd.* ☎ *508/347–0395* ▭ *AE, D, MC, V.*

Where to Stay

$–$$ ✕▭ **Publick House Historic Inn.** Each of the three inns and the motel in
Fodor'sChoice this complex has its own character. The 17 rooms in the Publick House,
★   which dates to 1771, are Colonial in design, with uneven plank floors

and canopy beds. The neighboring Chamberlain House consists of larger suites, and the Country Motor Lodge has more modern rooms. The Crafts Inn, about a mile away, has rooms with four-poster beds and painted wood paneling. The big, bustling Publick House restaurant ($$$–$$$$) serves traditional Yankee fare with an inventive spin— pecan-dusted scrod, pan-seared barbecued scallops with bok choy and blue cheese–shallot–mashed potatoes. Lighter fare is served in two taverns and a bake shop. ⊠ *Rte. 131, 01566* ☎ *508/347–3313 or 800/782–5425* 🖷 *508/347–5073* ⊕ *www.publickhouse.com* ⇖ *116 rooms, 9 suites* ⚘ *4 restaurants, tennis court, pool, shuffleboard, cross-country skiing, bar, playground, meeting rooms* ⊟ *AE, D, DC, MC, V.*

$$ 🏨 **Sturbridge Country Inn.** The atmosphere at this 1840s Greek-Revival farmhouse on Sturbridge's busy Main Street is between that of a country inn and a plush business hotel. Guest rooms—all with working gas fireplaces and whirlpool tubs—have reproduction antiques; the best is the top-floor suite. ⊠ *530 Main St., 01566* ☎ *508/347–5503* 🖷 *508/347–5319* ⊕ *www.sturbridgecountryinn.com* ⇖ *6 rooms, 3 suites* ⚘ *In-room hot tubs, hot tub, bar* ⊟ *AE, D, MC, V* ⫟◉⫠ *CP.*

$$ 🏨 **Sturbridge Host.** This hotel across the street from Old Sturbridge Village has luxuriously appointed bedrooms with Colonial decor and reproduction furnishings. Many rooms have fireplaces, and some have balconies or patios. Dinner is served nightly in Portobella's Italian Restaurant; the Oxhead Tavern serves a lunch and dinner pub menu, which includes club sandwiches and burgers. ⊠ *U.S. 20, 01566* ☎ *508/347–7393 or 800/582–3232* 🖷 *508/347–3944* ⊕ *www.sturbridgehosthotel.com* ⇖ *181 rooms, 39 suites* ⚘ *2 restaurants, miniature golf, pool, health club, sauna, boating, fishing, basketball, racquetball, bar, video game room, meeting room* ⊟ *AE, D, DC, MC, V.*

Nightlife & the Arts

Nightlife
Check out up-and-coming rockers and comedians trying out new material at **The Loft at Sturbridge Isle** (⊠ 400 Rte. 15 ☎ 508/347–2222 ⊕ www.sturbridgeloft.com). Weekend shows begin at 8:30 PM.

The Arts
Founded in 1994 by local English teacher Ed Cornely, the **Stageloft Repertory Theater** (⊠ 450A Main St. ☎ 508/347–9005 ⊕ www.stageloft.com), the region's lone professional theater guild, gives theater buffs a full lineup of comedies and tragedies, from Shakespearean classics to contemporary fare.

Sports & the Outdoors

When state officials decided a reservoir was needed to provide drinking water for the metropolitan Boston area, they scoped out a remote area in Western Massachusetts where the towns of Dana, Enfield, Greenwich, and Prescott stood. All four towns were subsequently taken by eminent domain and flooded using waters from the Swift and Ware rivers.

★ The **Quabbin Reservoir** was completed in the early 1940s, becoming the country's largest artificial lake. In addition to the reservoir (which spans

39 square mi), visitors can enjoy the beautiful views from the Quabbin Visitor Center, which documents the construction of the reservoir and contains historical documents about the flooded towns. There are numerous hiking trails, bird observation posts, and picnic areas as well. ⊠ *Rte. 9, Belchertown* ☎ *413/323–7221* ⊙ *Daily 9–4:30.*

Traversed by 10 mi of trails, the 1,400-acre **Wells State Park** is very popular with hikers. Walker Pond provides fishing and boating opportunities as well. ⊠ *Rte. 49* ☎ *508/347–9257* ⊕ *www.state.ma.us/dem/ parks/well.htm* ▨ *$2* ⊙ *May–Oct., daily.*

Shopping

A few miles west of Sturbridge, one of New England's top antiques-shopping destinations is **J&J Productions Antique & Collectibles** (⊠ U.S. 20, Brimfield ☎ 413/245–3436 ⊕ www.jandj-brimfield.com). It presents one of the region's most popular outdoor antiques shows three times per year: in mid-May, mid-July, and over Labor Day weekend. Quality antiques, fine estate jewelry, and precious glass from around the world can be found at **Showcase Antique Center** (⊠ U.S. 20 ☎ 508/347–7190 ⊕ www. showcaseantique.com)

The **Seraph** (⊠ 420 Main St. ☎ 508/347–2241) sells high-quality reproduction furniture, all fashioned using period materials and designs. You'll also find tin, pewter, and blown-glass accessories crafted in the Early America traditions. **Wild Bird Crossing** (⊠ 4 Cedar St. ☎ 508/347–2473) carries every imaginable accoutrement for bird-watching, including birdbaths, binoculars, and books.

HOLYOKE

❸–❽ *7 mi north of Springfield.*

The Lower Valley begins with the city of Holyoke, midway between Springfield and Northampton. The city takes its name from Captain Elizur Holyoke, the 17th-century explorer whose predominantly Irish followers established a settlement that would come to be known as Ireland Parish. Holyoke's proximity to the Connecticut River—in particular the swift current from nearby Hadley Falls—led to the construction of a series of dams and canals for the purpose of supplying water power to the region, touching off a major industrial boom. Well into the early 20th century, Holyoke prospered on the strength of its numerous manufacturing facilities, which produced, among other things, high-grade paper, for which Holyoke would earn it the nickname "Paper City."

In recent years, Holyoke has seen a strong economic comeback thanks to a robust local economy featuring microbreweries, publishers, and high-tech companies. Working hard to overcome its days as a textile-factory town, Holyoke has restored its downtown, which has one of the most impressive collections of 19th-century commercial architecture in the country. A stroll along the streets near Heritage State Park reveals some wonderfully innovative adaptations of vintage mill and factory buildings into condos, offices, and retail space. And the town continues

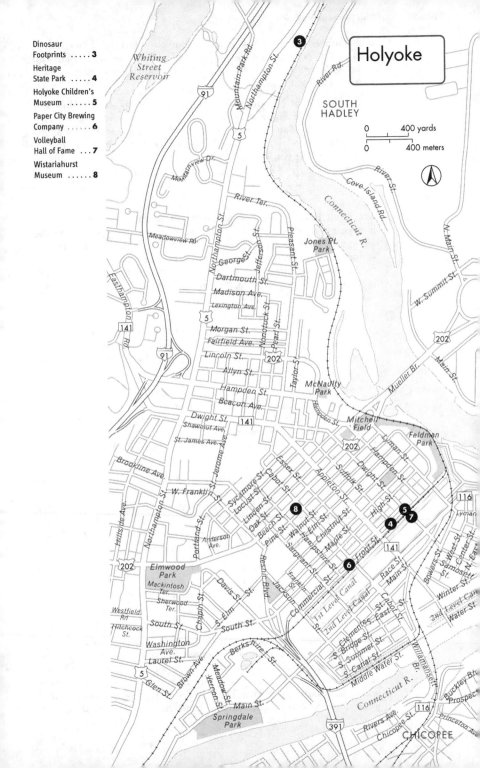

Holyoke

SOUTH
HADLEY

CHICOPEE

reimagining itself. Currently nearing completion is the Holyoke Canal-walk, a 2-mi pedestrian walkway that will traverse the city's canals and serve as a gateway to the Holyoke Arts Corridor, a consortium of local museums and galleries.

While Dr. James Naismith was busy inventing basketball down in Springfield, in Holyoke William G. Morgan was formulating his own sport, which he dubbed "volleyball." Today, Holyoke—known as the "birthplace of volleyball"—pays homage to Morgan with its Volleyball Hall of Fame. If you happen to be in town in mid-March, be sure to line up for the city's Holyoke St. Patrick's Day Parade.

What to See

☾ ❸ Check out 134 separate **Dinosaur Footprints,** dating back some 190 million years, which have been preserved in sandstone slabs along the banks of the Connecticut River. Western Massachusetts was a favorite stomping ground (pardon the expression) for prehistoric creatures like the *Eubrontes giganteus* and *Anchisauripus silliman*. ⊠ *U.S. 5, 2 mi north of Holyoke* ☎ *413/684–0148* ⊕ *www.thetrustees.org/dinosaurfootprints* ▭ *Free* ☉ *Apr.–Oct., daily sunrise–sunset.*

☾ ❹ The visitor center in **Heritage State Park** tells the story of this papermaking community, the nation's first planned industrial town. Kids can ride a vintage merry-go-round with 48 hand-carved, hand-painted antique wooden horses. ⊠ *221 Appleton St.* ☎ *413/534–1723* ▭ *Free* ☉ *Tues.–Sun. 10:30–4:30.*

☾ ❺ The **Holyoke Children's Museum,** which sits beside Heritage State Park in a converted mill, is packed with hands-on games and educational toys. Within the museum are a state-of-the-art TV station, a multitiered interactive exhibit on the human body, a giant bubble maker, and a sand pendulum. ⊠ *444 Dwight St.* ☎ *413/536–5437* ▭ *$4* ☉ *Tues.–Sat. 9:30–4:30, Sun. noon–5.*

❻ Founded a decade ago by local brewmeister Rick Quackenbush, **Paper City Brewing Company** brews a variety of homespun ales, from its flagship Ireland Parish Golden Ale to such rotating selections as Winter Palace Wee Heavy and Cabot Street Summer Wheat. Tours of the facility, complete with tastes of the merchandise, are given weekdays. ⊠ *108 Cabot St.* ☎ *413/535–1588* ▭ *Free* ☉ *Weekdays 9–5.*

❼ Volleyball was invented at the Holyoke YMCA in 1895, and the **Volleyball Hall of Fame** pays homage to the sport with informative videos and displays of memorabilia. Interactive games let you test your skills. ⊠ *444 Dwight St.* ☎ *413/536–0926* ⊕ *www.volleyhall.org* ▭ *$4* ☉ *Weekends noon–4:30.*

❽ The **Wistariahurst Museum,** the mansion once owned by silk magnate William Skinner, peers into the lives of one of Pioneer Valley's most prosperous citizens. This 1874 Second Empire home, with a sweeping Beaux Arts staircase and elaborately landscaped grounds, overflows with priceless antiques and artworks. The house's leather wall coverings and meticulous woodwork remain perfectly intact. ⊠ *238 Cabot St.* ☎ *413/*

534–2216 ✉ *Donation suggested* ⊙ *Apr.–Oct., Wed. and weekends 1–5; Nov.–Mar., Wed. and weekends noon–4.*

Where to Eat

$$–$$$ ✕ **Delaney House.** A meal at this popular eatery always feels like an event, partly because of the elegantly set tables and tasteful Victorian decor, and partly because of the music that flows from the comfortable lounge. The biggest plus is the food, beautifully presented in ample portions. Most choices are standard American fare: prime rib, sea scallops, and rack of lamb. Among the more ambitious creations are the shellfish lasagna and the veal sautéed with lobster, artichokes, mushrooms, and couscous. Well-known jazz musicians often play at the restaurant, which is about 5 mi north of downtown. ✉ *U.S. 5, Smith's Ferry* ☎ *413/532–1800* ☱ *AE, D, DC, MC, V* ⊙ *No lunch.*

$–$$ ✕ **Seamus O'Reilly's.** Pioneer Valley dwellers come from miles around to savor the flavor of this restaurant's no-nonsense Irish stew, hearty Pot 'o Gold Pie (creamy chicken stew with a light pastry crust), and many other Emerald Isle classics. And, of course, there's Guinness on tap. ✉ *80 Jarvis Ave.* ☎ *413/552–3311* ☱ *AE, MC, V.*

Where to Stay

$ ✕🏠 **Yankee Pedlar Inn.** Antique furnishings and four-poster beds fill many of the charming guest rooms at this sprawling country inn at a busy crossroads in Holyoke. The elaborate Victorian bridal suite is heavy on lace and curtains; the beamed carriage house has rustic appointments and simple canopy beds. Chicken potpie and hazelnut-crusted salmon with a raspberry vinaigrette are among the dishes served in the Grill Room ($–$$$), which has burgundy walls and is accented with stained glass. The more casual Oyster Bar hosts musicians many nights. ✉ *1866 Northampton St., 01040* ☎ *413/532–9494* 🖶 *413/536–8877* ⊕ *www.yankeepedlar.com* ⌨ *21 rooms, 7 suites* ⚐ *Restaurant, bar, nightclub, meeting room* ☱ *AE, D, DC, MC, V* ⚑ *CP.*

$ 🏠 **Carlson Inn & Suites.** Adjacent to the Delaney House, this attractive chain hotel has large and immaculate rooms, many with fireplaces and room to sleep four to six guests. A free morning paper is one of the niceties. The hotel, about 5 mi from both Holyoke and Northampton, is across from the Connecticut River and close to Mt. Tom State Reservation. ✉ *U.S. 5, Smith's Ferry, 01040* ☎ *413/533–2100 or 800/456–4000* 🖶 *413/539–9761* ⊕ *www.countryinns.com* ⌨ *36 rooms, 25 suites* ⚐ *Some kitchens, indoor pool, health club, hot tub, Internet* ☱ *AE, D, DC, MC, V* ⚑ *CP.*

Nightlife & the Arts

A favored haunt for regional jazz performers, the **Red Cat Café** (✉ 274 High St. ☎ 413/532–5559) presents live music on Thursday and Friday evening.

Sports & the Outdoors

A 3⅓-mi round-trip hike at the **Mt. Tom State Reservation** (✉ U.S. 5 ☎ 413/527–4805) leads to the summit, whose sheer basalt cliffs were formed by volcanic activity 200 million years ago. At the top are excellent views of the Berkshires. In winter, this is a favorite spot for cross-country skiers. The preserve is about 5 mi north of Holyoke.

Shopping

A restored 19th-century wood-and-brick factory building, **Open Square** (✉ 250 Open Square Way ☎ 413/532–5057) houses a number of charming boutiques and galleries. Enjoy a steaming cup of cappuccino in the Square Café. This was part of the first industrial complex in Holyoke's history.

SOUTH HADLEY

⑨ *5 mi north of Holyoke.*

South Hadley, like Amherst, was originally a portion of Hadley. It became the "South Precinct of Hadley" in the early 1700s, then finally the town of South Hadley in 1775. The southernmost section of town that faces the fast-moving Connecticut River is known as South Hadley Falls; it was here in the early 1800s that the nation's first-ever ship-worthy canal was established, making the region a busy shipping center well into the late 19th century. The canal gave birth to one of the most notable inventions in Pioneer Valley history: the so-called "inclined plane," a device that was used to transport boats across the falls from the lower canal into the upper basin (the inclined plane was retired after 10 years of service when proper locks were finally constructed).

A sprawling community at the base of the Holyoke Mountain Range, South Hadley is home to Mount Holyoke College. Formed in 1836 as the Mount Holyoke Female Seminary, Mount Holyoke (a member of New England's Seven Sisters schools) is the backbone of the local economy, a draw for the boutiques, theaters, restaurants, and other establishments within the Village Commons near the main campus on College Street. Popular performing artists regularly grace the stage at Mount Holyoke's Chapin Auditorium.

South Hadley's hilly terrain means there are plenty of wonderful vistas. Of particular note is Joseph Skinner State Park, midway between South Hadley Commons and Hadley, where visitors who ascend the famed Summit House atop Holyoke Mountain are afforded the finest view in the entire Valley.

At the top of Mount Holyoke, **J.A. Skinner State Park** provides some of the most stunning views of the Connecticut River Valley. The 390-acre park also is a prime spot for birding, picnicking, and hiking. After surviving several fires and the devastating hurricane of 1938, the Summit House, a former hotel, was donated to the state by owner Joseph Skinner. Today it serves as an observation deck with one of the most memorable views in all of New England. ✉ *Rte. 47* ☎ *413/586–0350* ⊕ *www.mass.gov/dem/parks/skin.htm* ☾ *Daily dawn–dusk.*

Founded in 1837, **Mount Holyoke College** was the first women's college in the United States. Among the college's alumnae are poet Emily Dickinson and playwright Wendy Wasserstein. The handsome wooded campus, encompassing two lakes and lovely walking or riding trails, was landscaped by Frederick Law Olmsted. ⊠ *Rte. 116* ☎ *413/538–2000.*

The **Mount Holyoke College Art Museum** contains some 11,000 works including Asian, European, and American paintings and sculpture. ⊠ *Lower Lake Rd.* ☎ *413/538–2245* ⊕ *www.mtholyoke.edu/offices/artmuseum* ☞ *Free* ☉ *Tues.–Fri. 11–5, weekends 1–5.*

Where to Eat

$–$$ ✕ **Fedora's Tavern.** A favorite place with college students between classes and shoppers perusing the shops at the Village Commons, this dark and cozy English pub serves up a wide range of pub grub. Try the Maine crab cakes, Portobello mushroom pasta, or a cup of what may be the best chili in the valley. ⊠ *25 College St.* ☎ *413/534–8222* ☐ *AE, D, MC, V.*

$ ✕ **Dockside Restaurant at Brunelle's Marina.** The Connecticut River and nearby Holyoke Mountain Range provide the backdrop for this enjoyable South Hadley haunt, which has a casual yet comfortable dining room. It serves up basic American fare, including steaks, seafood, and sandwiches. ⊠ *1 Alvord St.* ☎ *413/536–2342* ⊕ *www.brunelles.com* ☐ *MC, V.*

Where to Stay

$–$$ ☷ **An Old Indian Trail Bed & Breakfast.** A short drive from South Hadley, this sprawling bed-and-breakfast near the base of the Holyoke Mountain Range has three sun-drenched cottages replete with cozy quilts, comforters, and floral wall hangings. ⊠ *664 Amherst Rd., Granby 01033* ☎ *413/467–3528* ⇄ *3 rooms* ⌂ *Dining room, in-room VCRs, kitchenettes* ☐ *AE, D, DC, MC, V.*

$–$$ ☷ **Grandmary's Bed & Breakfast.** With three rooms from which to choose—the Primrose, the Princess Rose, and the Petit Rose—this soothing Victorian-era B&B fills up fast, especially during high season. The location, adjacent to the Mount Holyoke College campus and the shops of the Village Commons, couldn't be better. ⊠ *11 Hadley St., 01075* ☎ *413/533–7381* ⊕ *www.grandmarys.com* ⇄ *3 rooms* ⌂ *No kids under 10* ☐ *No credit cards.*

Nightlife & the Arts

Each summer at Mount Holyoke College, **Musicorda** (⊠ Wooley Circle ☎ 413/493–1544) presents a series of six chamber-music performances, with faculty and special guests performing works by Haydn, Debussy, many others. A two-part Young Artist Series spotlights the considerable talents of regional up-and-comers. Performances are held in the acoustically superb Chapin Auditorium.

Shopping

In addition to stocking more than 50,000 new and used titles, **The Odyssey Bookshop** (⊠ 9 College St. ☎ 413/534–7307 ⊕ www.odysseybks.

com) has a packed schedule of readings and book signings by locally and nationally known authors. It's open Monday to Saturday 10 to 8, Sunday noon to 5.

The **Hadley Antique Center** (✉ 227 Russell St. ☎ 413/586–4093) contains more than 70 different booths. The **Village Commons** (✉ College St.), across from Mount Holyoke College, is an outdoor mall with a movie theater, several restaurants, and many shops stocking everything from lingerie to handmade picture frames.

NORTHAMPTON

⑩–⑭ *10 mi northwest of South Hadley.*

The cultural center of Western Massachusetts is without a doubt the city of Northampton, whose vibrant downtown scene reminds many people of lower Manhattan (hence its nickname, "Noho"). No wonder John Villani ranked Northampton at the top in his book *The 100 Best Small Art Towns in America.* Packed with interesting eateries, lively clubs, and offbeat boutiques, the city attracts artsy types, academics, activists, lesbians and gays, and just about anyone else seeking the culture and sophistication of a big metropolis but the friendliness and easy pace of a small town.

Along a winding stretch of the Connecticut River, Northampton was settled in 1654 and became a trade and marketing center during the 18th century. Revivalist preacher Jonathan Edwards, whose ministry inspired the "Great Awakening" of the 1740s, became the first in a long line of historical figures to emerge from Northampton. In the mid-1800s, slave-turned-activist Sojourner Truth helped found the Northampton Association, a radical abolitionist group organized around the communal silk mills of nearby Florence that included movers like Frederick Douglass and Wendell Phillips.

Beginning in the mid-19th century, Northampton became a magnet for scores of artistic, literary, and political figures, among them poet Ralph Waldo Emerson and opera singer Jenny Lind, who dubbed Northampton the "paradise of America" following a visit in 1851 (inspiring the oft-used moniker "Paradise City"). The city's most notable inhabitant was Calvin Coolidge, a former city councilman who served as the country's 30th president from 1923 to 1928 and then returned to Northampton to live out his years in the the Beeches, a grand 12-room mansion on a hill overlooking downtown.

With its sidewalk cafés, interesting shops, street-corner musicians, downtown Northampton is a veritable feast for the senses. On weekends and holidays, finding a parking space can be a challenge (and the town's parking police are particularly vigilante, so beware), but you can usually find room in the downtown parking garage or in the many municipal lots surrounding Main Street.

On the corner of Main and King streets, where you can view the grand exterior of the Hotel Northampton, popular with travelers since it opened in the 1920s. Two of Northampton's most popular music

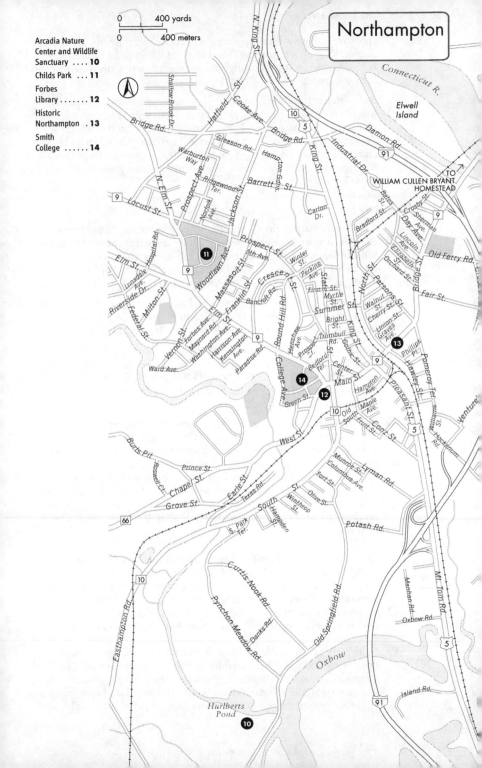

Northampton

0 — 400 yards
0 — 400 meters

spots are just a few blocks apart: the recently refurbished Calvin Theater on King Street, and the Iron Horse Music Hall on Center Street, both of which feature an ongoing retinue of nationally known performing artists.

Although you'll find an abundance of eating establishments in Northampton, it's the music scene that gives the town national prominence. Popular artists regularly make detours on their way from the Big Apple to Boston to perform locally at the Calvin Theater, the Pearl Street Nightclub, and the many other top venues. Where else can you watch Lucinda Williams let loose, then drive home through cow pastures after the show lets out?

What to See

At the wide place in the Connecticut River known as "The Oxbow" is
⑩ the Massachusetts Audubon Society's 700-acre **Arcadia Nature Center and Wildlife Sanctuary,** where you can try the hiking and nature trails and scheduled canoe trips. ⌂ *127 Combs Rd., Easthampton* ☎ *413/584–3009* 🖂 *$3* ☉ *Tues.–Sun. 9–3.*

⑪ Childs Park. A series of large lawns and two natural ponds covering 40 acres make up this public park, where an Italianate garden house overlooks a beautiful rose garden. ⌂ *Woodlawn Ave.* ☉ *May–Oct., 8–dusk.*

Northampton was the Massachusetts home of the 30th president, Calvin Coolidge. He practiced law here and served as mayor from 1910 to 1911.
⑫ At the **Forbes Library** (⌂20 West St. ☎413/587–1011 ⊕www.forbeslibrary. org/coolidge.html) the Coolidge Room contains a collection of his papers and memorabilia.

⑬ Historic Northampton maintains three houses that are open for tours: Parsons House (1730), Shepherd House (1798), and Damon House (1813). Together, they hold some 50,000 historical artifacts, including photographs, manuscripts dating back to the 17th century, fine furniture, ceramics, glass, and costumes. Exhibits in the main building chronicle the history of Northampton with some 50,000 documents, photos, and collectibles. ⌂ *46 Bridge St.* ☎ *413/584–6011* ⊕ *www.historic-northampton.org* 🖂 *$3* ☉ *Main building Tues.–Fri. 10–4; houses weekends noon–4.*

> **need a break?**

One of the many student-filled spots downtown, **Cha Cha Cha!** (⌂ 134 Main St. ☎ 413/586–7311) serves exceptionally tasty California-style burritos. On the lower level of Thorne's Marketplace, **Herrell's Ice Cream** (⌂ 8 Old South St. ☎ 413/586–9700) is famous for its chocolate pudding, vanilla malt, and cinnamon flavors of ice cream, as well as delicious homemade hot fudge.

⑭ Smith College, the nation's largest liberal arts college for women, opened its doors in 1875 (thanks to heiress Sophia Smith, who bequeathed her estate to the college's foundation). World renowned for its esteemed School of Social Work, Smith has a long list of distinguished alumnae, among them activist Gloria Steinem, chef Julia Child, and

IN THE MOVIES

N 2004, *MOVIEMAKER* MAGAZINE NAMED *Northampton one of the "Top 10 Cities for Moviemakers." This means that "Valleywood"—the name given to the town's burgeoning film industry—was suddenly a hot commodity. But the region has attracted filmmakers for decades. Leading the list of locally made films is the 1966 classic* Who's Afraid of Virginia Woolf?, *starring the volatile Elizabeth Taylor (in an Academy Award–winning role) and Richard Burton. The film was shot almost entirely in and around the faculty house at Smith College. (The building is still there, and is something of a mecca for film buffs.) Five years later, director Mike Nichols returned to make 1971's* Carnal Knowledge, *which found Candice Bergen, Art Garfunkel, Ann-Margret, and Jack Nicholson engaged in feats of sexual derring-do. Smith College once again served as backdrop.*

Lesser known was director J. Lee Thompson's 1975 film The Reincarnation of Peter Proud, *featuring Michael Sarrazin, Jennifer O'Neill, and Margot Kidder. The murder mystery included scenes shot at such local landmarks as Amherst's Lord Jeffrey Inn and Springfield's Memorial Bridge. Next came 1992's* Malice, *another dark tale shot in downtown Northampton and—you guessed it—Smith College. In 1999 Neil Jordan directed the thriller* In Dreams, *which centered on a murder committed near Quabbin Reservoir. The film includes underwater scenes of the "lost town" of Dana (flooded in the 1930s to make way for the reservoir), and footage taken inside Northampton State Hospital. A few months later the hospital would again serve as a setting, this time for* The Cider House Rules. *If you want to see what else is on the horizon, the Northampton Independent Film Festival showcases independently produced films each fall.*

writer Margaret Mitchell. One of the most serene campuses in all of New England, the college is also a leading center of political and cultural activity. Worth visiting are the **Lyman Plant House** (☎ 413/585–2740) and the **Botanic Gardens of Smith College,** which cover the entirety of Smith's 150-acre campus.

The **Smith College Museum of Art** (✉ Brown Fine Arts Center, Elm St. ☎ 413/585–2760 💲 $5, free 1st Sat. of month 10–noon ☉ Tues.–Sat. 10–4, Sun. noon–4) includes a new floor of skylighted galleries, an enclosed courtyard for performances and receptions, and a high-tech art history library. Highlights of the comprehensive permanent collection include European masterworks by Cézanne, Degas, Rodin, and Seurat. The fine representation of women's art ranges from Mary Cassatt to Alice Neel.

off the beaten path

WILLIAM CULLEN BRYANT HOMESTEAD – About 20 mi northwest of Northampton is the country estate of the 19th-century poet and author, William Cullen Bryant. In the scenic hills west of the Pioneer Valley, the wild 465-acre grounds overlook the Westfield River valley. Inside the Dutch Colonial 1783 mansion are furnishings and collectibles from Bryant's life, work, and travels. This is a great venue for bird-watching, cross-country skiing, snowshoeing, fishing, hiking, and picnics. ⊠ *207 Bryant Rd., Cummington* ☎ *413/634–2244* ⊕ *www.thetrustees.org* ⊠ *$5* ☉ *House: late June–early Sept., Fri.–Sun. 1–5; early Sept.–mid-Oct., weekends 1–5; grounds daily sunrise–sunset.*

Where to Eat

★ **$$$–$$$$** ✕ **Del Raye.** An upscale member of the esteemed Northampton dining empire that includes the more affordable but similarly outstanding Spoleto and Pizza Paradiso restaurants, this eatery is housed in a sexy, dimly lighted space with closely spaced tables and a swanky lounge. Among the world-beat creations are banana-encrusted sea scallops with dates, sweet tomatoes, and a cactus-fruit beurre rouge. Also tasty is the tangerine-glazed duck. ⊠ *1 Bridge St.* ☎ *413/586–2664* ⊟ *AE, MC, V* ☉ *No lunch.*

$$–$$$ ✕ **Spoleto.** A Noho mainstay since the '80s, busy Spoleto, in the heart
Fodor'sChoice of Northampton's downtown, delivers top-flight Italian fare. Try the veal
★ *forestierra,* sautéed veal with wild mushrooms in a peppercorn, cognac cream sauce—a can't-miss proposition. With an ever-changing menu and a cozy bar, this place is in a class by itself. Join the locals and stop by for the excellent Sunday brunch. ⊠ *50 Main St.* ☎ *413/586–6313* ⊟ *AE, DC, MC, V* ☉ *No lunch.*

$–$$ ✕ **Coolidge Park Café.** The big bay windows of the Coolidge Park Café, in the modern wing of the turn-of-the-20th-century Hotel Northampton, overlook downtown Northampton. On warm evenings, you can enjoy a cocktail from the outdoor patio; in winter you can relax by the fire in the old Wiggins Tavern while enjoying some classic American cuisine. ⊠ *36 King St.* ☎ *413/584–3100* ⊕ *www.hotelnorthampton.com* ⊟ *AE, D, DC, MC, V.*

$–$$ **Eastside Grill.** You might be 1,400 miles from Louisiana, but close your eyes while you're gobbling down this eatery's New Orleans–style barbecue shrimp and you'll swear you're in the heart of Crescent City. A Northampton mainstay, Eastside Grille presents a diverse bill of fare (which includes such old standbys as lobster corn chowder and pan-blackened rib eye); the service is consistent, and the martinis at the bar are always cold and dry. Be sure to try the superb Gorgonzola salad dressing. ⊠ *19 Strong Ave.* ☎ *413/586–3347* ⊟ *AE, D, DC, MC, V.*

$–$$ ✕ **Montana's Steak House.** Steer aficionados won't be disappointed by this steak house's serious cuts of beef. There's seafood and chicken as well. The restaurant is at the Clarion Hotel. ⊠ *1 Atwood Dr.* ☎ *413/ 586–1211* ⊕ *www.hampshirehospitality.com* ⊟ *AE, D, MC, V.*

$–$$ ✕ **Mulino's Trattoria.** In sleek quarters (which also contain the the Brasserie 40-A international restaurant downstairs and the Bishop's Lounge one flight up), this modern trattoria carefully prepares Sicilian-inspired home-style Italian food with authentic ingredients. You'll rarely taste a better carbonara sauce this side of the Atlantic, and don't overlook the smoked salmon in a lemon-caper-shallot sauce tossed with fettuccine. Portions are huge, and the wine list is extensive. ⊠ *41 Strong Ave.* ☎ *413/ 586–8900* ⊟ *AE, D, DC, MC, V* ☉ *No lunch.*

$–$$ ✕ **Northampton Brewery.** In a rambling building behind Thorne's Marketplace, this often-packed pub and microbrewery has extensive outdoor seating on an airy deck. The kitchen serves tasty comfort food, including black-bean dip, chicken-and-shrimp jambalaya, and the blackened blue burger (with blue cheese and caramelized onions). ⊠ *11 Brewster St.* ☎ *413/584–9903* ☐ *AE, D, DC, MC, V.*

Where to Stay

$$$–$$$$ 🏨 **Hotel Northampton.** Rooms at this 1927 downtown hotel include many reproductions of period antiques, including graceful four-poster beds. Many rooms have whirlpool tubs, and balconies overlooking a busy street or the parking lot. Wiggins Tavern serves standard American fare and an elaborate Sunday brunch; the Coolidge Park Café serves lighter fare. ⊠ *36 King St., 01060* ☎ *413/584–3100 or 800/547–3529* 🖷 *413/584–9455* ⊕ *www.hotelnorthampton.com* ➳ *99 rooms, 6 suites* ♿ *2 restaurants, gym, bar, meeting rooms* ☐ *AE, D, DC, MC, V* ⦿ *CP.*

$$ 🏨 **Clark Tavern Inn.** Some of the early customers at this 1742 inn included minutemen on their way to fight in Concord and Lexington. Two centuries later, when I–91 was slated to run right through the property, two dedicated preservationists saved the house by moving it. Braided rugs, canopy beds, and stencils create a homey atmosphere. Fireplaces warm two large but cozy common rooms; in summer, you can nap in the garden hammock or take a dip in the pool. Breakfast can be served fireside, on the screened-in porch, or in your room. ⊠ *98 Bay Rd., Hadley 01035* ☎ *413/586–1900* ⊕ *www.clarktaverninn.com* ➳ *3 rooms* ♿ *In-room VCRs, pool* ☐ *AE, D, DC, MC, V* ⦿ *BP.*

$ 🏨 **Autumn Inn.** Surrounded by the elegant Victorian homes of Northampton's Historic District, the Autumn Inn is an updated, two-story Colonial-style inn replete with traditional New England furnishings. It is within walking distance of Smith College (a quarter-mile down Elm Street) and is convenient to downtown Northampton locations. ⊠ *259 Elm St., 01060* ☎ *413/584–7660* ⊕ *www.hampshirehospitality.com* ➳ *29 rooms, 3 suites* ♿ *Dining room, pool* ☐ *AE, D, DC, MC, V* ⦿ *BP.*

¢–$ 🏨 **Twin Maples Bed & Breakfast.** Nearly 30 acres of fields and woods surround this 200-year-old farmhouse, which is 7 mi northwest of Northampton near the hilltop village of Williamsburg. Colonial and country antiques and reproductions furnish the small but enchanting rooms, which have restored brass beds. In winter you can watch maple-sugaring and attend a pancake breakfast. ⊠ *106 South St., Williamsburg 01096* ☎ *413/268–7925* 🖷 *413/268–7243* ⊕ *www.hamphillsbandb.com/ twinmaples* ➳ *3 rooms without bath* ♿ *No room phones, no room TVs* ☐ *AE, MC, V* ⦿ *BP.*

Nightlife & the Arts

Nightlife

For decades, the stately **Calvin Theater** (⊠ 19 King St. ☎ 413/586–8686) was a classic old-time movie house, but it fell on hard times in the '90s as a result of the megaplex trend. Thanks to a grand restoration project, the Calvin is back and better than ever, hosting a variety of nationally recognized performing artists throughout the year. A diverse collection

of pop, folk, jazz, and country artists from around the globe flock to
★ the cozy (capacity 180). **Iron Horse Music Hall** (✉ 20 Center St. ☎ 413/
586–8686 or 800/843–8425), Northampton's acoustically superb "listening room," which is one of the most intimate venues you'll find anywhere. The **Pearl Street Nightclub** (✉ 10 Pearl St. ☎ 413/584–0610)
presents a varied slate of theme nights, from 18-and-over and live rock
to dancing and top club DJs. **The Eleven's** (✉ 140 Pleasant St. ☎ 413/
584–4100) presents regional performers each weekend.

The spacious **Diva's** (✉ 492 Pleasant St. ☎ 413/586–8161) serves the
region's sizable lesbian and gay community with great music that draws
people to the cavernous dance floor. The reliable **Fitzwilly's** (✉ 23 Main
St. ☎ 413/584–8666) draws a friendly mix of locals and tourists for
drinks and tasty pub fare. The dimly lit **Hugo's** (✉ 315 Pleasant St. ☎ 413/
534–9800) has beer on tap, a rocking juke box, and all the local color
you'll ever want to see.

The Arts

The **Center for the Arts in Northampton** (✉ 17 New South St. ☎ 413/584–
7327 ⊕ www.nohoarts.org) hosts more than 250 gallery exhibitions and
theater, dance, and musical events each year, as well as the First Night
festivities New Year's Eve.

Sports & the Outdoors

☖ The **Norwottuck Rail Trail,** (☎ 413/586–8706 ⊕ www.hadleyonline.com/
railtrail) part of the Connecticut River Greenway State Park, is a paved
10-mi path that links Northampton with Belchertown by way of Amherst.
Great for biking, rollerblading, jogging, and cross-country skiing, it runs
along the old Boston & Maine Railroad route. Entry points include Route
9 in Northampton at junction of Damon Road (near Coolidge Bridge)
and Route 9 in Hadley at junction of River Drive. (Route 47 north).

For those who want the ultimate aeronautical experience (as well as the
best view of the Pioneer Valley), take a ride on one of the colorful hot-
air balloons operated by lighter-than-air experts at **Pioneer Valley Balloons** (✉ Old Ferry Rd. ☎ 413/584–7980). Pilots Richard Giusto, Lisa
Fusco, and Bill Hampton set sail seven days a week from the Northampton Airport.

Sportsman's Marina Boat Rental Company (✉ Rte. 9, Hadley ☎ 413/
586–2426) rents canoes and kayaks from summer through early fall.

Shopping

The massive **Antique Center of Northampton** (✉ 9½ Market St. ☎ 413/
584–3600) is home to more than 60 dealers. Among the different retailers that make up the **Hadley Village Barn Shops** (✉ 41 Russell St.
☎ 413/253–2515) is the Christmas Loft, which stocks Yuletide treats
all year long.

Thorne's Marketplace (✉ 150 Main St. ☎ 413/584–5582) is a funky
four-floor indoor mall in a former department store. Among the 35 shops
you'll find are Dynamite Records, which sells hard-to-find recordings,

TOURING THE HILLTOWNS

WITH SO MUCH GOING ON IN THE PIONEER VALLEY, *it's easy to overlook the sights along its western fringes. A trip to the tiny boroughs called "The Hilltowns" lets you explore old-style general stores, lantern-lit country inns, and white-steepled churches gleaming against a deep-blue sky.*

*From Northampton, head west along Route 9 to the town of **Williamsburg,** where you'll find the Williams House, an old-time tavern complete with wide-pine floorboards and a roaring fireplace. Continuing along Route 9, it's an uphill climb to **Goshen** (population 900), home to the D.A.R. State Forest, a favorite retreat for city dwellers. The road flattens before you reach **Cummington,** known for the William Cullen Bryant Homestead (named for the renowned 19th-century New England poet) and the Kingman Tavern, which displays two centuries' worth of local fact and figures.*

*From Cummington, head north along Plainfield Road to the hamlet of **Plainfield.** Its population of 580 may be among the lowest in the region, but the 2,165-foot summit of West Mountain ranks as the highest point in Hampshire County. Nearby Hawley State Forest has gushing streams and towering pine trees. From Plainfield, Route 116 takes you through charming **Adams,** where you'll find the down-home Adams Diner. To complete the loop back to Northampton, head east along Route 116, passing through the town of **Ashfield,** known for its maple-sugaring production, before reaching scenic **Conway.***

*Other points of interest lie just to the south. From Cummington, take Route 112 south to **Worthington,** home to one of the country's best small music festivals. Take Route 143 east to **Chesterfield** to a glimpse of the Chesterfield Gorge, a magnificent rock-lined waterway.*

and Different Drummer's Kitchen, a well-stocked culinary shop. **Williamsburg General Store** (✉ Rte. 9, Williamsburg ☎ 413/268–3036), a Pioneer Valley landmark, sells breads, penny candy, and gifts galore.

AMHERST

⑮–⑰ *8 mi northeast of Northampton.*

One of the most visited spots in all of New England, Amherst is known for its scores of world-renowned authors, poets, and artists. The above-average intelligence quotient of its population is no accident, as Amherst is home to a trio of colleges–Amherst, Hampshire, and the University of Massachusetts. The high concentration of college-age humanity bolsters Amherst's downtown area, which includes a wide range of art galleries, music stores, and clothing boutiques.

Amherst was initially part of Hadley (the town that separates Amherst from Northampton) before being incorporated in 1775. Amherst of the 19th century had a strong industrial base, with factories that produced wool, paper and, in particular, hats. However, education would become the town's chief attribute when, in 1821, Amherst College was formed

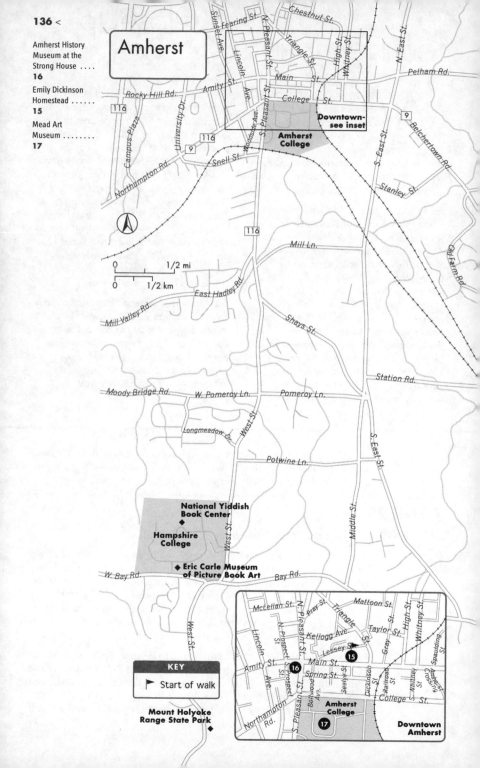

Amherst

Chestnut St.

Fearing St.

Sunset Ave.

N. Pleasant St.

Triangle St.

High St.

S. Whitney St.

N. East St.

Pelham Rd.

Lincoln Ave.

Main

College St.

St.

Downtown-see inset

9

Belchertown Rd.

Rocky Hill Rd.

Amity St.

Amherst College

Campus Plaza

116

University Dr.

9

116

Montague Rd.

Snell St.

Northampton Rd.

S. East St.

Stanley St.

Old Farm Rd.

116

Mill Ln.

0   1/2 mi

0   1/2 km

East Hadley Rd.

Mill Valley Rd.

Shays St.

Station Rd.

Moody Bridge Rd.

W. Pomeroy Ln.

Pomeroy Ln.

West St.

Longmeadow Dr.

S. East St.

Potwine Ln.

National Yiddish Book Center
◆

Middle St.

Hampshire College

West St.

◆ **Eric Carle Museum of Picture Book Art**

W. Bay Rd.

Bay Rd.

West St.

KEY

▶ Start of walk

◆ **Mount Holyoke Range State Park**

McLellan St.

N. Pray St.

Mattoon St.

N. Pleasant St.

Triangle St.

High St.

Whitney St.

Lincoln Ave.

N. Prospect St.

Kellogg Ave.

Taylor St.

Gray St.

Spaulding St.

Lessey St.

▶ **15**

Amity St.

16

Main St.

Spring St.

Dickinson

Railroad St.

S. Whitney St.

Amherst Crossing

S. Prospect St.

Bothwood

Northampton Rd.

S. Pleasant St.

College St.

Amherst College

17

Downtown Amherst

as an offshoot of Amherst Academy, a small preparatory school. Massachusetts Agricultural School—the predecessor of the University of Massachusetts—arrived 40 years later.

More than any other Pioneer Valley locale, Amherst typifies the cultural diversity of the region. Though Amherst occasionally makes front-page news for its stubbornly liberal political viewpoints (such as canceling a high-school production of *West Side Story* due to its depiction of Latinos), one thing's for certain: the creative environment that is Amherst's hallmark has inspired countless individuals who've dedicated their lives to the arts and humanities, among them filmmaker Ken Burns (a Hampshire College grad), author Tracy Kidder, and Pulitzer Prize–winning poet James Tate.

Given the ebb and flow of the immense student population, Amherst has a highly changeable environment. During summer months, visitors can enjoy a tranquil lunch at a sidewalk café; in fall, football games and foliage viewing make the town one of the busiest in the entire Northeast.

a good walk

Start downtown adjacent to the **Amherst Commons,** the sprawling lawn that divides the shops of North Pleasant Street from Amherst College. Just ahead on the other side of the street is the **Emily Dickinson Museum ⑮ ▶,** which provides an in-depth overview of Amherst's beloved poet. Backtrack up Main Street until you reach the center of Amherst, then turn right onto North Pleasant Street, where you'll find a quarter-mile of college-style book and record stores, clothing boutiques and eateries. Making the loop back to the corner of Main and Amity streets, turn right onto Amity, where next to the Jones Library you'll find the **Amherst History Museum at the Strong House ⑯.** Head toward the other side of Amherst Commons, and you're now on South Pleasant Street, where you can view the contemporary artwork on display at R. Michelson Galleries before crossing the Commons on your way to Amherst College and the **Mead Art Museum ⑰.**

What to See

⑯ **Amherst History Museum at the Strong House.** Housed in a mansion dating from the mid-1700s, this museum displays an extensive collection of household tools, furnishings, and clothing that reflects changing styles of interior decoration. Most items are Amherst originals, dating from the 18th to the mid-20th centuries. ✉ *67 Amity St.* ☎ *413/256–0678* ⊕ *www.amhersthistory.org.* ⌨ *$4* ☉ *Feb.–Nov., Wed.–Sat. 12:30–3:30.*

▶ ⑮ **Emily Dickinson Museum.** The famed Amherst poet lived here her entire life (1830–86), and the many of the poet's belongings are contained within (though her manuscripts are housed elsewhere). The museum is outfitted with period accoutrements including original wall hangings and lace curtains. Next door is **The Evergreens** (✉ 214 Main St. ☎ 413/253–5272), an imposing Italianate Victorian mansion in which Emily's brother Austin and his family resided for more than 50 years. Tours of both buildings are conducted. ✉ *280 Main St.* ☎ *413/542–8161*

⊕ *www.emilydickinsonmuseum.org* ⊟ *$8* ⊙ *June–Aug., Wed.–Sat. 10–5, Sun. 1–5; Sept.–Nov. and Mar.–May, Wed.–Sat. 1–5.*

need a break? Newspapers and books are strewn about the tables at the **Black Sheep** (⊠ 79 Main St. ☎ 413/253–3442), a funky downtown café specializing in flavorful coffees and creative sandwiches such as the C'est la Brie (a baguette smothered with Brie, roasted peppers, spinach, and raspberry mustard) and the French Kiss (truffle pâté, Dijon mustard, and red onion on a baguette).

☾ **Eric Carle Museum of Picture Book Art.** This museum celebrates and preserves not only the works of renowned children's book author Eric Carle (who penned *The Very Hungry Caterpillar*) but also such luminaries as Maurice Sendak, Lucy Cousins, Petra Mathers, and Leo and Diane Dillon. Puppet shows, lectures, and storytelling are all part of the museum's ongoing calendar of events. ⊠ *125 W. Bay Rd.* ☎ *413/586–8934* ⊕ *www.picturebookart.org* ⊟ *$5* ⊙ *Tues.–Sat. 10–4, Sun. noon–4.*

Mount Holyoke Range State Park. A favorite of outdoor enthusiasts, this park has plenty of of hiking and cross-country skiing trails. The Notch Visitor Center, on Route 116 in Amherst, has displays and interpretive programs. ⊠ *Rte. 116* ☎ *413/586–0350* ⊟ *Free* ⊙ *Daily.*

⓱ **Mead Art Museum.** On the campus of Amherst College, Mead houses six different galleries filled with prints, drawings, photographs, textiles, and furnishings from around the globe, many dating back to the early 19th century. Rotating exhibitions are presented in the Fairchild Gallery. ⊠ *Rtes. 9 and 116* ☎ *413/542–2335* ⊕ *www.amherst.edu/mead* ⊟ *Free* ⊙ *Sept.–May, Tues., Wed., and Fri.–Sun. 10–4:30, Thurs. 10–9.*

★ **National Yiddish Book Center.** The effort to save Yiddish literature and preserve Jewish culture has become a major movement here. The center, on the campus of Hampshire College, is housed in a thatched-roof building that resembles a cluster of houses in a *shtetl*, or traditional Eastern European village. Inside, a contemporary space contains more than 1½ million books, a fireside reading area, a kosher dining room, and a visitor center with changing exhibits. The work here is performed out in the open: hundreds of books pour in daily, and workers come across everything from family keepsakes to rare manuscripts. ⊠ *Rte. 116* ☎ *413/256–4900* ⊕ *www.yiddishbookcenter.org* ⊟ *Free* ⊙ *Sun.–Fri. 10–3:30.*

Where to Eat

$–$$ ✗ **Judie's.** Since 1977, academic types have crowded around small tables on the glassed-in porch, ordering chicken ravioli with walnuts, shrimp tempura, gumbo popovers, Gorgonzola-and-mushroom burgers, and probably the best bowl of French onion soup the town has to offer. The atmosphere is hip and artsy; a painting covers each tabletop. ⊠ *51 N. Pleasant St.* ☎ *413/253–3491* ⊟ *AE, D, MC, V* ⊙ *Closed Mon.*

Fodor'sChoice
★

¢–$ ✗ **Antonio's.** Who says you have to be in New York to get a late-night slice? Long after the other eateries have folded up the awnings, Antonio's is still dishing out thin-crusted pies piled with both traditional and unusual toppings. ✉ *31 N. Pleasant St.* ☎ *413/253–0808* ⊟ *MC, V.*

★ ¢–$ ✕ **Bub's Bar-B-Q.** Back in 1979, Bub Tiley came up with the idea of opening an authentic Southern-style barbecue joint in Sunderland. A quarter-century later, Bub's—which serves up ribs, chicken, and catfish with a slew of side dishes—is more popular than ever. Maybe it's the sauce, Tiley's's own tangy concoction. Pick up a jar before you leave. ✉ *Rte. 116, north of Amherst town line, Sunderland* ☎ *413/548–9630* ⊟ *MC, V* ⊗ *Closed Mon.*

¢–$ ✕ **Hangar Pub & Grill.** Hot stuff awaits at this popular University Drive hangout, where wings of all types—from boneless to Buffalo—are served up day and night. Be careful when you choose your sauce; the intensity levels range from "wimp" to "afterburner." ✉ *55 University Dr.* ☎ *413/549–9461* ⊟ *MC, V.*

¢–$ ✕ **Rafters Sports Bar & Restaurant.** Watching the Patriots power their way to another Super Bowl—or the Red Sox making miracles at Fenway—has become a ritual for college students at this local hangout. You can also order big burgers, steaks, and salads and wash them down with a frosty pint from the well-stocked tap. There are also pool tables and other diversions. ✉ *University Dr. and Amity St.* ☎ *413/549–4040* ⊟ *AE, DC, MC, V.*

Where to Stay

★ $–$$ ✕▢ **Lord Jeffery Inn.** This gabled brick inn sits regally overlooking the village green. Many of the guest rooms have a light floral decor; others have stencils and pastel woodwork. In the formal dining room ($$–$$$$), with its dark paneling and prodigious fireplace, you might sample such favorites as baked scrod or grilled loin of venison. Burgers, salads, and the like are served at Boltwood's Tavern, which has a small bar and a wraparound porch. ✉ *30 Boltwood Ave., 01002* ☎ *413/253–2576 or 800/742–0358* 🖶 *413/256–6152* ⊕ *www.lordjefferyinn.com* ☞ *40 rooms, 8 suites* ♿ *2 restaurants, bar* ⊟ *AE, DC, MC, V.*

$–$$$ ▢ **Allen House Victorian & Amherst Inns.** A rare find, these late 19th-century inns a block apart from each other have been gloriously restored with precision to the aesthetic of the Victorian era. Busy, colorful wall coverings reach to the high ceilings. Antiques include a burled-walnut headboard and dresser set, carved golden-oak beds and wicker steamship chairs. Lace curtains and hand-stenciling grace the rooms, which have supremely comfortable beds with goose-down comforters. It's a short walk to downtown. Rooms in the Amherst Inn tend to be larger and even more plush. Some rooms have decorative fireplaces. ✉ *599 Main St., 01002* ☎ *413/253–5000* ⊕ *www.allenhouse.com* ☞ *14 rooms* ♿ *Massage, business services; no room TVs, no kids under 10, no smoking* ⊟ *No credit cards* ⦿| *BP.*

¢–$ ▢ **Campus Center Hotel.** On the University of Massachusetts campus and convenient to all of Amherst, this modern hotel has pleasant motel-style rooms with large windows overlooking the surrounding countryside. You can use university exercise facilities—as well as the pool and tennis courts—with prior reservation, and dine at several campus restaurants. Because the hotel is part of the college, there's no hotel tax. ✉ *Murray*

THE TOWN IN BETWEEN

MIDWAY BETWEEN AMHERST AND NORTHAMPTON IS *the town of Hadley, a bucolic community that stands in stark contrast to the chic shops and lefty politics of its college-town peers. One of the country's older towns (founded in 1659), Hadley has its share of history. It is the birthplace of Major General Joseph Hooker, a kindly Civil War leader who during his tour of duty opened his camps to all sorts of needy individuals, even prostitutes (hence the common nickname for the world's oldest profession). A leading producer of corn brooms during the early 19th century, Hadley developed a strong farming base in later years; today it has the largest amount of agricultural acreage in the entire region. Hadley is known throughout the world for its springtime harvest of asparagus (or "'spara-grass," as the locals call it), and is a key supplier of broadleaf tobacco for major cigar-manufacturing firms.*

Like Northampton and Amherst, Hadley has attracted its share of urbanites looking to start anew. But moving here is no easy task; the town keeps a tight grip on residential growth. As a result, about 80% of the town's vast countryside remains untouched, affording residents ample space and visitors some spectacular scenery. A short distance from the center of town, the West Street Commons—the largest village green in all of New England—is framed by rows of vintage Colonial-style homes. To the north along Route 47 is North Hadley Village, a quarter-mile stretch of quaint homes along the banks of the Connecticut River. (These are included in the National Register of Historic Places.) The Old Hadley Cemetery has several markers dating back to the late 17th century.

D. Lincoln Tower, 1 Campus Center Way, 01003 ☎ *413/549–6000* 🖷 *413/545–1210* ⌕ *114 rooms, 2 suites* ♿ *Business services, meeting rooms* ▭ *AE, D, DC, MC, V.*

Nightlife & the Arts

Nightlife

Live local bands perform Monday, Thursday, and Saturday nights at the place locals refer to as the "ABC," the **Amherst Brewing Company** (✉ 24–36 N. Pleasant St. ☎ 413/253–4400). The pub has a decent-size dance floor and, as the name implies, a vast selection of beers brewed right on the premises. It also serves sandwiches, burgers, and salads.

The earthy aroma from nearby Cowls Lumber fills the air as you stroll into **The Harp** (✉ 163 Sunderland Rd., North Amherst ☎ 413/548–6900), a small but cozy tavern where regional rock and acoustic acts perform Thursday to Sunday nights. The place also serves seafood, sandwiches, and snacks until midnight.

The Arts

Each summer at the Hartsbrook School, the **Hampshire Shakespeare Company** (✉ 193 Bay Rd., Hadley ☎ 413/548–8118 ⊕ www.

hampshireshakespeare.org) stages a selection of plays under the stars, the way the Bard meant it to be.

Major ballet and modern dance companies appear at the **University of Massa-chusetts Fine Arts Center** (⊠ Whitmore Circle ☎ 413/545–2511 or 800/ 999–8627). The **William D. Mullins Memorial Center** (⊠ Commonwealth Ave. ☎ 413/545–0505) hosts concerts, plays, and other live events.

Sports & the Outdoors

Biking
Valley Bicycles (⊠ 319 Main St. ☎ 413/256–0880) rents bikes and dis-penses advice about the best places to hit the road.

Fishing
The Connecticut River sustains shad, salmon, and several dozen other fish species. From May to October, at **Waterfield Farms** (⊠ 500 Sunderland Rd. ☎ 413/549–3558), you pay $3 per person to drop your line. Poles and bait are available.

Hiking
The Metacomet–Monadnock Hiking Trail (⊠ Rte. 9, Belchertown ☎ 413/562–9863) is part of the 117-mi trail that runs from Connecticut to New Hamp-shire. This longtime favorite is beloved for its flowing streams and abun-dant foliage. Look for the gorgeous waterfall near the halfway point of the 4-mi trek. Parking is available along the westbound side of Route 9.

Shopping

An institution in the Pioneer Valley, the **Atkins Farms Country Market** (⊠ Rte. 116, South Amherst ☎ 413/253–9528 or 800/594–9537) is surrounded by apple orchards and gorgeous views of the Holyoke Ridge. Hayrides are offered in fall, and children's events are hosted throughout the year. There's also a bakery and a deli. A few miles north of Amherst, the **Leverett Crafts & Arts Center** (⊠ Montague Rd., Leverett ☎ 413/548–9070) is home to 20 resident artists who create jewelry, ceramics, glass, and textiles.

DEERFIELD

⑱ *10 mi northwest of Amherst.*

In Deerfield, horse-drawn carriages clip-clop past perfectly maintained 18th-century homes, neighbors tip their hats to strangers, kids play ball in fields by the river, and the bell of the impossibly beautiful brick church peals from a white steeple. This is the perfect New England vil-lage, though not without a past darkened by tragedy.

Settled more than 8,000 years ago, Deerfield was originally a Pocum-tuck village—deserted after deadly epidemics and a war with the Mo-hawks that all but wiped out the tribe. English pioneers eagerly settled into this frontier outpost in the 1660s and 1670s, but two bloody mas-sacres at the hands of the Native Americans and the French caused the village to be abandoned until 1707, when construction began on the buildings that still exist today in what is known as Deerfield Village.

The Pioneer Valley's ultimate blast from the past, Deerfield Village is an impeccably preserved community of 14 museum houses from the 18th and 19th centuries surrounded by acres of fertile farmland, a stone's-throw from the Connecticut River. Here visitors are treated to a glimpse into daily life during the years leading up to the Revolutionary War and beyond. Historic Deerfield is also home to 200-year-old Deerfield Academy, one of the nation's leading prep schools.Though a popular destination for fall-foliage trippers, Deerfield (and adjacent communities South Deerfield, Whately, Hatfield, and Sunderland) is easy on the eyes any time of year. Businesses along U.S. 5 and Route 10 provide a smorgasbord of New England treats, from native apples, peaches, and sweet corn to maple syrup produced and bottled at local sugaring houses. The observatory deck atop Mount Sugarloaf provides one of the most extraordinary views in the valley.

Fodor'sChoice ★ Although it has a turbulent past, **Historic Deerfield** now basks in a genteel aura. With 52 buildings on 93 acres, this village provides a vivid glimpse into 18th- and 19th-century America. The tree-lined avenue has 14 homes that are open to the public year-round. Well-trained guides are happy to chat about the region's history. Purchase a ticket that lets you visit all the houses at the **Flynt Center of Early New England Life** (⊠ 37-D Old Main St.), which contains two galleries full of silver and pewter as well as needlework and clothing dating back to the 1600s. At the **Wells-Thorn House,** various rooms depict life as it changed from 1725 to 1850. The adjacent **Frary House** has arts and crafts from the 1700s on display; the attached Barnard Tavern was the main meeting place for Deerfield's villagers. Also of note is the **Hinsdale and Anna Williams,** the stately home for this affluent early New England couple. Native American artifacts, quilts and furnishings from early settlers, and other objects are on display at the **Memorial Hall Museum** (⊠ 8 Memorial St. ☎ 413/664–3768), one of the oldest museums in the country. Plan to spend at least one full day at Historic Deerfield. ⊠ *Old Main St.* ☎ *413/774–5581* ⊕ *www.historic-deerfield.org* ⊠ *$14* ⊘ *Daily 9:30–4:30.*

Fodor'sChoice ★ ☾ Since it opened in fall 2001, **Magic Wings Butterfly Conservatory & Gardens** has rapidly become one of the region's most popular attractions. The facility has an indoor conservatory garden where you can stroll among thousands of fluttering butterflies, as well as an extensive three-season outdoor garden filled with plants that attract local species. You can also observe the butterfly nursery, where throughout the day newborns experience the joy of flight. An extensive garden shop sells butterfly-friendly plants; there's also a snack bar and gift shop. ⊠ *281 Greenfield Rd., South Deerfield* ☎ *413/665–2805* ⊕ *www.magicwings.net* ⊠ *$8* ⊘ *Daily 9–5.*

The **Yankee Candle Company** not only displays a full review of its product line—including scented candles in such outlandish aromas as cantaloupe and banana-nut bread—but an array of live exhibits. In a small candle-making museum off the main showroom you can watch costumed docents practicing the art of candle-dipping, using historically accurate implements. Highlights for younger kids include the Bavarian Christmas Village and Santa's Toy Factory, where electric trains chug by over-head and faux-snow falls lightly. You can have lunch at either the pleas-ant café or the full-service restaurant. ⊠ *U.S. 5 and Rte. 10, near junction of Rte. 116, South Deerfield* ☎ *413/665–2929* ⊕ *www. yankeecandle.com* ◪ Free ☉ *Daily 9:30–6.*

Where to Eat

$$$ ✕ Sienna. The atmosphere here is soothing and the service well man-nered, but it's the food that really shines. Choices on the ever-changing menu might include a wild-mushroom crepe served with Roquefort cheese or pan-seared sea bass on a bed of Swiss chard accompanied by fingerling potatoes and a sweet corn flan. After an irresistible dessert such as a coconut panna cotta with persimmon compote, your evening ends with the personal touch of a handwritten bill on a sheet of stationery. ⊠ *6 Elm St., South Deerfield* ☎ *413/665–0215* ▭ *MC, V* ☉ *Closed Mon. and Tues. No lunch.*

$$–$$$ ✕ Chandler's. Adjacent to the Yankee Candle Company, this restaurant's menu includes seafood standouts such as pan-seared diver scallops and Maryland crab cakes and hearty meat dishes such as roast prime rib and grilled sirloin. The old-fashioned dining room is illuminated by (unscented) candles from next door. ⊠ *Greenfield Rd., South Deerfield* ☎ *413/665–1277* ▭ *AE, MC, V.*

Ⓒ $ ✕ Tom's Long Hot Dogs. Forget the golden arches—this is where locals go for a fast-food fix. Sure, you can order burgers and fries, but if you're a frankfurter fanatic, dive in to one of Tom's "footlongs" (featuring world-famous Blue Seal Franks, made down the road in Chicopee). Don't spare the sauerkraut. ⊠ *37 State Rd.* ☎ *413/665–2931* ▭ *No credit cards.*

Where to Stay

$$$$ ✕▣ Deerfield Inn. Period wallpaper decorates the rooms at this lovely
Fodor'sChoice lodging, which was built in 1884. Rooms are snug and handsomely ap-
★ pointed with both period antiques and reproductions; some rooms have four-poster or canopy beds. The restaurant ($$$–$$$$) showcases such creative American fare as pan-seared pheasant with crushed peppercorns and wild mushrooms in a cognac cream sauce with a truffle risotto cake. The tavern ($$–$$$) serves lighter fare. ⊠ *81 Old Main St., 01342* ☎*413/774–5587 or 800/926–3865* ◪ *413/773–8712* ⊕ *www.deerfieldinn. com* ◪ *23 rooms* ♿ *2 restaurants, coffee shop, bar; no smoking* ▭ *AE, MC, V* ▯◁ *BP.*

$ ✕▣ Whately Inn. Antiques and four-poster beds slope gently on old-wood floors of the guest rooms at this informal Colonial-era inn. The dining room ($$–$$$; no lunch) has a fireplace and exposed beams; it's dimly lighted, with candles flickering on the tables. Prime Angus steaks, baked lobster with shrimp stuffing, rack of lamb, and other traditional entrées are served here or in the more casual lounge. There's no lunch during the week, but on Sunday dinner is served beginning at 1 PM. Enjoy the gorgeous east-facing view of the valley from the front veranda. ⊠ *Chest-nut Plain Rd., Whately Center 01093* ☎ *413/665–3044 or 800/942–8359* ⊕ *www.whatelyinn.com* ◪ *4 rooms* ▭ *AE, D, MC, V.*

¢–$ 🖼 **Sunnyside Farm Bed & Breakfast.** Maple antiques and family heirlooms decorate this circa-1800 Victorian farmhouse's country-style rooms, all of which are hung with fine-art reproductions and have views across the fields. A full country breakfast is served family-style in the dining room. The 50-acre farm is about 8 mi south of Deerfield, convenient to cross-country skiing, mountain biking, and hiking. ⊠ *21 River Rd., Whately 01093* ☎ *413/665–3113* 🛏 *5 rooms with shared bath* ⚴ *Dining room, pool* ⊟ *No credit cards* ⍥ *BP.*

Nightlife & the Arts

Just a short trip up the Mohawk Trail, the attractive **Charlemont Inn** (⊠Rte. 2, Charlemont ☎ 413/339–5796) hosts jazz artists on the weekends. Every weekend at the hotel-turned-roadhouse called **Hot-L-Warren** (⊠ 19 Elm St., South Deerfield ☎ 413/665–2301) you can hear some of the best rock and country bands in the region. There are pool tables and a dance floor that's packed by 11 PM.

Sports & the Outdoors

Take a drive up the winding, tree-covered road, or better yet, hike up the short but challenging trail that leads to the twin peaks of North and South Sugarloaf, the centerpiece of **Mt. Sugarloaf State Reservation.** Here you'll find picnic tables, charcoal grills, and a multitiered observation deck offering a spectacular view of the entire valley. ⊠ *Rte. 116, South Deerfield* ☎ *413/545–5993* ⊙ *Road open dawn–dusk, excluding winter months.*

Shopping

A short drive from Historic Deerfield, **Richardson's Candy Kitchen** (⊠ 500 Greenfield Rd. ☎ 413/772–0443) makes and sells luscious cream-filled truffles as well as other handmade chocolates and confections.

GREENFIELD

⑲ *4 mi north of Deerfield.*

In the 1990s, Greenfield made national news by stubbornly refusing to let Wal-Mart open a superstore downtown. Ironically, Greenfield, unlike other Pioneer Valley villages, is hardly a hotbed of political activism; its big-box opposition was merely an effort to preserve the sanctity of its downtown. Today, Main Street remains one of the few locales that time has been left largely untouched, as evidenced by downtown mainstays such as Wilson's Department Store or the old-style Garden Cinemas.

A prosperous trade and industrial center for much of its first 300 years, Greenfield declined during the latter half of the 20th century but has since become increasingly popular again for its bustling downtown streets and its residential neighborhoods dotted with immense Victorian mansions. Venture into the highly walkable downtown and you'll find independently owned shops, pubs, and eateries. The town is also a good base for exploring the northern half of the valley. At the junction of Route 2 and I–91, Greenfield serves as the gateway city to the Mohawk Trail. There are great opportunities to explore the landscape, including the spectacular views from Poet's Seat Corner.

☺ A centrally located outdoor space, **Greenfield Energy Park** has exhibits about creative ways of using energy and demonstrations about alternate modes of transportation. There's also a children's train. ⊠ *50 Miles St.* ☎ *413/774–6051* 🎫 *Free* ⊙ *Daily.*

☺ Just west of downtown is **Old Greenfield Village,** a replica of an 1895 New England town. Among the 15 buildings are a general store, a church, a schoolhouse, and a print shop. ⊠ *Rte. 2, Greenfield* ☎ *413/ 774–7138* 🎫 *$5* ⊙ *Mid-May–mid-Oct., Wed.–Mon. 10–4.*

A generous display of historical artifacts that trace the development of Greenfield are housed at the **Historical Society of Greenfield.** ⊠ *Church and Union Sts.* ☎ *413/774–3663* 🎫 *Free* ⊙ *June–Aug., Sat. 8–noon.*

off the beaten path

MONTAGUE – Due east of Greenfield, this artist enclave is divided into a series of communities—Turners Falls, Millers Falls, Lake Pleasant, Montague City, and Montague Center—known as the "five fingers on one hand." The Millers River divides Turners Falls from Millers Falls; Montague City is along the Connecticut River. Montague Center is where you'll find most of the town's noteworthy shops.

Where to Eat

$$–$$$ ✗ **Blue Heron.** In a red clapboard mill dating from the 1830s, this hard-to-find eatery looks out on a rushing, evergreen-shrouded river southeast of Greenfield. The kitchen turns out contemporary southern European and North African–inspired fare, such as scallion potato pancakes with house-cured gravlax and Moroccan vegetable tagine with free-range chicken served over couscous. ⊠ *Greenfield Rd., 7 mi southeast of Greenfield* ☎ *413/367–0200* ☐ *MC, V* ⊙ *Closed Mon. and Tues. No lunch Wed.–Sat.*

¢–$$ ✗ **Famous Bill's.** Well known for such classic American fare as savory slabs of prime roast rib of beef, Famous Bill's also serves a sumptuous surf-and-turf dinner. The casual restaurant is a few blocks from Greenfield's downtown. ⊠ *30 Federal St.* ☎ *413/773–9230* ⊕ *www. billsrestaurant.com* ☐ *AE, MC, V.*

$ ✗ **Taylor's Tavern.** Inside this atmospheric pub, the no-frills menu includes pasta dishes, burgers, and other fare. ⊠ *238 Main St.* ☎ *413/773– 8313* ☐ *AE, D, MC, V.*

Where to Stay

$–$$$ 🏨 **Brandt House Country Inn.** This turn-of-the-20th-century Colonial Revival mansion is set on 3½ manicured acres. The owner is an interior decorator, and her touch is evident throughout. The sunlit, spacious common rooms are filled with plants, plump easy chairs, and handsome contemporary furnishings; the elegantly appointed guest rooms have featherbeds. The emphasis is on comfort and hominess. The stunning penthouse, with a full kitchen and sleeping loft, sleeps up to five. ⊠ *29*

Highland Ave., Greenfield 01301 ☎ *413/774–3329 or 800/235–3329* 🖷 *413/772–2908* ⊕ *www.brandt-house.com* 🖘 *7 rooms, 6 with bath, 1 suite* ♨ *Some in-room hot tubs, refrigerators, some in-room VCRs, tennis court, meeting room, some pets allowed* ⊟ *AE, D, MC, V* ⦿ *BP.*

$–$$$ ▦ **The Hitchcock House.** Each room in this stately Victorian-style bed-and-breakfast, built in the late 1800s, is outfitted with old New England furnishings; beautiful quilts and comforters keep you cozy during long winter nights. ⊠ *15 Congress St., Greenfield 01301* ☎ *413/774–7452* ⊕ *www.thehitchcockhouse.com* 🖘 *5 rooms* ⊟ *AE, MC, V.*

Nightlife & the Arts

Nightlife

A microbrewery in the center of town, the **People's Pint** (⊠ 24 Federal St. ☎ 413/773–0333) serves a robust handcrafted ales and porters, as well as freshly baked breads and healthy pub fare. It also books a wide range of folk and rock acts. About 3 mi east of Greenfield, the honky-tonk **Route 63 Roadhouse** (⊠ Rte. 63, Millers Falls ☎ 413/659–3384) delivers the region's top rock bands.

The Arts

A cultural mainstay in the Pioneer Valley, the **Pioneer Valley Symphony** (☎ 413/773–3664) presents orchestral and choral works performed by regional musicians. Concerts are at Greenfield High School and Smith College in Northampton.

Sports & the Outdoors

High on a ridge overlooking the Connecticut River, **Poet's Seat Tower** is one of the Pioneer Valley's most rewarding short jaunts. From the summit of Rocky Mountain there are inspiring 360-degree views of the countryside. To get to there, follow directions from Maple Street.

Shopping

The **Longview Tower Specialty Shoppes** (⊠ Rte. 2 ☎ 413/772–6976) carries a great selection of jam and candies. There's an eye-popping view of the valley from the top of a massive steel observation tower.

The **Battelle Harding Gallery** (⊠ 267 Main St. ☎ 413/834–2359 ⊕ www.battellehardinggallery) specializes in the works of Provincetown artists. In a former bank building, **Pushkin Gallery** (⊠ 332 Main St. ☎ 413/774–2891 or 413/549–4564) carries the works of prominent Russian painters, both contemporary and vintage.

SHELBURNE FALLS

❷⓿ *14 mi west of Greenfield.*

A tour of New England's fall foliage wouldn't be complete without a trek across the famed Mohawk Trail, a 63-mi section of Route 2 that runs past picturesque Shelburne Falls. The community, separated from neighboring Buckland by the Deerfield River, is filled with little art galleries. It's best known for the Bridge of Flowers, an immense former trolley bridge covered with an enormous floral display. Some 35,000 visitors travel each year to view the bridge as well as the nearby Glacial Potholes, an exquisite rock formation in the Deerfield River at Salmon Falls (once a favorite fishing spot for Native Americans).

Founded in 1768, Shelburne Falls became a prominent railroad hub during the latter part of the 19th century, serving Boston & Maine and New Haven lines. For years, the Shelburne Falls & Colrain Street Railway bolstered the local economy by shipping produce and lumber to other communities in the region. Today, the Shelburne Falls Trolley Museum keeps the memory of the railway alive with a real working artifact from the rail era, the Shelburne Falls & Colrain Street Railway Combine No. 10.

With its streets lined with graceful Victorian homes, Shelburne Falls is the quintessential New England village. The foothills surrounding the town provide stunning views of Massachusetts, Vermont, and New Hampshire. It is here that the town's most notable resident, comedian Bill Cosby, built his home after receiving his doctorate in education from the University of Massachusetts.

★ From May to October, an arched, 400-foot trolley bridge is transformed into the **of Flowers** (⊠ At Water St. ☎ 413/625-2544), a promenade was bursting with color.

In the riverbed just downstream from the town are 50 immense **Glacial Potholes** (⊠ Deerfield Ave. ☎ 413/625-2544 ⊕ www.shelburnefalls. com ⊠ Free ☉ Daily). These geological wonders were ground out of solid granite during the last Ice Age.

Shelburne Falls Trolley Museum. Take a ride on this real working tribute to the old Colrain Street Railway Combine No. 10, the trolley car that served businesses in and around Shelburne during the early part of the 20th century. ⊠ *14 Depot St.* ☎ *413/625-9443* ⊕ *www.sftm.org* ⊠ *$2.50* ☉ *May–Nov., weekends 11–5.*

The late 19th-century building that is home to the **Shelburne Historical Society** displays many historical artifacts pertaining to the region, some dating back to the 1700s, including numerous New England genealogical records. ⊠ *Church and Maple Sts.* ☎ *413/625-6150* ⊠ *Free* ☉ *Wed. 10–4.*

Where to Eat

$–$$ ✕ **A Bottle of Bread.** An inviting, homey atmosphere and simple yet creative menu (including delicious smoked-turkey sandwiches and salmon cakes) make this a fine choice for lunch or dinner. ⊠ *18 Water St.* ☎ *413/625-6264* ⊟ *D, MC, V* ☉ *Closed Mon. and Tues.*

$–$$ ✕ **Café Martin.** The menu at this little eatery is incredibly diverse—the steak Gorgonzola and shrimp scampi are superb, but if you're after something with a slightly different accent, try the kung pao chicken. Burgers and sandwiches are available for lunch. ⊠ *24 Bridge St.* ☎ *413/625-2795* ⊟ *MC, V* ☉ *Closed Mon.*

$-$$ ✕ **Copper Angel.** Near the Deerfield River, the Copper Angel specializes in vegetarian cuisine but also serves plenty of poultry and fish dishes. The organic produce–based menu includes lentil cutlets with vegetable gravy, tofu stir-fry with peanut sauce, stuffed chicken breast with garlic-mashed potatoes, and orange-pepper shrimp. A deck overlooking the Bridge of Flowers is a pleasant place for summer dining. ⊠ *2 State St.* ☎ *413/625–2727* ⚞ *Reservations not accepted* ▤ *MC, V* ☽ *Closed Tues.*

$-$$ ✕ **Stillwaters.** Locals swear by the Stroganoff, but there are other tender treats on tap at this atmospheric eatery overlooking the Deerfield River, including chicken picatta and that old New England stand-by, Yankee pot roast. ⊠ *1745 Mohawk Trail, Charlemont* ☎ *413/625–6200* ⊕ *www.protoelf.com/stillwaters* ▤ *MC, V* ☽ *Closed Tues.*

Where to Stay

$ ▦ **Bear Haven Bed & Breakfast.** If you love stuffed bears, consider this cozy three-room bed-and-breakfast near the center of Shelburne Falls. A small army of cute creatures awaits you. The inn is within walking distance of many downtown shops and galleries. ⊠ *22 Mechanic St., 01370* ☎ *413/625–9281* ⊕ *www.bearhaven.com* ⇔ *3 rooms* ⚒ *No smoking, no kids under 12* ▤ *AE, D, MC, V* ⑩ *CP.*

¢-$ ▦ **Johnson Homestead Bed & Breakfast.** This scenic estate is on 80 acres of beautiful Shelburne countryside. Beautiful wide floorboards, a cheery sitting room, and homemade breakfasts guarantee a tranquil stay. ⊠ *79 E. Buckland Rd., 01370* ☎ *413/625–6603* ⊕ *www.flybyfrog.com/johnson.html* ⇔ *3 rooms* ⚒ *No kids under 12* ▤ *No credit cards* ⑩ *CP.*

¢-$ ▦ **Penfrydd Farm.** In the middle of a 160-acre working farm, this serene B&B occupies a rejuvenated 1830s farmhouse with exposed beams, wide floorboards, skylights, and a big hot tub. The ideal place to get away from it all, Penfrydd Farm is in the middle of fabulous fall foliage and plenty of snow for snowshoeing and cross-country skiing in nearby Cook State Forest. The inn is 8 mi north of Shelburne Falls. ⊠ *105 Hillman Rd.* ⚐ *R.R. 1, Box 100A, Colrain 01340* ☎ *413/624–5516* ⊕ *www.penfrydd.com* ⇔ *4 rooms, 3 with shared bath* ⚒ *Some in-room hot tubs, hot tub; no kids under 10* ▤ *AE, MC, V* ⑩ *BP, CP.*

Nightlife & the Arts

Chamber music lovers can enjoy Schubert, Liszt, Handel, and many other great composers during the **Mohawk Trail Concert Series** (⊠ Rte. 2, Charlemont ☎ 413/625–9511). Performances at the Federated Church include both regional and internationally renowned artists. A meet-and-greet with the players follows each concert.

Richie Havens and Ferron are just a few of the folk favorites who've graced the stage as part of the concert series called **Hilltown Folk** (⊠ 51 Bridge St. ☎ 413/625–9362). The monthly events are held in the recently refurbished Memorial Hall Theater.

Long for those old movie houses where you can find Humphrey Bogart one week, Monty Python the next? Head to Shelburne Falls, where **Pothole Pictures** (⊠ 51 Bridge St. ☎ 413/625–2526) screens classics every weekend.

Sports & the Outdoors

White-water rafting in the Class II–III rapids of the Deerfield River is a popular summer activity. From April to October, **Zoar Outdoor** (✉ 7 Main St., Rte. 2 ☎ 800/532–7483 ⊕ www.zoaroutdoor.com) conducts day-long rafting trips along 10 mi of challenging rapids, as well as family-friendly floats along gentler sections of the river. The outfitter also rents equipment and leads canoe and kayak tours and rock climbing expeditions.

Shopping

With works by more than 175 local artisans, the **Salmon Falls Artisans Showroom** (✉ 1 Ashfield St. ☎ 413/625–9833 ⊕ www.penguin-works.com/sfas) carries sculpture, pottery, and glass (including hand-blown pieces by Josh Simpson). **North River Glass/Young & Constantin Gallery** (✉ Deerfield Ave. ☎ 413/625–6422 ⊕ www.ycglass.com) has a stunning display of hand-blown glass.

Shelburne Falls Coffee Roaster (✉ 635 Mohawk Trail ☎ 413/625–6474 ⊕ www.ibuycoffee.com) sells a variety of beans, including organic and custom blends. Cards, books, paintings, jewelry and other heavenly works of art are on view at **Wings of Light** (✉ 20 Bridge St. ☎ 413/625–0144 ⊕ www.clearangel.com).

NORTHFIELD

㉑ *24 mi northeast of Shelburne Falls.*

Northfield, as the name implies, sits along the northern edge of Massachusetts. In fact, the community sits just across the border from New Hampshire and Vermont. The center of town is an impressive sight, a 2 mi stretch of Route 63 dotted with massive maple and elm trees and well-preserved colonial homes and quaint country stores (including an old-fashioned IGA grocery store). A drive along Route 63 through Northfield and the adjacent communities affords some of the region's most spectacular views. Approaching from the south, where the terrain is higher, you can see the Connecticut River as it winds its way through the rolling hills.

Northfield was established in 1671 by settlers from the Northampton area who moved here following an Indian uprising. Any misgivings they had were alleviated by the region's rich soil. More than 300 years later, Northfield continues to make much of its living from agriculture. The pastoral town is also home to one of the valley's many notable educational institutions, the Northfield Mount Hermon School. For culture, there's the Bolger Arts Center, with an ongoing schedule of theatrical productions. During the summer months, take in a double feature at the Northfield Drive-In, one of the few surviving drive-in theaters in the Northeast.

Northfield is handy to many popular southern vacation destinations, including Keene, New Hampshire, and Brattleboro, Vermont, both tranquil college communities just a half-hour drive from the center of town. Some of the region's best skiing areas, including Vermont's Mount Snow, Bromley, and Stratton, are within striking distance of Northfield.

Erving State Forest provides a wide variety of recreational pursuits including, boating, swimming and fishing at Laurel Lake. From Northfield, take Route 63 south to Route 2 east to Erving center. ⊠ *E. Main St., Erving* 🕾 *978/544–3939* 🖺 *$2 per car* ⊙ *May–Oct., daily 9* AM*–10* PM.

The **Northfield Mountain Recreation & Environmental Center** has 26 mi of trails for biking, hiking, and horseback riding, and you can rent canoes, kayaks, and rowboats at the campground at Barton Cove. From here you can paddle to the Munn's Ferry campground, accessible only by canoe. The center also runs 1½-hour riverboat tours of the Pioneer Valley along a 12-mi stretch of the Connecticut River between Northfield and Gill, where you'll pass through a dramatically narrow gorge and get a close look at a nesting ground for bald eagles. The tours, offered between mid-June and mid-October, are Wednesday to Sunday at 11, 1:15, and 3. The cost is $9. In winter, the center rents cross-country skis and snowshoes and offers lessons. ⊠ *99 Miller's Falls Rd.* 🕾 *413/863–9300 or 800/859–2960* ⊕ *www.nu.com/northfield* 🖺 *Free* ⊙ *Daily 9–5.*

off the beaten path

MT. MONADNOCK – Every year, thousands of visitors ascend the winding foot trail that leads to the 3,165-foot summit of Mt. Monadnock, purported to be the second-most scaled mountain in the world. When conditions are clear, the skyline of Boston is easily visible to the east, as are hundreds of miles of mountain ranges and valleys in all directions. During winter months, cross-country skiing enthusiasts use 12 mi of trails, situated on 5,000 acres of protected highlands. From the Northfield area, follow Route 10 north into New Hampshire; at Winchester Center, take a right onto Route 119 east, after about 10 mi, head left on U.S. 202 north to Jaffrey. ⊠ *Rte. 124, Jaffrey, NH* 🕾 *603/532–8862* ⊕ *www.nhstateparks.org* 🖺 *Free* ⊙ *Daily.*

Where to Eat

★ **$$–$$$** ✕ **Putney Inn.** Sumptuous entrées like lamb shank cassoulet and charbroiled filet mignon, a pastoral New England setting, and jazz pianist Patty Carpenter performing "Moonlight in Vermont" make this establishment in the nearby town of Putney well worth the trip. ⊠ *Putney Landing Rd., Putney, VT* 🕾 *802/387–5517* ⊕ *www.putneyinn.com* 🖃 *AE, DC, MC, V.*

¢–$ ✕ **Riverview Café.** Grab a window seat at this casual eatery in the nearby town of Brattleboro, Vermont, and you'll be treated to views of downtown to the west and the rolling hills of New Hampshire to the east. The menu includes a selection of steaks, sandwiches, and soups. ⊠ *36 Bridge St., Brattleboro, VT* 🕾 *802/254–9841* 🖃 *AE, DC, MC, V.*

¢ ✕ **Big Kitchen Café.** It's not every day you get to eat in a barn, but the proprietors of the Big Kitchen Café converted one into a restaurant. Full of rustic charm, the eatery delivers a plethora of choices ranging from

American fare to Mexican. There's no alcohol, so bring your own bottle. ⊠ *61 Main St.* ☎ *413/498–5593* ▤ *MC, V.*

Where to Stay

$ ▣ **Centennial House.** Once home to presidents of the Mount Hermon School, this 1811 Colonial B&B has three spacious, antiques-filled guest rooms (two of them can be booked with additional adjoining bedrooms) and a third-floor suite with a kitchen that makes it perfect for families. The inn's large, glassed-in sunroom is a delightful place to curl up with a book; the pine-paneled living room has a huge fireplace. There are 2½ acres of grounds where guests gather to watch the sunset. ⊠ *Main St., 01360* ☎ *413/498–5921 or 877/977–5950* ☒ *413/498–2525* ⊕ *www.thecentennialhouse.com* ⋑ *3 rooms, 1 suite* ⅋ *Internet; no room phones, no TV in some rooms* ▤ *AE, MC, V* ⑩ *BP.*

Nightlife & the Arts

Nightlife

Southern Vermont's live-music mainstay for decades, the **Mole's Eye Café** (⊠ 4 High St., Brattleboro, VT ☎ 802/257–0771) brings in live bands from the region each weekend. Just south of Northfield, the honky-tonk **Route 63 Roadhouse** (⊠ Rte. 63, Miller's Falls ☎ 413/659–3384) is a spacious, pine-paneled music room hosting regional rock groups.

The Arts

The year was 1949, and the **Northfield Drive-In** (⊠ Rte. 63, Winchester, NH ☎ 603/239–4054 ⊕ www.northfielddrivein.com) was packed with Buicks and Oldsmobiles for a debut screening of Orson Welles' *The Third Man*. More than five decades later, the french fries and the atmosphere are still exactly the same. It's open late May to Labor Day and screens double features nightly. Admission is $8.

THE PIONEER VALLEY A TO Z

AIRPORTS

Bradley International Airport, in Windsor Locks, Connecticut, is the most convenient airport for flying into the Pioneer Valley. It's about 20 mi south of Springfield. American, America West, Continental, Delta, Midwest Express, Northwest, Southwest, United, and US Airways serve Bradley.

⨯ Airport Information **Bradley International Airport** ⊠ U.S. 20 [take Exit 40 off I-91] ☎ 860/292-2000 ⊕ www.bradleyairport.com.

BUS TRAVEL

Peter Pan Bus Lines links most major Northeast cities with Springfield, Holyoke, South Hadley, Northampton, Amherst, Deerfield, Greenfield, and Sturbridge and provides transportation to Bradley and Logan airports. Pioneer Valley Transit Authority provides service in 24 communities throughout the Pioneer Valley, including a Downtown Trolley that loops through Springfield on two vintage streetcars on weekdays.

⨯ Bus Information **Peter Pan Bus Lines** ☎ 413/781-2900 or 800/237-8747 ⊕ www.peterpanbus.com. **Pioneer Valley Transit Authority** ☎ 413/781-7882 ⊕ www.pvta.com.

CAR TRAVEL

A car is your best way for exploring the region, as distances between attractions can be significant and public transportation impractical for most visitors. Interstate 91 runs north–south through the valley. Interstate 90 links Springfield to Boston. Route 2 connects Boston with Greenfield and, via U.S. 5, Deerfield.

EMERGENCIES

🔢 Hospitals & Emergency Services **Baystate Medical Center** ⊠ 759 Chestnut St., Springfield ☎ 413/794-0000. **Cooley Dickenson Hospital** ⊠ 30 Locust St., Northampton ☎ 413/582-2000. **Holyoke Hospital** ⊠ 575 Beech St., Holyoke ☎ 413/534-2500.

LODGING

BED-AND-BREAKFASTS Berkshire Folkstone Bed & Breakfast Homes is a reservation service. 🔢 Reservation Services **Berkshire Folkstone Bed & Breakfast Homes** ☎ 413/268-7244 or 800/762-2751 🖷 413/268-7243 ⊕ www.berkshirebnbhomes.com.

TRAIN TRAVEL

Amtrak serves the Pioneer Valley with stops in Amherst and Springfield, with free parking at both stations. Express trains to New York City take three hours or less. Advance ticket purchases are often required, so book ahead.
🔢 Train Information **Amtrak** ☎ 800/872-7245 ⊕ www.amtrak.com.

VISITOR INFORMATION

The Greater Springfield Convention & Visitors Bureau serves the entire Pioneer Valley; it also operates the Riverfront Visitor Information Center, next to the Basketball Hall of Fame. Both the Northampton and Amherst chambers of commerce have useful visitor centers and Web sites. Additionally, the Franklin County Chamber of Commerce has more specific information about the northern end of the valley at its visitor center by the Route 2 exit of I–91. The Sturbridge Area Tourist Association is your best resource for that area.
🔢 Tourist Information **Amherst Area Chamber of Commerce** ⊠ 409 Main St., 01002 ☎ 413/253-0700 ⊕ www.amherstchamber.com. **Franklin County Chamber of Commerce** ⊠ 395 Main St. ☎ Box 898, Greenfield 01302 ☎ 413/773-5463 ⊕ www.franklincc.org. **Greater Northampton Chamber of Commerce** ⊠ 99 Pleasant St., Northampton 01060 ☎ 413/584-1900 or 800/238-6869 ⊕ www.northamptonuncommon.com. **Greater Springfield Convention & Visitors Bureau** ⊠ 1441 Main St., Springfield 01103 ☎ 413/787-1548 or 800/723-1548 ⊕ www.valleyvisitor.com. **Sturbridge Area Tourist Association** ⊠ 380 Main St., Sturbridge 01566 ☎ 508/347-7594 or 800/628-8379 ⊕ www.sturbridge.org.

INDEX